WILT

JUST
LIKE ANY OTHER
7-FOOT
BLACK MILLIONAIRE
WHO LIVES
NEXT DOOR

Wilt Chamberlain
and David Shaw

MACMILLAN PUBLISHING CO., INC.

NEW YORK

COLLIER MACMILLAN PUBLISHERS

LONDON

Macmillan Publishing Co., Inc.
866 Third Avenue, New York, N.Y. 10022
Coller-Macmillan Canada Ltd., Toronto, Ontario

Library of Congress Catalog Card Number: 73–2124

SECOND PRINTING 1973

Printed in the United States of America

Most of the people whose cooperation and encouragement helped make this book possible are mentioned in the text itself. But there are others whose assistance was invaluable. For their aid in opening doors and jogging memories, special thanks to Don Baker at the University of Kansas, Marie Linehan of the Harlem Globetrotters, Rick Smith of the Golden State Warriors, and Mary Lou Liebich, Jeff Temkin, and the entire staff of the Los Angeles Lakers.

And, for her patience and understanding, our gratitude and appreciation to Alice Shaw.

Preface

When I first met Wilt Chamberlain, in the spring of 1971, I had written only one sports story in the previous five years—and that was about football, not basketball. But I had been around athletes most of my life, and I had long since been disabused of the stereotype of the athlete as simpleton. I counted several athletes among my close friends, and I knew them to be bright, sensitive, articulate human beings—men of discriminating taste and catholic interests.

Still, even I wasn't fully prepared for the breadth and depth of Wilt Chamberlain's concerns—nor for his omnivorous appetite for information . . . and his 24-hour-a-day compulsion for what he likes to call "argumentation."

In the 14 months we worked together on this book—in his living room, in his den, in his kitchen, in his dining room, in his bedroom, in his hotel room, in my living room, in my office, on buses, on airplanes, in taxicabs, in airport waiting rooms, in sports arena locker rooms—I found myself engaged in heated discussions with him over more varied subjects than I can recall. We argued about everything from the Watts riot and the war in Vietnam to the relative difficulty of making chocolate *soufflé* and lemon meringue pie; we disagreed on the comparative intelligence of Richard Nixon and John Kennedy, and the propriety of addressing strangers by their first names; we talked about euthanasia, dress standards, lifestyle, marriages, funerals, racism, exploitation, materialism, Presidential politics, movies, music—and the supposed differences between a woman's clitoral and vaginal orgasms.

And we made bets. Oh, how we made bets. If you yawn around Wilt Chamberlain, he's likely to say, "Bet you $2 on it." We made bets on football games, on the population of São Paulo, on the name of the biggest-circulation newspaper in the world, on cotton production in California, on potato production in Maine, on. . . .

In between our philosophical discussions—and our trivial wagers—we somehow found time to work on this book.

We intended, we said, to write a book that was not just another sports book, not just another black book, not just another celebrity book—and not just another one of those first-person books in which the protagonist attributes all his success to good luck and the help of everyone he's ever known, from the newspaper vendor on the corner to the boy who shined his shoes last time he was in Newark Airport. We wanted a book that would capture and reveal Wilt Chamberlain, the man, as he really is—a complex, diverse, unique, immensely self-assured and self-possessed human being.

Alex Hannum, who coached Wilt in San Francisco and again in Philadelphia, used to like to answer the question "What's Wilt Chamberlain *really* like?" with a comment as perceptive and illuminating as it was glib:

"Wilt," he would say, "is just like . . . any other 7-foot, black millionaire who lives next door to you."

That's the Wilt I came to know—a man who is, above all, unique, truly one of a kind, in his frailties and his inconsistencies, as well as in his insights and his accomplishments and his response to the constant pressure he's been subjected to for almost 20 years.

When I submitted this manuscript to my editors, they looked at a few polysyllabic words and intriguing observations and asked me, "Are you sure Wilt said that?"

Yes, I am. The words are Wilt's words. The thoughts are Wilt's thoughts.

And the book is Wilt's book.

DAVID SHAW

WILT

1

IT WAS ONE OF THE MOST curious sensations I'd ever experienced in my entire life. The Lakers had just beaten the Chicago Bulls, 95-92, to win the first round of the 1973 playoffs in Los Angeles. We had won in the final seconds of the final quarter of the final game, when I blocked a jump shot near the top of the key, grabbed the ball and fired a full-court pass to Gail Goodrich for a lay-up. And yet, when it was all over, and I found myself, quite literally, with tears in my eyes, the tears were not tears of triumph and joy and exultation—or even relief—for myself and my teammates. The tears were tears of anguish—and they were for the Chicago Bulls.

The Bulls had outplayed us and outhustled us in almost every game. They had given us just about the most physically punishing and emotionally exhausting seven-game series I can recall in my 14 years of NBA play. Chicago, to be honest about it, had deserved to win. The Lakers didn't. In fact, as terrible as it sounds, there were times in the fourth quarter of that seventh game—when we were playing poorly and falling behind—that I was actually hoping we would lose. It just didn't seem fair to Chicago for us to win,

1

and when the game was over and we *had* won, I put my arms around two of the Chicago players—Norm Van Lier and Chet Walker—and went to their dressing room with them, even before I went to the Laker dressing room. I told Chet and Norm and Jerry Sloan and all the other Bulls how great they were and how I really thought they had deserved to win.

I told them I knew how they felt then because I had been through the same shattering, frustrating experience so many times myself—playing my heart out, giving every last ounce of physical and psychic energy, clearly deserving to win . . . and yet, somehow, finally losing.

I knew that in a matter of days—if not hours—Chicago's brilliant, valiant effort would be forgotten. The next round of the playoffs would be underway, and Chicago would be out of it— runners-up, also-rans, losers. Losers. How I had come to despise that word. In sports, there is only one winner and a million losers; one team wins the NBA championship or the Super Bowl or the World Series, and every other team is a "loser," no matter how great they played all season.

God, how I empathized with the Bulls that night. To play so well and come so close, against such insuperable odds, and still lose. For most of my career, of course—right up until the Lakers won the NBA championship in 1972, in fact—I'd been called a "loser," too. For damn near half my life, I'd lived with that "loser" label stuck on me like some big, ugly scar from an operation I'd never had. But I was no more a loser all those years than Chicago was a loser that night in Los Angeles.

Loser, shit! If I'd been a loser, so were such so-called basketball "immortals" as Bob Pettit and Dolph Schayes—to say nothing of such sports heroes as Hank Aaron and Willie Mays and Joe Namath and Jim Brown. No one ever called those guys "losers," but do you know how many world championships each of them won? I'll tell you exactly how many—one! And that's the same number I'd won before the Lakers won that 1972 championship. (Funny, isn't it? Most people forget my first world championship, back in 1967, when I was with the Philadelphia 76ers). Even with just one championship going into the 1971–72 season, I'd won more than Elgin Baylor or Oscar Robertson or Jerry Lucas or Jerry West—or John Brodie or Roman Gabriel or Sonny Jurgenson or Bob Feller or Ted Williams or Juan Marichal—had ever won.

Not only that, but people always seemed to forget that back when I was a kid, I led my YMCA team to the national championship. They forgot that in three years, my high school team lost only three games—and won two all-city and three all-public school championships. In college, at Kansas, where all that loser crap really got started, my team won more games when I was a sophomore than it ever won before—and we came closer to winning the national championship than Kansas has ever come since.

Ah, but the pros, you say, the NBA. What about all those seventh-game losses to Bill Russell and the Boston Celtics? Well, I want to get into that more later on, but let's look at a few simple facts right now, OK?

Fact No. 1: My team beat Boston in the playoffs once, in 1967, and that's once more than any other team beat them during all those years they had what all the experts say was the greatest basketball team in history—the greatest sports dynasty of all time.

Fact No. 2: Winning doesn't just mean winning seventh games. I played for three teams in my pro career, and every one of them won more games and did better in the playoffs while I was with them than they ever did before or since.

Fact No. 3: Most knowledgeable observers readily agree that Boston almost invariably had better players, better coaching and better luck than my teams did. The astonishing thing was not that my teams lost, but that we came so close to winning so often.

I know all this sounds like a horribly egotistical exercise in sour grapes and self-aggrandizement. Well, I remember reading somewhere, probably when I was in grade school, that some eighteenth-century British playwright once said, "Modest men are dumb." That's probably overstating the case just a bit, but I never have been known for my humility. Besides, that's not the point. I don't have to stand on the rooftops and shout, "I'm great!" In the first place, my individual records and statistics speak for themselves, and in the second place, I'm big enough for everyone to see me without my having to climb up on any rooftop and maybe break a leg. I only recounted all those winning records and told you what happened before I came and after I left each team to get you to thinking a little. Sure, I made my share of mistakes,

3

and I have to share the blame for all those championship losses; but maybe the records I've just told you about will give you a subtle hint that it wasn't always all my fault, that maybe I didn't always have all-time all-pros for teammates—or tactical geniuses for coaches.

Surprisingly, I didn't hear so much of that loser bullshit after the Knicks beat us for the NBA championship this past season. Maybe it was because we had beaten them the previous year, and that tended to lay the loser thing to rest, at long last. Or maybe it was just because this 1973 Knick-Laker playoff was so strange.

They beat us in four out of five games, but all five games were in doubt until the final seconds, and we could easily have won any—or all—of them; everyone, I think, realized that. In fact, I've never seen a series in which one team (the Knicks) always seemed to get the one crucial break they needed at just the right moment in each game. This was particularly true on almost-identical plays in the last two games of the series. In the fourth game, the Lakers came back from a 21-point deficit, and trailed only 94-92 with 48 seconds left. The Knicks' Dave DeBusschere took a rebound that I had been fighting for with his teammate Willis Reed, and Dave just threw the ball up in the air, hoping to draw a foul, but—as he later admitted—never dreaming the ball would go in the basket. It went in, though, and that destroyed our momentum. When Dave hit his free throw, the Knicks had the game wrapped up.

In the very next game, the Lakers rallied from a 14-point fourth-quarter deficit to cut the Knicks' lead to 84-80 with three and a half minutes to play. When Jerry West missed an easy jump shot for us, the Lakers' Bill Bridges grabbed the rebound in close and put the ball in the basket—just as DeBusschere had in the previous game. I had a good view of the play, and it looked to me like Bill was fouled on the play—just as I had fouled DeBusschere in the previous game. But the official called it the other way; he said Bill committed the foul. Instead of the Lakers trailing just 84-83 (assuming that Bridges made one of his two free throws), the Knicks got two free throws, Bill Bradley made them both, and the Knicks took an 86-80 lead. The official's call turned out to be a five-point play—a six-point Knick lead, instead of a one-point

4

Knick lead—and that was the game . . . and the 1973 NBA championship.

Not that I mean to take anything away from the Knicks. They played good defense and smart team basketball, and they took advantage of the breaks—something we just didn't do. They deserved to win; we didn't. But basketball is a funny game sometimes. If you look at the record books ten years from now and see that the Knicks beat us, four games to one, in 1973, you probably won't remember just how close the series really was—and how deceptive that final four-to-one margin was. But that, I guess, is part of the mystique that has made pro basketball such an enormously popular sport. And since basketball is primarily responsible for so many of the personal pleasures and material comforts I enjoy today, I can't very well complain about it, can I?

2

NOW THAT I LIVE IN A
million-dollar house and own my own boat and go to Europe every
summer and drive a Bentley and a Maserati and enjoy all those
other simple necessities of life, I suppose it would make a better
story if I could say it all began in a dimly lit log cabin or a rat-
infested slum tenement. Sorry, no rags-to-riches story here. Not
that my family was rich—or even well-to-do—while I was growing
up. We didn't have any *pâté de foie gras* or *chateaubriand* for dinner. Pot roast and pork chops would be more like it. But I never
missed a meal or had to make do with a skimpy portion or a meal
lacking in the essential nutrients. And I never went to school without shoes or clean clothes, or came home crying because I didn't
have a nickel to buy an ice cream cone. Oh, sure, I wore my older
brother's hand-me-downs when I was little, and my younger
brother wore my hand-me-downs, and all my sisters wore their
older sisters' hand-me-downs. But when you come from a family
of nine kids, there's a helluva lot to hand down. It would've been
foolish not to use some of the clothes again—about as foolish (and

6

as wasteful) as giving the Venus de Milo a pair of gloves for Christmas.

Actually, my parents had eleven children, but the first two died real young, when they were one or two, I think—before I was born, anyway. I was just about in the middle of the other nine—two girls, then a boy, two girls, then a boy (me), two girls, then a boy. I rather doubt that my parents planned it that way, but the sequence of the children had a nice symmetry about it, don't you think? Almost like a good poem.

I was born at 11:27 P.M., August 21, 1936, which—for you astrology buffs—makes me a Leo. I wouldn't even bring it up except I just missed being a Virgo by 33 minutes, and considering how many times later on, in my basketball career, I would "just miss" something—usually a championship—that seems a fittingly ironic way to have come into the world.

The most amazing thing about my childhood, when I look back on it, is how my parents managed to provide so well for all us kids. My father had about three different full-time jobs at various times, as I remember. He was a welder in a shipyard first, and then he worked for 20 years or so at Sears and Roebuck, doing handyman work. During most of my childhood, though, he was a janitor and handyman for Curtis Publishing Co., and I frankly doubt that he ever took home more than $62 a week. And yet, we lived in a fairly nice lower-middle-class to middle-class area, the west end of West Philadelphia, and we had a good, big row house. It was almost 15 or 20 years old when we moved in in 1938, but it was a corner house with a living room and a dining room and a cellar and a fenced-in roof on top of the garage where we all played a lot.

There were four bedrooms in the house, so we doubled up on the sleeping—even quadrupled up when the girls were younger. But there's 14 years between my oldest sister, Dolores, and my youngest brother, Oliver, so we weren't all around at the same time and it wasn't really that crowded. About the only really bad thing I can remember about that house was that the trolley car barn was a block away, and the trolleys used to come roaring by our bedroom windows about 5:30 every morning when they started their daily runs. We had some maple trees on that side of the house, but they didn't shut the noise out, and until you got used to it, those predawn trollies could really shake you out of bed in a hurry. After awhile, we didn't even need any clocks or watches. We just told time by the trollies; they ran in cycles, taking people to and from work, and they were pretty damn dependable.

We used to joke about them a lot when we had company—and we always had company. My mother and father were good hosts, fun to be with, and the kids all got along pretty well together, too. We were a real close family. Still are. Besides, my mother was an excellent cook, and she and my father were both soft touches for friends and visiting relatives who wanted to borrow a few bucks. In fact, it seems friends and relatives were always eating with us and staying overnight with us. And they were always welcome. I didn't eat at other kids' houses very often, but they sure ate at my place a lot. I particularly remember our Sunday morning breakfasts, with orange juice and eggs and toast and our choice of sausage and bacon and some kind of fish.

So how did my parents manage? Well, my father was the neighborhood handyman, and he made a little money on the side, doing paint-up, fix-up work for friends and neighbors. And my mother hired herself out as a domestic, right up until my second or third year in pro ball. That brought some money in, too, but they were both so generous, they often did the work for nothing, just to help out people they liked. Of course, their abilities saved us a lot of money. My mother (and, later my sisters) did all the cooking, cleaning, laundry, ironing, and sewing, and my father did all the painting, electrical work, plumbing, carpentry, and miscellaneous repair jobs around the house, so we saved quite a bit of money there. And, for all their generosity, my parents were both good money managers.

They couldn't spend all their time working, though. They were very much in love and very much devoted to each other and to the children. I think their record—if you can call it that—speaks for itself. They were married 46 years—until my father died in 1968—and all nine of their living children made something of themselves. At least, none of us has had any trouble with drugs or booze, and none of us has wound up in jail or on welfare.

I guess the one thing that helped the family make it financially was the way all the kids pitched in and went to work as soon as they could. No one had to ask us. We just started working—and contributing some of our earnings to the household, even when they were only pennies and nickels. Later, when we started making decent money (decent for kids, anyway), we'd all pool our money and buy a sofa or a chair or something for the kitchen when it was needed.

For a variety of reasons, I was probably the biggest worker among the kids. I always hustled, always looked for a way to make a few cents. Hell, I had my first job when I was five years old. I delivered papers and washed windows and shoveled snow and cleaned cellars. Sometimes, I'd deliver prescriptions for the doctor down the street or take my wagon down to the grocery store and help people take their groceries home. When I was six or seven or so, I'd get up at five o'clock in the morning and help the milk-man unload wooden crates of full milk bottles and then help him pick up the empty bottles and carry them back to the truck. As I recall, he'd give me a penny or two every day. Or was it every crate? Or every block? It doesn't matter. Whatever it was, it didn't add up to much. And it didn't last long. My mother woke up and came out early one morning and saw me hauling those big crates around and chased the milkman halfway down the block. When she got through with him, about all he could do was point to me and mumble, "But I thought he was 12."

I was already about eight or ten inches taller than most kids my age, so I guess it was an easy mistake for him to make. Not that I worried a whole lot about losing the job. Finding work was always pretty easy for me. This was in the early 1940s, remember, during World War II, and there were a lot of shortages, a lot of commodities that were valuable because they were scarce. So I became a scavenger—the neighborhood junk collector. I'd find bits and pieces of iron, tin, brass, old rags, even newspaper and card-board. I'd look anywhere and everywhere—trash cans, vacant lots, store disposal areas, the gutter. A lot of the stuff I got by going door to door, asking for scraps and discards, and before long, everyone got to know me, and they'd save things for me. Once I started going to school, I did this on Saturdays, and I could collect maybe 200 pounds or so in a single morning if I started early and really worked at it. You could take all that stuff to the junkyard and get eight or nine cents a pound for it, and after I gave my mother half the money, I'd still have more than enough

9

left to take my closest sister, Barbara, and my youngest sister, Yvonne, to the movies and buy some popcorn and ice cream.

By the time I was ten, I was a regular businessman—a budding Rockefeller. But even a Rockefeller makes an occasional business mistake, right? Well, I made a few, too. The most disastrous one came one winter when I was eight or nine, and I went down into the basement, looking for old rags and junk to sell. I sorted through a whole bunch of boxes and bags and picked out the stuff I thought I could get the best price on. None of it really looked too good, but I figured I could make a little something on it anyway, so I threw it all in a big pile and hauled it to the junkyard. I got $2 for it and promptly forgot about the whole thing. A good deal, but nothing special, you know.

That's what I thought.

A few months later, about Easter time, my mother was doing her spring cleaning and putting the winter clothes away and getting the spring and summer clothes out. Well, she went down to the basement—and came up screaming like she'd seen a rat on the Sunday breakfast table. It seems like all those "rags" I'd sold had been about 95 percent of the family's summer clothes. That was the most miserable Easter of my life; I wasn't allowed to go anywhere for two weeks. I didn't learn my lesson, though. The very next year, I took a bunch of old rugs out of the basement and sold them to the junkman for 75¢. About Christmas time, my mother went looking for one special rug she wanted to put down. She'd paid $75 for it. Yup, you guessed it. It was one of the rugs I'd sold.

About the only thing that saved me from really severe punishment when I did those things was that I meant well—and I wasn't the first one in the family to make those mistakes. A couple of years earlier, my sister Shirley had sold the piano to a junkman driving down the street—for $5. I think she had an ulterior motive, though. She hated the piano lessons my mother made her take.

Anyway, when I got older—11, 12, somewhere in there—I gave up my career as a junkman and started going down to 2nd Street, the Philadelphia produce district, and buying watermelons and cantaloupes and tomatoes and hauling them through the streets in my wagon, shouting, "Watermelon Man," and selling them door to door at a good profit. About the same time, my

10

father taught me how to paint and took me on some of his jobs in the neighborhood. It didn't take me very long to put my own crew together, with other boys in the neighborhood, and hire us out to do our own paint jobs. I remember one of our first jobs real well. Me and a friend named George were painting away on this house, right across the street from where my dad was painting another house, working alone, and we thought we were really doin' it, really smokin'. About lunchtime, we looked over, and my father had damn near the whole front of his house done. Compared to him, we looked like we just started ten minutes ago.

From painting, it was natural for me to get into other kinds of construction and contracting work, and I had one job with a real son-of-a-bitch of a contractor. I was supposed to take this sixteen-pound sledgehammer and break up the old pavement in front of this house. Then I was supposed to pick up all the old pavement, haul it away, mix new cement, and pour it out. When I was done, he'd come along with his trowel and level it off and draw the curb lines in it. He'd get paid $125 or so for the job and keep $120. I'd do all the back-breaking work and get a lousy $5.

With all the work I did as a kid, I think I can remember only about one other time that I really got screwed. I was about 13 or 14 then, the summer between ninth and tenth grades, and I went away to camp—Pine Forest Camp. I'll never forget it. The man who ran the place told me and these four good friends of mine how much fun it would be. We could play basketball and ride horses and just have ourselves a helluva time. All we'd have to do, he said, was work in the kitchen a little. Shit! We wound up working 17 hours a day, washing dishes and pots and pans, and we never did get to see a basketball court. We were supposed to stay there eight weeks, and he'd pay us $125 each. That figures out to about thirteen cents an hour. Boy, were we pissed. Well, one night, two of us went out horseback riding—late at night was the only time we had free—and he heard about it and fired us for "fooling around."

I got a chance to pay him back, though. My first year in pro ball, with the Philadelphia Warriors, the guy who ran the camp contacted the Warriors' owner, Eddie Gottlieb, and asked if I could come up there to run a basketball clinic for the kids who were there.

11

"Screw him," I said.

Then I got to thinking.

"How much will he pay?" I asked Eddie.

"They usually pay $200 or $300 for something like this. We might get $500, if you want to push it, since you worked there once, and he can get his money's worth bragging about how one of 'his boys' made it big."

That did it. "Tell him I'll do it—for $2,000."

The guy agreed to it, and when I got to the camp, I went up and drank some juice with the cats he had working in the kitchen, doing my old job. Then I gave him his damn clinic—three hours for $2,000. That figures out to $666.66 an hour—or about $666.53 an hour more than he paid me as a dishwasher. I'm not sure I ever got more pleasure out of taking another man's money, believe me.

Despite an occasional misadventure, like the one at that camp, all the work I did as a young kid was invaluable; it taught me the value of a dollar—and the value of my own work. I learned how to bargain and negotiate and how to judge people and prices and services, and I think all the owners I later played pro basketball for—men like Abe Saperstein and Eddie Gottlieb and Franklin Mieuli and Irv Kosloff and Jack Kent Cooke—would tell you I learned my childhood lessons well (perhaps too well the way they see it).

Not that I was all tycoon as a young kid. I had one habit that was distinctly untycoonish: I sucked my thumb. Yeah, I know, most babies suck their thumbs. But for some reason, I kept sucking my thumb until I was out of elementary school, into junior high school. I remember when I was about two years old and was sick in the hospital, and this nurse tied my hand to the side of the crib to stop me from sucking my thumb and I got so mad I bit the hell out of her. I don't know if I kept sucking my thumb after that out of some subconscious desire to show her she couldn't stop me or what, but I sure must have looked weird when I got to be 12 years old and about 6 foot 3, walking around with this big thumb jammed in my mouth, my head rocking rhythmically from side to side.

Thumb sucking didn't cost me any jobs, though, and I've often wondered why I worked so damn hard when I could have

12

been out playing with the other kids. I guess there are several possible explanations. With our big family, the money came in handy, of course. And I sure liked having some change in my pocket all the time so I could buy things I wanted—and, not incidentally, show off to the other kids. My mother and father set a good example by working so hard themselves, so that's another reason—they just got me into the habit young, and I've never broken it. If I was going to work at all, there was no sense doing it halfway. It was like my mother used to say:

"Whatever you do, large or small, do it well, or don't do it at all."

I believed that and I tried to live by it. I still do. Whether it was painting houses and selling junk as a kid, or playing basketball and making love as an adult, I want to do it well, do it right—be the best at it, if I possibly can.

Even when I was collecting rags and scrap metal, I'd always try to get more this week than last week—and more every week than any other kid in the neighborhood. That's why I'd get so pissed, later on, when I became a basketball star, and some dumb fans and jerks in the press would say I was only good because I was tall and that I had everything fall in my lap without working for it. Dick Young, a crotchety old man who writes for the New York *Daily News,* said that as recently as last May, during the Laker-Knick playoffs. He said I not only wasn't a great basketball player, I wasn't even a "good basketball player . . . simply a big basketball player." Young, who was a pretty fair sportswriter 20 years ago, seemed to take it as a personal affront when the Dodgers and Giants left New York for California, and he has been using his column to vent his spleen ever since.

Sure, I had some natural advantages—my height and a good home and good parents and a whole lot of other things—but I worked my ass off to capitalize on those opportunities. Like when I started shotputting. Every day, I'd spend two or three hours putting the shot. It didn't matter if it was raining or snowing or hailing. I'd wallow in the mud if I had to, but I'd practice and practice and practice, the year round. That's why I beat those other guys and won shotput championships in high school and college. They just practiced in season, but I was willing to make sacrifices, to practice when they were going out on dates or going to the movies or just loafing and fooling around with friends. Once I got into basketball, I was the same way; I'd practice afternoons and evenings and weekends, and during the summer I'd practice all day long, working on my moves and my shots and my passing and my rebounding.

It helped, of course, that I had the ability to really concentrate on whatever I was trying to master. That's probably been one of the keys to my success in anything I've ever tried. Some guys can concentrate hard for a short time, but then their attention wanders. I've always been able to concentrate on something for as long as I had to, put my mind to it and shut everything else out—whether it's driving across the country in record time or practicing the shotput or figuring a play in a high-stakes card game. I just hang in there till the other guy is beat—literally and figuratively.

I'm sure some measure of my competitive instinct and urge to excel comes from my father—whether it's in the genes or just absorbed from being around him so much. He was very competitive, too, a great checkers and pinochle player, and he worked hard at it, studying his every play, studying his opponent . . . and he didn't lose very often. We were very close, and we used to play each other all the time, when I was a kid and an adult, and I got so I could beat him at pinochle. But I never did beat him at checkers, not once in all the thousands of times we played.

After I'd been playing pro basketball a while, some of the amateur psychiatrists in the press started analyzing me and decided I always wanted to be the best because I was so tall. They said I wanted to prove that I could win at things where my height was no advantage. One sportswriter, I remember, said I wanted to be the best basketball player, the best card player, the best track man, the best football player and the best cook. Well, what's wrong with that? Why shouldn't a guy want to be the best at anything he does? I mean, it'd be different if I wanted to be the best at something crooked or impossible or immoral. If I wanted to be the best safecracker or the best pimp, you might be justified in locking me up. Or if I said I wanted to be the best jockey, you sure as hell would be justified in laughing at me. But track? Cards? Cooking? If you have ability in a certain area, why not capitalize on it and improve it and use it?

Of course, a fierce competitive instinct can sometimes lead you into excesses. Being the best at many things and wanting to be the best at many others might make you exaggerate your own exploits just a trifle. I get carried away sometimes and say I can pass a football better than Joe Namath and drive better than Dan Gurney and cook better than Graham Kerr. To be perfectly truthful, probably only two of those three statements are true.

In my zeal to win, I've probably also, well, not exactly cheated, but if you and I are playing cards and you dip your hand a little, I'm going to take a quick peep. If you're not particularly perceptive—and if the stakes aren't too high—I might even fool around a little when I deal, just for fun, you know? I like to win and I'll do anything I can, take advantage of every opportunity I get, to beat you.

I imagine the sportswriters are right, to a certain extent, about this drive stemming from some inner need to prove I'm good—and smart—not just big. My height has become such a dominant, overwhelming factor in my life—much more so than my blackness—that I'm sure I subconsciously, if not consciously, try to beat guys at things where my height not only doesn't help me but sometimes handicaps me. I won't deny there's a certain satisfaction in being the only center ever to lead the NBA in assists—or in consistently outshooting Jerry West from 20 or 25 feet out when the Lakers have shootaround games in practice. The same was true of my performance in other sports—outrunning guys who were smaller and supposedly faster than me or beating high-jumpers and shotputters who were supposed to be better coordinated than me. Big guys aren't supposed to be able to water ski either, but you ought to see me out there. Whoooeeee! And this winter, I hope to take up snow skiing! But excelling in other athletic endeavors, however diverse and challenging they may be, has not been enough for me. I have a broad range of social and intellectual interests, and I've tried to excel in them as well. I negotiate most of my own investment deals now, and I love to cook and gamble and pick up pretty girls and debate anything from politics to prepubescent fertility rites. Being seven feet tall sure as hell isn't much of an advantage in any of those (except, maybe, picking up pretty girls), but I do pretty damn well at all of them, if I do say so myself.

15

Still, I think it is simplistic and misleading to attribute my competitive instinct in all these areas to a compulsive desire to prove I'm not just some seven-foot freak who can dunk basketballs. After all, I wanted to be the best at what I was doing long before I even knew what a basketball was. I didn't play basketball until I was in junior high, and that was well after my days as a junk man, card player and undisputed neighborhood Monopoly champion had begun.

Ours wasn't a very sports-minded family back then, except for my father being a big boxing fan, and I guess my first real competitive sport was track. Well, just plain running, really. As a young kid, I always ran. I ran to the market, to school, to friends' houses, back home—everywhere. I had these four real close friends—Vince Miller, Marty Hughes, Howard Johnson, and Tommy Fitzhugh—and we ran all over the place together. We wound up playing basketball together eventually, all five of us starting on the same team in high school, but then we were just grade-school runners—the fastest in Philadelphia, if not the entire world, we thought.

When I was in the fourth grade, I was selected to run the anchor leg on the 300-yard shuttle in the 1946 Penn Relays. It was one of the first sports events ever telecast live, and all the other guys on my team were in the sixth grade, so you can imagine how proud I felt. One of the guys on the team was considered the fastest guy in our school, Georgia Brooks Elementary School, and I challenged him to a race and we ran from one end of the schoolyard to the other and back and finished in a dead heat.

I remember the fourth grade for another reason, too. I got pneumonia and almost died. I suppose if I had, it would've made life a little easier for a few NBA centers, but after slipping in and out of a coma for several months, I finally recovered. The bout with pneumonia was actually my second serious health problem. When I was two, I ruptured myself and had to have a hernia operation and wear a truss until I was five or six. Can you believe that? Going from diapers to a truss? There's supposed to be about 60 or 70 years between those two stages, isn't there?

I had another weird health problem as a kid—festering mosquito bites. I'd get them in the summers, when I'd go down to Virginia to visit my uncle on his farm, and my shins would

16

be red and raw, all the way from the ankle to the knee. My mother took me to clinic after clinic trying to find a cure, but none of the salves we tried did much to ease the pain—probably because I'd never give the sores much chance to heal. Between playing and working, they were always getting aggravated, and I can remember not being able to swim sometimes because the chlorine was so bad for the sores. I've got ugly scars on my shins from those bites now, and that's why I wear long socks and those huge knee pads when I play—the socks to cover the scars up, the knee pads to protect them from getting kicked. They don't bother me much anymore, but up until a few years ago, they'd really hurt in cold weather.

For all the lingering pain and discomfort of the mosquito bites, the pneumonia was clearly my most serious childhood disease, though. By the time I recovered, I'd lost a whole year of school, and I was back in the same grade as my sister Barbara, who was a year younger. But I was glad to be back, and the first thing I wanted to do when I got my strength back was start running. I even taught Barbara how to run. I'd grab her hand as soon as the school bell rang at the end of the day and practically drag her, running, all the way to our house. It wasn't a very good teaching technique, and I somehow suspect I'll never make much of a track coach, but Barbara sure as hell learned how to run fast. She got to be the fastest girl in school and I was the fastest boy, and we'd beat everyone around, individually and as a brother-and-sister team.

All that running did two things for me—it gave me stamina and it gave me speed. Later, when I became a pro, I was able to go the full 48 minutes almost every game, and lead my team in minutes played every year of my career (except 1969–70, when I hurt my knee and missed almost the entire season). I'm sure all the running I did as a kid for fun and in formal competition made that possible. You probably won't believe this, but I'm still pretty damn fast. I know it's hard to imagine a guy who stands seven feet tall and weighs close to 300 pounds being fast, but I do have a nine-foot stride, you know. Hell, I used to race all the quick little guards on the various pro teams I played for, and—except for Al Attles, who ran a dead-heat with me—I beat them all. I'd take a guy like Hal Greer and spot him the distance from the end

17

line to the free-throw line, and still beat him to the other end of the court. One time, I remember, while I was still a junior in college, Elgin Baylor and Oscar Robertson and I were in New York, and Elgin started riding me and Oscar about being "the slowest guys I've ever seen." Elg always loved to needle guys, so we didn't let it get to us for awhile, but finally I suggested we all have a race and see just who was slow and who wasn't. We were walking up Seventh Avenue, near 46th Street, and Elg said, "OK. I'll say 'Go,' and when I do, let's all take off." Well, Elg was a great basketball player, but he was no track star and he knew it. When he said "Go," me and Oscar took off, and Elg just stood there, laughing. I guess it was a pretty funny sight—two college students in coats and ties, Oscar about 6 foot 5 and me 7 foot, racing down the middle of Seventh Avenue in broad daylight. I whipped Oscar's ass, though. Really beat him. That was the last I ever heard about any racing from him or Elg. Another time, I even beat Jim Brown in a foot race once. No, twice—three times! It was at a party in Los Angeles one summer about ten or twelve years ago, and he came in and said something about how he had heard I was supposed to be fast and he was going to run me into the ground. I was dressed pretty well, wearing a suit, with a fine looking chick and all, so I wasn't hot for no foot race.

"You got your sneaks on, Jim. It wouldn't be fair," I told him.

He wouldn't give up. "Aw, Wilt, take your shoes off and run. You know you're nothing but a country boy anyway."

Well, I finally let him talk me into it, and we went out, and I took my shoes off, and the rest of the guests at the party —probably 100 people or so—came out to watch. We raced 40 yards, and I beat him by two yards. He couldn't believe it, man. He'd run the 100 in 9.6 or so in college, and there was no way I was that fast. So he said, "Let's go again." We did. He's really straining this time, but I beat him again—by about a yard. Well, it's just about killing poor Jim. "One more time," he says. We go again, and I win again—by inches—even though I step on a piece of glass and damn near cut my toe off just before I finish.

Jim walked away talking to himself—and my toe hurt so bad I couldn't get my shoe back on. I had to miss the rest of the damn party.

I could regale you with a few more tales of my winged size

14½ Ds, I suppose—things like racing Chet Walker through the streets of Rome in the summer of 1971—but I have a hunch you wouldn't be all that impressed, even if I had sworn affidavits that I'd beaten Jesse Owens and Bob Hayes in back-to-back 100-yard dashes. It's my seven feet in the air, not my two feet on the ground, that did the most to get me where I am today, so before I start talking in detail about my basketball career, it's about time to tell you a little of what it's like being seven feet tall.

3

ONE SUMMER, AFTER I'D started high school, I went down to Laneview, Virginia, where my father's brother had a farm. I was about 6 foot 11 then, and when one of the neighbors down there took me out driving, the people he'd stop and talk to would always point to me and say, "Pickett Nelson, Pickett Nelson." I heard that name practically all summer, and finally, one day, I asked him who Pickett Nelson was.

He sorta smiled and leaned back and said, "Well, I'll tell you, son. A few years back, 20, 30 years ago maybe, there was a man around here called Pickett Nelson, and I guess you kind of remind folks around here of him since you're so tall."

I asked him how tall Pickett Nelson was, and he said, "Oh, eight feet, maybe eight-and-a-half feet. He was really up there. In fact, that's how he got his name. We used to pick peaches around here as youngsters, to make spending money, and Nelson was so tall, he could just take his bushel basket and reach up and pull a limb of the tree down and shake those old peaches right into his basket.

20

grade and about five of us
trolley car barn I was tellir
cops. Our mothers had to
lecture, and—wouldn't yo
directed at me and my mot
that because I was the bigg
I was the youngest one th
the other guys wanted to

I'll admit I had a littl
to grow so fast. My legs h
for my body (I wear a 4
look pretty weird to som
and skinny. I can rememl
in Philadelphia, and havi
motion and everyone not
ment than the inconven
to this day.

For more than 20 ye
and smart-ass question
variety. It's something I
wise intelligent people
restaurant or on the stre
"Gee, you're sure tall."
of going up to an obvi
pounds, and say, "Ho
sure fat."

It really gets annc
walk in and right aw
everyone starts talkin;
6 foot 7" or "My bro
daughter dates a big,
sure as hell wouldn't
ance salesman who l
office."

I suppose the di
ugly, even nasty, bu
to be tall—or, at lea
advantages to being
—and, sure, I've ex

"It was a sight to behold, I tell you. People would come from miles around to watch him, and when they saw old Nelson start to work, they'd call out, 'Go ahead on, Nelson. Pick it, Nelson, pick it.' That's how he became Pickett Nelson, and I don't guess anyone 'round here even remembers his real first name."

So I said, "Pickett Nelson, huh? Wow, that's a groove. Where is he now?"

"No one knows. One morning, everyone looked around, and Pickett Nelson was gone. He'd just up and left. We went looking for him, you know. He lived down the road a piece, and he'd sleep on a mattress on the living room floor, with the front door open and his feet hanging outside because no room in the house was big enough for him. One morning, his mother came in to wake him up so he could go pick some peaches and he was gone. They never saw him again. But the folks around here thought of him when they saw you."

It was a great story, I thought, and I always wondered if the old guy made it up so I wouldn't feel self-conscious about those people pointing at me, or if there really had been a Pickett Nelson and just how tall he really was. Whatever, it was my first real introduction to the impact my size could have on people and the way they'd notice me immediately.

When I was real young, I remember hearing stories about my mother's grandfather, Jake, who was supposed to have been 6 foot 10 or 7 foot 2 or something like that. I never saw him or saw any pictures of him and I always half-suspected he never existed either. If I did inherit my height, though, it sure must have come from my mother's side of the family: she was 5 foot 9½, and my father was only 5 foot 8¾. One of my brothers, Wilbert, is 6 foot 5, but my other brother, Oliver, is barely 6 foot even. In fact, they'd both get mad sometimes when some guy about 5 foot 7 would say something to them about me, and then ask, "What happened to you?" Oliver finally took to saying, "I'm the youngest. They just ran out of inches by the time they got to me."

All my sisters were pretty normal size, too, except Selina, who was 5 foot 8½, and used to play basketball on the girls' teams in high school and the local church league.

I was 29 inch
inches—but I onl
just about average
career—hell, I o
kept growing all
the other kids, th
and . . . I was 6
school, but it w
I really started t
went down to
four inches in s
almost didn't r
the front door.

When peop
lot about the ir
the end of the
buying clothes
troublesome. I
end of the be
the time. Or h

I'll bet I
bangs his he
place with a
doorways, air
out of habit—
that I can af
by-nine-foot
with "norm
for me).

There a
larly when
your ability
I used to
old and I'c
for childre
weren't su
the ticket
to be olde

I also

reasoning that while it would be improper to ask the lady next door what size her bust is, it would be perfectly proper to ask the same question of Raquel Welch or Liz Taylor. Like me, they exploit and benefit from their natural assets. But I just don't think that's sufficient justification for a perfect stranger asking what amounts to a very personal question—whether it's height *or* bust size (or weight or age or salary, for that matter).

Besides, until we wrote this book, I really didn't know exactly how tall I was. I had myself measured specifically for this book. A doctor did the job, with me lying down (standing up, the human body tends to compress slightly), and I came out 7 feet 1 1/16 inches—exactly what I've been telling people for 15 years! (Now you won't have to ask me how tall I am if we ever meet.) That was actually the first time since high school that I'd been measured. People never believed me when I told them I didn't know exactly how tall I was, but I never really saw any sense in measuring myself. What good would it have done? What could I do about it? Someone who's overweight can diet or exercise to lose weight, so there's a good reason for them to want to check their weight periodically. But what was I supposed to do if I suddenly decided I didn't want to be 7 feet tall anymore? Cut my feet off, maybe? Chop my head off? Have a transplant surgeon graft my waist to my ankles?

At first, I just tried to ignore people when they'd ask their stupid questions. But I'm too garrulous a guy to just say nothing; I like to talk and joke and put people on. When someone asks how tall I am, I might say, "6 foot 13," and if someones says, "You must be a basketball player," I may shake my head gravely and say, "No, I'm a jockey." If I'm in a particularly good mood, I'll roll my eyes and gaze up at the heavens and say something like, "If you think I'm tall, you should see my brother."

One time when I was with the Globetrotters, a guy came up to all of us in the street, in Italy, and asked us if we were basket-ball players. Now, what else would a half-dozen big, black guys walking through Milano be? So I told the guy, "No, we're with Count Basie's band." And he said, "Oh, is he in town?" And I went on, rapping about the concert that night and how we hoped all the tickets would be sold and would he like to come as our guest and all.

I did something that was even more fun about a year later, in Toronto, when a traffic cop stopped a friend and me on our way to a football game and asked my friend if I was a basketball player. I shook my head and my friend said, "No, man, he's a wrestler—Juan El Gigante, Johnny the Giant. Haven't you ever heard of him?" The cop shook his head, so my friend kept putting it to him. "Yeah, he's the No. 1 wrestler in America. He's going to be on TV here in a couple of weeks." We damn near had that guy ready to buy a couple of ringside tickets for my next match.

It's amazing what people will believe—no matter how preposterous it sounds or how clearly it contradicts what they can see with their own eyes. Hell, just last season, in Phoenix, I was talking to two girls in a parking lot outside a nightclub, and one was saying I was 7 feet and the other said I couldn't be more than 6 foot 7 or 6 foot 8. I put on my best straight-face and told the second one, "You sure know your stuff. I'm 6 foot 7½." You should've seen the look of triumph she gave the other girl.

Sometimes—not often, but sometimes—a comment about my height will leave me speechless . . . like the time a drunk in San Francisco staggered by, took one look at me and backed away in terror, mumbling, "Please don't fall this way."

But I'm not always in a playful, pleasant mood when someone asks about my height. Maybe I'm tired or we just lost a game or maybe I'm just busy with another person. Then I can get snotty. If they ask, "How's the weather up there?" I'll snap, "The same as it is down there" or "Why don't you come up and find out." Or, if they just say, "God, you're big," I'll say, "Not nearly as big as your mouth."

One time I was with a friend in a restaurant in Philadelphia, and this little old lady came up to me and said, "Excuse me, son, how tall are you?" She was so polite about it, I told her. Then she got nasty. I tried to walk away from her, but she just kept ranting and raving and yelling, "You're a liar, you're a liar. You're at least 9 feet tall." People stopped eating and started looking around, and I got embarrassed and had to leave.

You get accustomed to things like that after a while, and you learn to consider the source and not let it bother you. But the cumulative impact of all these questions and comments about my height contributes to the general public stereotype of the big man as brainless goon or sideshow freak—and that's an insidious sort of thing that's virtually impossible to combat.

The press doesn't help any either. We've got a sports columnist on the *Los Angeles Times* named Jim Murray, and he has a quick wit and literary flair not common among sportswriters. But he doesn't always let facts get in the way of a good phrase. Sometimes I think he writes things just so he can read his own column the next morning and tell himself how clever he is. Here are just a few things he's written about me over the years:

> He was put together in a laboratory by a mad doctor with a pair of pliers, a screwdriver and a Bunsen burner. If you look close, you can see the bolts in the forehead. You don't feed it, you oil it, baby.

Another one:

> Even in summer, Wilt has snow on top. If he ever gets tired of basketball, he could rent himself out as a community antenna. To rush him to the hospital, you'd need a hook and ladder.

Another:

> Sir Edmund Hillary was introduced to Wilt, and promptly organized an expedition to climb it. . . .

I know Murray has a job to do, so I always tried not to get too upset. In 1971, when I had a party to open my new house, I even invited him. You know what he wrote the next day?

> It's not a house, it's a nursery rhyme in brick . . . The lord of the house should go around saying, "Fe, fi, fo, fum!" It's the kind of place you'd expect to see a lot of little kids in mouse hats riding plastic elephants. . . . The rooms are South American batcave.

He went on like that—a whole column full of lewd shit. Several prominent architects had spoken very highly of my house,

26

but here was this character who probably wouldn't know Frank Lloyd Wright from Flash Gordon repaying my courteous invitation by making fun of my house—and trying to make me look like a freak. Then the guy has the gall to come up to me in an airport and introduce his wife and son as "great fans of yours, just like me."

Maybe Murray's readers think he's hilarious, and maybe you think I'm too thin-skinned, but I've seen the subconscious effect that kind of writing can have on the general public. If I'm with a friend, for example, and a stranger wants to know how tall I am, he won't ask me; he'll ask the person I'm with. Even if there's just the stranger, my friend and me in an elevator, he'll ask my friend, not me. I'm sure part of that is because my size is so intimidating, but I really think he's primarily motivated by what I call the "freak factor"; subconsciously, he figures a big goon like me can't possibly have enough brains and coordination to chew gum and walk at the same time, much less answer an intricate, complex question like "How tall are you?" And people like Jim Murray help perpetuate that false impression. Hell, I've even had people show me quotations from literature with lines like, "Tall men are like houses of four stories, wherein commonly the uppermost room is worst furnished" or "Nature did never put her precious jewels into a garret four stories high, and therefore exceeding tall men had ever very empty heads."

I guess the main reason people have so much trouble accepting a 7-footer as just another guy, though, is that they have absolutely no way to relate to him. You can sit in your living room and watch Joe Namath throw touchdown passes on television and maybe fantasize yourself in his shoes. If you close your eyes for a few minutes and take an extra guzzle or two of beer, it's not too hard to see yourself wearing No. 12, prancing around in those white tennis shoes, flinging 60-yard passes downfield, winning the Super Bowl. But how are you gonna fantasize being 7 feet tall? You might be about Joe's size yourself. If not, you probably have guys that size for neighbors and friends and relatives. But how many of you are 7 feet tall—or even close to it? How many 7-foot friends and neighbors and brothers and cousins have you got? Hell, even Willie Shoemaker doesn't have my problem. At least everyone was his size once; they know what it's like to be small. They can remember the particular problems they had when they were that size. But there is just no way the average guy can envision what it's like being a 7-footer. And when that 7-footer is also black, rich, famous, and dominates his sport as no other man in history has dominated any sport, well, you can see how unique my situation is and how difficult it is for people to relate to me. Since ignorance breeds discomfort, people take the easy way out; they mask their ignorance and assuage their discomfort by thinking of me—and treating me—as an aberration, a walking abnormalcy, a goon, a freak.

The nickname I picked up in high school, "Wilt the Stilt," is part of that image; it makes me sound like an attraction in a carnival sideshow—and not a very good one at that. Jack Ryan, a sportswriter back in Philadelphia, hung that one on me when I first started playing basketball, but I didn't like it and none of my friends ever use it. All my friends and my brothers and sisters called me "Dip" or "Dippy." They still do. They never call me "Wilt." Even my sister Barbara's little boy calls me "Uncle Dip." A kid in the neighborhood where we grew up gave me that name. He had nicknames for everyone—names like "Bruno" and "Hiker" and "Brother" and "Noblehead." Some of the names were logical, others were just nonsensical. Mine was logical—I was so tall, I had to dip under things. In time, "Dip" and "Dippy" evolved into "Dipper" and "Big Dipper," and I always kind of liked that —or its Latin equivalent, *Ursa Major*. That's the name I have on my boat and my house. It has a special ring to it, a certain beauty and power and grace and majesty—and it represents something real, enduring, eternal. It's not just a nursery rhyme reference to my height or some inanimate object. It tells a story. It's bigger than life itself. I just think it fits me far better than "Wilt the Stilt."

As you can see, I feel pretty damn strongly about this whole height question. But I don't want to give you the idea that I'm unhappy being 7 feet tall. I'm not. I'm only distressed by those who make such a big deal out of it, using it to intrude on my privacy and demean and degrade my dignity as a human being.

One sportswriter was writing a few years ago about some of my frustrations and ambitions, and he said, "He wants, when you come right down to it, to be 6 feet tall." Nothing could be further

28

from the truth. Given a choice, I wouldn't be any other height —except maybe 7 foot 4. Being tall has been fun. When I was a kid, I always found work easily because my height made me look older than I was. And my height enabled me to play all kinds of jokes on my brothers and sisters—like pretending I could see their Christmas presents hidden on the top shelf of the bedroom closets. Every year, I'd tell them about these incredibly fancy presents they were getting—black patent leather shoes and new coats and expensive toys—and they'd always believe me, right up to Christmas Day. Then I'd do the same thing again the next year.

Clothes look better on tall men, too, and I like good clothes. And girls, well, girls just fucking freak out over really tall guys for some reason, and I'm sure my height has played as great a role in my success with the ladies as my brilliant mind, my rapier-like wit, my devilish good looks, my color, my reputation—and my money.

My height has been primarily responsible for my success in life and I know that. Oh, sure, if I were 6 foot 2, I might have made a few millions dollars as a Philadelphia lawyer—which I always wanted to be—or as a race car driver or stockbroker or football star. But that's all conjecture. I owe almost everything I have now to basketball, and it's damn certain I wouldn't have all this if I were a 6 foot 2 basketball player. It's not that I lacked the skills to make it as a guard (more on that later). It's just that I probably wouldn't even have considered going into basketball if I were that small. It wasn't even my idea to play basketball in the first place. I told you—I was a runner. I was going to be an Olympic Games track champion. But when I got to junior high school, the kids started razzing me and saying, "Man, as tall as you are, you should play basketball."

Frankly, I always thought basketball was a sissy game. I'd watch my brother Wilbert and his friends pick up stones and play like they were hooking them into a basket, or I'd see kids play in the schoolyard, and it just didn't seem like a very physical game to me. It wasn't like running or playing football, and I just wasn't very interested in it. The kids kept on me, though, and I finally decided to give basketball a try, just to get them off my back. So these friends I told you about—Vince and Marty and Tommy and Howard—and me started to fool around with a basketball.

29

We didn't have a real track at our junior high or anywhere close by, so that was added incentive to find something else competitive to do, and basketball was it. We'd run from house to house picking each other up after school every day. Then we'd run to the basketball court and play until dark, run home for dinner, and run back and play some more inside. During the summer, sometimes we'd just lock ourselves in the gym and play all day. Once I tried to play at home in the basement, but I broke up the plumbing, and it cost us $85 to fix it, so we usually played at Haddington Recreation Center, a few blocks from my house. We'd also play kids from other parts of the city in their play-grounds, and after about a year, basketball was the most important thing in our lives, and we all vowed we'd play together in high school, at Overbrook. We played instead of working, and I played in school leagues, church leagues, and the Police Athletic League. Paul Arizin, who was already a star with the Philadelphia Warriors, had played in the PAL. So had Tom Gola and Hal Lear and Guy Rodgers, and they were all college all-Americans by then. There were still some hellaciously good players in PAL, most of them much older and far more experienced than me, and playing against them really hastened my development as a basketball player. It was either that or get eaten alive.

I had college and pro scouts looking at me by the time I was in the ninth grade, and some people from West Catholic High School, a perennial high school powerhouse in Philadelphia, tried to convince me to go there, even though I was a Baptist. Another Catholic high school, St. Thomas More, gave me my first taste of high-power, big-money recruiting tactics. They offered to pay my bus fare and give me lunch money if I'd enroll there. But I decided to go to the public high school in my area, Overbrook, and my first year there I was picked to be on the Philadelphia YMCA team that went to High Point, North Carolina, for the YMCA national championships.

When my team, the Christian Street "Y," won the championship, three guys on the team were named YMCA all-Americans. Two of us, me and Claude Gross, were the only high school guys on the all-American team—everyone else was already in college—so you can imagine how proud we were. But that same year, Claude's high school team, Benjamin Franklin, beat Overbrook.

To show you what a kind-hearted fellow I am and how I don't hold grudges, I should tell you that a few years later, I let Claude marry my sister Selina. Well, I guess I didn't really have much to say about it, one way or the other. But they did get married. And they're still married. (I was even best man at the wedding.)

Overbrook lost only one other game my first year—to West Catholic, in the city championship game, after we'd already won the public school championship. West Catholic put four guys on me almost the whole game, and I still got something like 29 points. But my teammates couldn't capitalize on being left wide-open most of the time, so we lost, 54-42. I found out later that the West Catholic coach had his team practice for us by having one guy stand on a chair in the center position, near the free-throw line, with four guys swarming all around him on defense. It was typical of what I'd encounter so often the rest of my high school and, particularly, my college career—special ganging defenses that climbed and pushed and shoved and just plain surrounded me and virtually ignored my teammates.

I think that's one of the reasons I developed this habit of holding the ball in one hand and really smacking it against my other hand when I came down with a rebound. It sounded like a gunshot, and it gave me a sense of power, of fighting back against these guys who were harassing me. I guess I was like some cavalry captain with just a few men in a fort being besieged by thousands of Indians, shooting off his cannon in the middle of the night at no one in particular. In a sense, I was saying, "This is my kingdom; stay out." I did the same thing then when I blocked shots; I just swatted them as hard as I could, solely for the psychological effect of the sound and sight of it. My coach, Cecil Mosenson, didn't teach me that you should pass the ball out quickly on rebounds, not waste time banging it in your palm, or that you should try to keep shots in-bounds when you block them, to give your teammates a chance to get the ball, so I just went my merry way, smacking the ball on rebounds and knocking it into the bleachers on blocked shots. I don't imagine Coach Mosenson really knew what to make of me anyway. You should've seen the look on his face the first time I dunked the ball. Remember, this was almost 20 years ago, and hardly anyone was dunking then. It wasn't the status thing it is now, when even 6 foot 1 guards try to do it. Hell,

31

my first dunk was just an accident. I got the ball on a fast-break and I was too close to the basket to shoot, so I just jumped up and jammed it in, without realizing just what I was doing. The crowd went crazy, and the old coach looked like I'd just jumped through the basket myself, feet first.

My three years at Overbrook were tremendously exciting, particularly once the college and pro scouts started coming to watch me play, and all the sportswriters started saying I was already better than George Mikan of the Lakers and Tom Gola, the LaSalle all-American. I scored 32 points in my first varsity game, and averaged about 30 for the whole year. As I said, we won 20 games and lost just 2, winning the public school championship, but losing the city championship to West Catholic.

Catholic schools had dominated city basketball in Philadelphia since before World War II, and with me just a sophomore, we were still a pretty inexperienced team. But in my junior year, we went undefeated 20 straight games and won both the public school and city championships, and I averaged 37.3 points per game. When I was a senior, we lost just one game—59-58 in a Christmas tournament—and again won the public school and city championships.

In three years, we won 58 and lost 3, and I scored 2,252 points (a 36.9 average) to break Tom Gola's state scoring record. (Gola, then an all-American at LaSalle and later a teammate of mine on the Philadelphia Warriors, had set his record in four years.) I could have scored even more, but we usually won by such lopsided scores that the coach took me out after about 20 or 25 minutes. We'd win by scores like 90-39, 94-38, 127-59, 113-58, and the coach didn't see any reason to pour it on, so he'd pull me and the other starters. Hell, I scored 74 points in one game and played only 24 minutes. (High school games are just 32 minutes anyway. Colleges play 40 minutes, the pros 48 minutes.) I scored more than 40 points 22 times. My senior year, I averaged 50 points for our first 16 games—a total of 800 points, just 12 less than the combined total of all our opponents in those games.

A lot of teams tried to stall on us, so I couldn't embarrass them by scoring so many points, but I still had some wild games—61 points once, 71, 73, 74, 90. The 90-point game was really unbelievable, and I still get a kick out of joking about it with friends 'cause they never believe me. Just last season, in Omaha, I was jivin' in the locker room with the Lakers about that game, and everyone was laughing; it just didn't sound possible the way I told it.

It was in my senior year, against Roxborough, and for some reason I'd always scored well against them. In my freshman year, I tied the state record by getting 71 points against them. When we played them in my junior year, I got 74 to break the record. Then, as a senior, I got the 90—and I got 60 of those points in about 10 minutes . . . *even though Roxborough was holding the ball and stalling!*

I scored 26 points in the first half, despite sitting out almost three minutes, and when I got a couple of more baskets early in the third quarter, the fans started screaming for me to break my record. We were way ahead, so my teammates started feeding me. That's when Roxborough started holding the ball, just passing it around, not taking any shots. They didn't want me to break the record again, and they didn't want Overbrook to humiliate them. They failed on both counts. We won, 123-21, and I scored 31 points in the third quarter (27 of them in the last four or five minutes) and 33 points in the fourth quarter (before I was taken out of the game with more than two minutes to play). I hit 36 of 41 from the field and 18 of 26 from the free-throw line, and I think I also got about 40 rebounds.

There were a lot of other games when I got about two-thirds of my team's points, too, and that gave some people, particularly outside Philadelphia, the idea that I was a one-man team. They'd see wire service stories with me getting 46 of Overbrook's 75 points or 48 of our 78, and automatically assume I was playing with a bunch of stiffs. But that wasn't true. We had several other good players—including my four friends, Vince and Marty and Tommy and Howard. Like we vowed in the eighth grade, we all went to Overbrook and all of us were starters my senior year.

Vince, in particular, was a great player. He was a forward, about 6 foot 5, and he could really shoot and rebound. In our city championship game my senior year, we slaughtered West Catholic, 83-42—the first time they'd ever lost a city championship game; I scored 35 and Vince got 31. Marty was probably the most popular guy on the team, though. He was 5 foot 8½, a slick ball-handler and fancy dribbler, a damn good guard. But he wasn't nearly as good a player as Vince, and I guess that was my first lesson in what I later came to call my "Nobody roots for Goliath" theory.

Though Vince was well liked by his teammates and fellow students and most of the fans, it was Marty who became the darling of just about everyone. I—and, to a lesser extent, Vince—were Goliaths in a society that is composed predominantly of Davids. I didn't see it in those terms then, of course, but as time passed, it helped explain why players like Marty and Gail Goodrich and Jerry West are so popular with the fans, while guys like me and Kareem Abdul-Jabbar get booed.

Part of the small guy's appeal is that he's playing what has increasingly become a big man's game. That's probably one reason so many girls in Los Angeles tell me how "cute" Gail is. But, more than that, the fan—as I said earlier—can identify with the shorter players; he can vicariously experience the little guy's triumphs over us big brutes. So he starts out rooting for the little guy, and then—subtly at first, but with mounting fervor—he begins rooting against the Goliaths, even booing and jeering us.

It's interesting to see how the press responds to this dichotomy. Often, they start saying the big guy is even bigger than he really is, and the small guy is even smaller than he really is. They'll say Kareem must be 7 foot 4 or 7 foot 5, instead of 7 foot 2, for example, but they'll slowly whittle Elgin Baylor's height down from 6 foot 6 to 6 foot 5 to 6 foot 4. That makes Kareem's accomplishments seem that much less significant ("after all, he's so tall, he should be able to score") and Elgin's accomplishments that much more significant ("he's so short; I don't see how he scores all those points against those big guys").

Because of this David-and-Goliath situation, players like Kareem tend to be branded with grossly inaccurate stereotypes. People assume that because he's the tallest player in the league, he must be the best rebounder—and a poor shooter. In actuality, Kareem is a fine shooter, with a soft, delicate touch. But he isn't nearly as good a rebounder as he should be. He's good, all right, maybe great, but not as great as Nate Thurmond or Bill Russell or a few other guys.

I've had even more misinformation circulated about me in this regard. A lot of sportwriters have insisted I'm 7 foot 3 or 7 foot 4. One guy in Philadelphia, Jack Kiser, a good friend as well as a good sportswriter, has always referred to me in print as 7 foot 3, no matter what I told him. So, for years, people said all I could do was score from in close. They said I couldn't play defense or handle the ball or shoot from the outside. Then, when I led the league in assists with the Philadelphia 76ers in 1968, people started talking about the "new" Wilt Chamberlain, as if—at the age of 32—I suddenly learned to do something I'd never done before . . . and did it so well I beat such brilliant, career-long ball-handlers as Oscar Robertson, Guy Rodgers, Jerry West, and Lennie Wilkens for the assist title. Four years later, when the Lakers won the championship, the same thing happened all over again. My primary responsibility on the Lakers was defense, so all of a sudden, people discovered I could play defense and block shots. But I'd been blocking shots and passing off ever since I began playing basketball. It's just that no one noticed those things as long as I was scoring 40 or 50 points a game. Scoring is the most exciting part of basketball for the average fan, and if someone scores like I did, the fan isn't likely to pay much attention to anything else.

I remember one game in my senior year at Overbrook when I decided I'd been scoring too many points, so I passed off almost every time I got the ball. I scored only 16 points, but I had about 20 assists, and we won, 93-56. Even when I was scoring more, though, I was also passing off. And I was always a good outside shot. I still am, for that matter. Bill Sharman has a game called "21" he has the Lakers play in practice. It's three-on-three, with the first team to hit 21 baskets the winner. You have to shoot from 18 to 22 feet out—and the losers have to run three laps. Well, I was almost always on the winning team, no matter how the teams were organized. One week last season, we played "21" ten times, and I was on the winning team in all ten—even though we changed the teams around after every game.

I'll be the first to admit that I wouldn't be a great outside shooter under game conditions now; I haven't done it for too long. Oh, sure, I could take two or three outside shots a game, but you don't hit a very good percentage if you shoot that infrequently. To keep your eye and your touch, you have to take at least 10 or 15 outside shots a game, and if I did that, I'd just hurt my team. I'm supposed to be under the boards for rebounds and follow-shots. That's what I'm paid for. And I can't very well do that if I'm in the corner or at the top of the key shooting one-handers.

But when I did shoot regularly from outside, in high school and college, I could really hit. In fact, my high school coach always said my jump shot from the foul line was my best shot; some of the national sportswriters who came to Philadelphia to see me play back then said the same thing. There was a story in *Sport* magazine, during my senior year at Overbrook, that said:

> He has basic court savvy, he can hit with a one-hander from the corner . . . or with a two-handed set from the outside. He passes well out of the pivot, learns and develops quickly and thinks in sound basketball terms.

(This past spring, during the NCAA championship game on television, they showed film clips of some present-day pro stars back when they played for the NCAA championship. Some Laker fans were astounded to see skinny old Wilt dribbling the full length of the court, leading the fast break, and whipping a behind-the-back pass to another guy for a lay-up. They were also amazed to see me hitting jump shots from the top of the key.)

I think one reason I was able to do all those things was that I continued running track, even after I became a basketball star. Running and high jumping and putting the shot in high school helped immeasurably with the timing and coordination and judgment necessary to be a good playmaker or shooter or rebounder —or anything else—in basketball. I high-jumped about 6-6 and put the shot about 47 feet for my high school team, and ran the 440 in 48.6 and the 880 in 1:58.6 for the local AAU team. My senior year, after we won the city basketball championship, I was the only double winner in the public school championship track meet, taking firsts in the high jump and the shot put.

Track always was more fun for me than basketball, and one of the things I always liked to do in a meet was wait till everyone else had jumped or put the shot before I'd even take my first turn. I'd just tell the guy running the high jump competition to let me know when everyone had taken their best jumps, "then put the bar up another inch or two and I'll jump." I'd do the same thing with the shot—wait till everyone had all their puts, then go out and win the event with one throw.

I didn't have much competition in track, but I had all I could handle in basketball—and that's really what helped me develop and polish my skills at such an early age. I'd play in every game I could find. Men in Philadelphia like Bill Berry and a Mr. O'Farrell started their own amateur leagues, financed out of their own pockets, just to give young boys like me a chance to play ball and stay out of trouble. I played in those leagues and in the PAL and the Narbeth League and the AAU, and I played almost every day in schoolyard pickup games. Some of the best basketball players in the country have come out of the West Philadelphia schoolyards, you know. In my neighborhood alone, one high school—Overbrook—got guys like Walt Hazzard (now Abdul Rahman), who led UCLA to its very first NCAA championship and played last season with the Golden State Warriors; Wali Jones, who formerly starred with the Philadelphia 76ers and Milwaukee Bucks; Wayne Hightower, an all-American at Kansas and later a star with the San Francisco Warriors; Jackie Moore, an all-American at LaSalle and later a star with the world champion Philadelphia Warriors; and, of course, myself.

I remember going down to Washington, D.C., too, to play against the best high school players there (including Elgin Baylor), and going to New York during my senior year at Overbrook for a game between the Philadelphia high school all-stars and the New York high school all-stars. (Philadelphia won, of course—94-85; I got 51 points.)

But my stiffest competition usually came during the summers, when I played up at Kutsher's Country Club in the Catskills, the so-called "Borscht Belt" of mostly Jewish-owned resorts in the mountains, about 100 miles north of New York City. Haskell Cohen, the public relations man for the NBA, had seen me play at Overbrook, and he got me a job at Kutsher's as a bell-hop (for $26.00, plus tips, every two weeks). When I wasn't working, I was

37

playing on the hotel basketball team, with—and against—some of the top college and professional stars in the country.

One of the top pro stars up there was Neil Johnston, who led the NBA in scoring all three years I was in high school. I don't think Neil took too kindly to having a skinny high school kid outplay him game after game in two-on-two scrimmages, with all those people watching, and that may help explain why he and I didn't get along particularly well five or six years later when I joined the NBA myself. Who was my first NBA coach? Right. Neil Johnston.

I can't take all the credit for outplaying Neil, of course. I had some help from my teammates. And we had a pretty good coach at Kutsher's. Fellow named Red Auerbach. He came to Kutsher's from Boston almost every summer, and he really worked us, boy. I wanted to do a lot of different things up there—practice the shot, ride horses, fool around some, make some money toting bags. But old Red always kept on me to practice—usually during the hottest part of the day, too, right after I got through working five or six hours as a bell-hop. About the only time Red didn't talk basketball to me was when he was playing poker. I always serviced the games —bringing them water and cards and drinks—and Red would usually give me a $5 or $10 tip. I could usually tell whether he'd won or lost by how hard he'd make us practice afterward—and by how much he'd needle me about how good some of the other guys playing in the Catskills were and how they were going to really show me something when we played against them. Once he had this guy from Oregon coming in—his No. 1 draft choice with the Celtics for the next year—and he kept telling me how this guy, Chet Noe, was going to teach me a lesson. Sure enough, Chet came in one day and we scrimmaged. Poor Chet. Poor Red. Poor Celtics. I moved his ass out like he was in high school and I was the No. 1 draft choice. I scored over, under, around, and through him, and blocked so many of his shots, he must have thought I was the backboard. Chet never did make the NBA. (In all honesty, I must admit I don't think Red ever missed him. The Celtics got another pretty good college center a year or two later . . . Bill Russell.)

Red didn't let my performance against Chet stop him from

38

riding me, and he must have spent three or four weeks warning me about one of our upcoming opponents, Shawanga Lodge, and their star, B. H. Born. "I think it is only fair to tell you, Chamberlain, that B. H. Born has just made all-American from the University of Kansas, and B. H. Born is going to make chopped chicken liver out of you."

Well, in the first half of the game against Shawanga, I scored 26 points off B. H. Born. He got two points off me. I was really feeling cocky when I came back to the dressing room at halftime, and I sort of strolled in and flopped myself down on the training table, with my arms folded behind my head, and started whistling and looking sideways at old Red. He just glared at me for what seemed like ten minutes. Then he grinned a little and said, "Now, Mister Chamberlain, may I please have your attention for a moment. We do have a second half to play, even if *you* seem to think the game is all over." He was right. I was riding on a cloud, and I don't really remember much about the second half, except that we won and I wound up with 45 or 50 points and B. H. wound up with six or eight.

Later, Red talked to me about my future.

"You've got pretty good grades, don't you?"

I said I did—about a B average, taking French, algebra, trig, the geometries, statistics, and some business courses. As a young kid, thrilled with horseback riding and visits to my uncle's farm in Virginia, I'd always said I wanted to be a farmer. Now, in high school, I was trying to decide between business and law school.

"Why don't you go to Harvard when you get out of high school?" Red asked me.

It took me a minute to understand. Then I remembered the NBA had a territorial draft rule that gave every pro team first choice among all the college players within 50 miles of its home base. Foxy old Red. If I'd go to Harvard, he could exercise Boston's territorial draft rights to get me for the Celtics.

But before I got out of high school, Eddie Gottlieb, the owner of the Philadelphia Warriors, pushed through a rules change, permitting teams to use their territorial draft rights on high school players, too. The new rule—like so many I would later encounter in college—had been clearly intended to apply to only one person

. . . Wilton Norman Chamberlain. So, when I was still at Over-brook, the Warriors drafted me. Good-bye, Harvard. Good-bye, Boston. Good-bye, Red.

But B. H. Born had been impressed by my play, too, and he wrote his coach at Kansas about me, and they started scouting me and recruiting me almost immediately.

4

OMEONE AT OVERBROOK WHO
kept track of such things once told me there were more than 200
colleges and universities after me by my senior year—77 "major"
schools and 128 "minor" schools. It got so bad, with all the recruiters coming to town and wanting me to come visit them, that
I had to turn the whole thing over to my high school coach, Cecil
Mosenson. Even so, the pressure became unbearable. I guess I
was the first of the big, black, high school superstars, and everyone—recruiters, coaches, fans, everyone—was new to this kind of
chase. By the time guys like Elvin Hayes and Sidney Wicks and
Artis Gilmore and Bob Lanier and, especially, Lew Alcindor (as
he was then known) came along, the coaches and recruiters all
knew what to say and how to act; it made things easier for the
guys who followed me. But with me, everyone was still experi-
menting, feeling their way, learning a new game, and I was the
unwitting—but not unwilling—guinea pig.

In the beginning, I'll admit, it was a lot of fun. It seemed like
every college in the country wanted to fly me to their campus for
a weekend to see their gym and meet their coach and tour their
city. I had offers from damn near every state in the union—plus

41

Hawaii, which wasn't even a state yet. Alphabetically, the schools ranged from Arizona State to Xavier of Ohio. Geographically, well, I had offers from the West (UCLA, University of San Francisco, Washington State), the Midwest (Michigan State, Purdue, Ohio State), the South (Florida, North Carolina, Oklahoma), the East (Temple, Holy Cross, St. Joseph's)—everywhere, anywhere, you name it.

I took my first trip—to Dayton—when I was in the tenth grade, and by my senior year at Overbrook, I was just about the best customer the Philadelphia Airport ever had. It got so everyone there—the ticket agents, the stewardesses, the janitors—all got to know me and expect to see me come in every Friday night and return every Sunday night. The alumni would send their tickets down to the airport, and I and, sometimes, Coach Mosenson would pick them up and take off. When we got to each city, some alums would be waiting for us at the airport to take us to dinner and give us the grand tour and, if possible, take us to see their team play.

I remember one sportswriter, Jim Enright in Chicago, who also officiated at basketball games, telling me he saw me so often, at so many different college games, he thought I was a fan of his, following him around. On successive weekends, he said, he saw me at Dayton, Cincinnati, Illinois, and Indiana.

We had several college basketball powers right in Philadelphia, in the Big Five, of course, and a lot of people assumed I'd enroll in one of them—St. Joseph's, Penn, Villanova, Temple, or LaSalle. Jackie Moore, a hotshot at Overbrook a few years before me, had gone to LaSalle, so some sportswriters figured it would be natural for me to follow him. Tom Gola, another Philadelphia schoolboy star, had also gone there. But I wanted to get out of Philadelphia. I thought it was time I got away from home, on my own, and going to college—the first really big decision of my life—would provide the opportunity to do just that.

I ruled out the Pacific Coast, right from the start. I was convinced they didn't really play good basketball out there, despite the back-to-back NCAA championships USF had won in 1955 and 1956. I was wrong, of course—stupidly, horribly wrong, as John Wooden and UCLA have since proven so clearly and incontrovertibly.

42

I didn't much want to play in the South either. This was 1955, man. I didn't want the Ku Klux Klan burning any crosses in my chest. In fact, I was surprised by all the letters I got from Deep South schools who said they had heard all about me, but obviously didn't know I was black. Jesus Christ, can you see Alabama or Georgia or Mississippi offering me a scholarship back then if they knew I was black? Sheee-it! That was seven years *before* ole Ross Barnett damn near started another Civil War, just because one black man, James Meredith, wanted to enroll at the University of Mississippi. I can imagine what those cats would've done to *me*. I probably would have been shipped back to Philadelphia in pieces—if anyone could find the pieces. No, thanks. I wasn't about to be a big, brave—dead—pioneer.

I remember one time the coach from Missouri, Wilbur Stalcup, met me at the airport in Kansas, trying to cut in on the Kansas recruiters. Like all other recruiters, he spent half his time telling me how great he was and how influential his friends were and all. Then he put on his best Abraham Lincoln face and said, "Boy, how'd you like to be the first Negro to play at the University of Missouri?"

Well, I put on my best William Buckley face and told him, as drolly as an unsophisticated 17-year-old could manage, "I think I'd rather be the second one."

Actually, I'd decided fairly early that I wanted to go to college in the Midwest. All through my teenage years, I'd heard that's where they played the best basketball in the country, and I wanted to play with—and against—the best. Two Midwest schools that rushed me the hardest were among the first I rejected—Notre Dame and Michigan State. I just figured they put too much emphasis on football, and I wasn't the least bit interested in playing second fiddle to some musclebound dudes who ran around in shoulder pads and helmets, grunting and hitting each other.

When you get right down to it, I really only considered four schools seriously—Michigan, Indiana, Dayton, and Kansas. After two weekend trips to Ann Arbor, I eliminated Michigan, for much the same reason I had eliminated Michigan State and Notre Dame —football.

For a while then, Indiana was the frontrunner. It had a great basketball tradition, and there were a couple of sensational high school kids who had already enrolled there. "If you come too, Wilt, we'll go undefeated for three years," the Indiana recruiters told me. Indiana had something else going for it as well. Two friends—Wally Choice, a basketball player, and Milt Campbell, a football player and decathlon man—were already at Indiana, and they both told me they were very happy there.

I'm not exactly sure why I ruled out Indiana, but I suspect the first seeds of my disenchantment were planted by a few members of their own basketball team. They told me the coach, Branch McCracken, didn't make all the important decisions—his wife did. Somehow, I just couldn't see myself playing for a woman coach. I mean, how could she possibly know a pick-and-roll from a box-and-one? And how could I tell her I'd lost my jockstrap? Hell, I wouldn't even know what to call her . . . "Mrs. Coach"? "Coach-ess"? "Coachita"?

I'd also heard some disturbing rumors that McCracken wasn't all that fond of blacks, so even when his recruiters relayed word, through Wally Choice, that they would double whatever Kansas offered me, I decided against Indiana. (Later on, after I enrolled at Kansas, Coach McCracken went around making nasty cracks about how I would've come to Indiana "but we couldn't afford him." Wasn't that a laugh!)

Anyway, with Indiana down, that left Dayton and Kansas. Dayton tried hard. So did the whole state of Ohio. One wealthy alum told me he'd like to see me go to Dayton, but he'd take care of me just the same if I went to Ohio State or Cincinnati. You wouldn't believe the offers Dayton made me. They had to be kind of vague about them, of course, because the NCAA was acutely aware of how much all these colleges wanted me. No matter where I finally enrolled, there was sure to be a big investigation, so the recruiters had to be careful what they said.

They told me just enough to let me know money would be no object, but not enough to incriminate themselves should the NCAA bloodhounds start asking questions—which they did, even before I left Overbrook. I spent four hours with one NCAA official, answering his questions about what Dayton had offered me. Because the recruiters had been so calculatingly circumspect, I could honestly answer that all they'd offered me was what the NCAA allowed—tuition, room, board, and $15 a month spending money.

But they'd hinted at much, much more—like $100 a week or so spending money, a new car, and a job, as well as a new home for my parents. That was about par for most of the big schools that came after me—and the "jobs" they said they'd give me were a real riot. A school in Southern California or the Southwest would say they'd pay me to shovel snow off the president's lawn; a school in the middle of the farm country would say they'd pay me to keep seaweed out of the football stadium; a school in the middle of a big city would say they'd pay me to see that no mountain-climbing equipment got mixed up with the basketball uniforms.

Surprisingly, with all the basketball games I saw on my recruiting trips to the various colleges, I can only remember one. It was at Dayton, and they had a seven-foot center named Bill Ewell, who was typical of the early seven-footers in basketball, players like Swede Halbrook, Charlie Share, and Larry Faust—big but clumsy, barely able to jump out of their own way, not at all able to pass or shoot. I've always thought it was kind of stupid to measure basketball players by head-to-toe height anyway. There are a lot of tall guys, like Ewell and Dukes and Halbrook and a lot of others, who just aren't much good. They ought to list reach as well as height—like they do with boxers. If you have long arms and can jump well, you can compensate for four to six inches in height easily. I'm a couple of inches taller than Nate Thurmond, but his arms are longer than mine; I'm five inches taller than Connie Hawkins, but our arms are about the same size, and his hands are actually bigger than mine. Even some little guys—Jerry West is one—have such disproportionately long arms that it's really misleading to think of them as being small, just as it's misleading to assume any seven-footer will automatically be good. I remember thinking, when I saw Ewell on that trip to Dayton, "Boy, if Dayton thinks he's good, wait till they see me play."

Only they never did get to see me.

What finally soured me on Dayton was my sudden realization that I'd encounter severe racial prejudice there. I'd grown up in an ethnic neighborhood—black, Jewish, and Italian—and I'd never really seen much discrimination as a kid. In fact, I can only remember one "incident," and that was when I was three or four and I got on the bus to come from Virginia to Philadelphia with my mother and she wouldn't let me sit in the front of the bus. I kept

45

saying, "No, mama, this seat right here is open," and she'd keep trying to steer me to the back. Finally, the driver had to come over and say, "No, sonny, you go back there with your mother like a good little boy."

By the time I got to college, I knew about the KKK and the lynch mobs down South and all, but I was unbelievably naive about the more subtle forms of discrimination in the North (and South); when I went to Dayton on a recruiting trip and they fixed me up with a fancy hotel room and told me I could order all my meals from room service, I had no idea they were trying to hide me and keep me from finding out I couldn't get served in the hotel dining room—or any other restaurant in town. I've probably had 9,000 meals from room service now, and I'll be just as happy if I never have another one, but that was one of my first opportunities to try it, and I thought it was a pretty big deal. I had a ball, calling up and ordering damn near everything on the menu and not having to pay for any of it.

When I told recruiters from other schools about my room service splurge, they fell all over themselves telling me what it really meant. They were, understandably, only too happy to tell me things that would cut down another school. So, scratch Dayton. That left Kansas.

Dr. Forrest C. Allen—Phog Allen, as he was known—had been head coach at Kansas since 1920, and he was a legend in American college basketball. He'd won almost 600 games (and lost only about 200) and he'd won 22 conference championships and one national championship. Just about everyone agreed he was one of the greatest coaches in history. He'd forgotten more about basketball than most coaches would ever know. But Dr. Allen was more than a master strategist; he was a brilliant psychologist, too, and he was just as effective at recruiting kids as he was at coaching them. He visited me and my family in Philadelphia, and my mother just flat fell in love with him. He was kind and courteous and considerate, and he didn't come on strong with how important and influential he was, and he talked about my academic program, not just basketball.

Dr. Allen was also smart enough to play the black angle for all it was worth. He had several prominent blacks visit our home to extol the virtues of an education at Kansas. There was Dowdal

Davis, general manager of a black newspaper, the Kansas City *Call,* Etta Moten, a concert singer who was fairly well known back then, and Lloyd Kerfords, a wealthy Kansas industrialist. They all told me I could help the black man by attending Kansas—and they said they were living proof that Kansas could help me.

Needless to say, I was impressed. When I saw the campus, in Lawrence, and the big, new fieldhouse they were just finishing, I was even more impressed. The calls and letters and visits from Kansas officials and alums kept coming. Kansas, they reminded me, had a rich basketball heritage; Dr. James Naismith, the man who invented the game of basketball, had been Kansas' first basketball coach, around the turn of the century. I would be happy at Kansas, they said; I would get a good education, play for the best basketball coach in America *and* be going to a perennial track powerhouse.

On May 14, 1955, I announced my decision: I would go to Kansas on a basketball and track scholarship.

Then the roof fell in. The NCAA wanted to talk to me. So did the FBI. And the IRS. Even the press jumped on me. One guy wrote:

> Why would a boy from Philadelphia, with five of the best basketball schools in the country just a short ride from his house, decide to fly half way across the United States to go to college . . . unless he was getting paid plenty to do it?

Another writer, Lenny Lewin, in New York, was even more skeptical and snotty. He wrote:

> I feel sorry for The Stilt. When he enters the NBA four years from now, he'll have to take a cut in salary.

Everyone was convinced I was getting half of Fort Knox to play for Kansas. I was grilled and badgered and hounded and cross-examined like I was some rapist or murderer. During one all-day meeting in Kansas City, they deliberately tried to trick me and confuse me by asking me the same questions over and over, worded just a shade differently each time. But I told them all the same thing:

"I'm getting a scholarship for tuition, room, and board, plus $15 a month for laundry and incidentals."

47

They couldn't shake my story, and when I left, the guy in charge of the interrogation told me:

"It was nice talking to you, but I don't believe a word of it."

Neither did I.

The big rumor in those days was that wealthy Kansas alums had put up a $30,000 slush fund to be turned over to me when I graduated, and the NCAA asked me a lot about that. I told them, quite honestly, that just wasn't true. And it wasn't. The figure was probably less than $20,000. And it wasn't a slush fund. The arrangement was that once I was a sophomore, playing for the varsity, I'd get spending money whenever I needed it. No specific sums were mentioned. That's why I was able to tell the NCAA what I did. The alums gave me a few names, and said, "Go see these guys when you need a few bucks." I rarely had to ask for anything, though. The team won so many games and I scored so many points, they were always coming up to see me afterward and shoving wads of bills into my hands or my pockets. It might be $5 or $10 or $100, and it just kept coming. I guess I got about $15,000 or $20,000 while I was there, but I really don't know for sure; I never kept any records.

How did I justify taking the money? Well, in the first place, just about every other top star was being taken care of; why not me? I needed the money more than the guys who gave it to me anyway. Besides I was getting much less from Kansas than I could've gotten at almost any of the other big schools that tried to recruit me. But the main reason I took the money was pure economics: With me playing basketball, Kansas University, the city of Lawrence, the state of Kansas, and all of these alums got richer. People bought tickets to see me play, and they ate meals and bought clothes and rented motels while they were there. The publicity attendant on my play brought even more money to Kansas, both directly and indirectly. Why should I let them exploit me, without reaping at least a little of the profit myself? I figured it was a fair trade—particularly later on, when I heard people talking about the new Kansas Turnpike they built while I was there, and said it was "the turnpike Wilt built" because so many thousands of fans used it to come to see me play.

I wasn't the only one who benefited from my decision to go to Kansas. I always thought that my high school coach, Cecil Mosenson, came away with a little more than the satisfaction of seeing one of his boys make good. Of course, most schools dangled some bait in front of Coach Mosenson. Usually it was a job—in some cases, even the chance to be head basketball coach if he could bring me with him. With Phog Allen around, Kansas wasn't about to make that offer, of course, but they "helped" him out in other ways.

Kansas did one other thing for Coach Mosenson. Like I said earlier, we had several damn good players on my team at Overbrook, particularly my friends Vince Miller and Marty Hughes. Either of them could easily have made the team at Kansas. But Kansas wouldn't take them. Instead, they took another one of my teammates—Doug Leamon. Doug was a nice guy and a fairly decent ballplayer, but he couldn't carry Vince's jock.

He was white, though, and Vince and Marty were black.

I honestly don't remember if I realized it back then, but that was my first real lesson in one of those reprehensible but immutable truths about American society—a black man has to be twice as good as a white man just to get an even break. A superstar like me might not have trouble, but match any black beneath superstar status with a white guy of equal or even inferior ability, and the white guy will get the job every time. This is less often true now than it was then, I know, but it's still standard operating procedure in many areas of life, including sports and entertainment, where blacks are supposed to have made the greatest progress. (Hell, I think Glen Campbell, for example, has less talent than dozens of black comics and singers I could name. He has about as much voice and personality as one of my dogs. But he makes millions of dollars. A black man would have to be a combination Sammy Davis/Flip Wilson/Lou Rawls to make anywhere near that much.)

I suppose Kansas' recruitment of Doug, instead of Vince or Marty, should have tipped me off that I might run into the same prejudice in Lawrence that had helped convince me to eliminate Dayton and Indiana and the whole South. But, like I say, I was pretty naive about those things—until the day I actually came to Kansas to start school.

Doug and I drove out from Philly together, planning to share the driving time. He told me he was a good driver, but after about the first four miles, he ran the car off the highway into a ditch, and I had to take over. So I drove 1,154 miles all by myself, and we got into Kansas City, about 35 miles from the campus in Lawrence, late one evening, and we decided to stop for dinner. It seemed everyone in the restaurant knew me. They'd been reading about Kansas recruiting me and all, and we talked about basketball for a few minutes. Then the waitress came over, kind of mumbling and stumbling, and told me she couldn't serve me at that table. I thought maybe she meant it was reserved for someone else, so Doug and I got up and moved to another table.

"We can't serve you there either," she said.

I was pretty groggy from having driven 16 or 17 straight hours, so I still didn't know what she meant. I started to move again. She told me to come back in the kitchen, and she would give me whatever I wanted. The owner came out then, too, and he said the same thing: They'd serve me in the kitchen, but not in the restaurant proper.

Fortunately, Doug realized what the problem was before I did. He grabbed my arm, and said, "Let's go, Dip. We can get a bite somewhere else."

I don't know if it's just because I was so tired or because I had been so sold on Kansas, but I didn't understand what the hell was going on until we got outside and Doug explained it to me. Then I really got pissed. I jumped back in my car and I must've driven to Lawrence in record time. I drove right up to Dr. Forrest C. Allen's house. It was about midnight by then, but I went storming up to his front door, and started banging on it so hard, I almost knocked the damn thing down. When he answered, I said, "Do you know what the hell just happened to me?" Then I told him.

He said:

"Aw, just forget about those people. Come on in here and go to sleep. You can stay with us tonight."

I told him I wasn't interested in no sleep. I was hungry. He said he'd call the Chi Omega fraternity house, and have someone go down to the local greasy spoon and get me some hamburgers. I asked him to tell me where the greasy spoon was, "and I'll go myself," but he came on real solicitous about how tired I probably was and how it was the least they could do for me and all. Well, I found out later why he was so eager to have someone else get the hamburgers for me; even the greasy spoon was segregated, and he knew if I found that out, I'd probably say, "Fuck Kansas," and head back to Philadelphia before the first day of classes.

Well, it took me about a week to realize the whole area around Lawrence, except for one black section in Kansas City, was infested with segregation. I called on a few of the alums who had recruited me, and I told them in no uncertain terms what they could do with Kansas if things didn't get straightened out in a hurry. A couple of them told me, "Look, Wilt, you just go wherever you want. You sit down in those restaurants and don't leave until they serve you."

That's exactly what I did. It took me about two months, but I went into every damn place within 40 miles of Lawrence, even places I didn't want to go into. I'd just sit there and glower and wait. Finally, they'd serve me. I never got turned down or bad-mouthed or anything, and when I got through, other blacks would follow me. I singlehandedly integrated that whole area, and I guess that's one reason I get so angry now when some of the young, militant blacks call me an "Uncle Tom"—like when I backed Richard Nixon for President in 1968, and a lot of my friends, people like Harry Belafonte and Elgin Baylor and Walt Hazzard (now Abdul Rahman), really jumped on me for "letting your race down."

I guess the black whose antipathy hurts me the most is Kareem Abdul-Jabbar. Back when he was Lew Alcindor, in high school, he came over to my apartment in New York all the time. We never played much basketball together, but we played a lot of cards, and I'd take him down to Greenwich Village to a lot of jazz spots. I was able to get him into a few places he was actually too young for—including a couple we went to with dates when I took him out on the town as a kind of high school graduation present. I took him up to Kutsher's with me, too, and on a few other upstate trips. I could see he was getting the same kind of recruiting pressure I'd gotten, probably more, and he just needed a sympathetic friend and a sanctuary where he could visit with people who understood and wouldn't hassle him. But when he got to UCLA and then turned pro and got so heavily into the black pride/black power thing, he started to snub me. He seems to think that because I haven't changed my name and still have a lot of white friends,

51

I've abandoned the black man. Hell, he hardly even talks to me anymore. He won't even look at me when the Lakers play the Bucks and we jump center.

But I'm just as aware of the injustices done to the black man as anyone. I just don't believe you help things by running around, saying how evil Whitey is. I figure I've done my share—the restaurants I integrated in Kansas, the busloads of black kids I used to take to summer camp from Harlem, the contributions I make, in name and money, to various black causes and programs. Just because I don't call a press conference every time I do something like that doesn't mean I'm insensitive to the black man's plight.

Like I think the biggest disgrace in 20th century America was having segregated troops right up until 1948. I mean, if a guy can go out and fight and die for his country, how in God's name can you treat him differently than any other soldier? That's blasphemous; that's inhuman. I'm upset about some of the other obvious forms of discrimination, too, like in education and employment, and I could never understand why the government can't solve the problem of segregated housing. They don't seem to have any difficulty when it comes to tearing down black neighborhoods for urban renewal; why can't they put up some nice, partially subsidized housing for blacks in good white neighborhoods?

But I realize that's not the way things are done in America. There are certain priorities and certain stereotypes, and they are adhered to, no matter who gets hurt.

Stereotypes? Try being a black athlete traded to a new team. The first thing everyone wants to know is whether you plan to help the black underprivileged kids in that city. I got asked that question every time I was traded or my team moved—in San Francisco, in Philadelphia, and in Los Angeles. What do you want to bet that no white player gets asked if he plans to work with the underprivileged white kids? Do you think anyone asked Pete Maravich that when he got drafted by Atlanta? Or Steve Carlton when he got traded to the Philadelphia Phillies? Or Fran Tarkenton when the Giants traded him back to Minnesota? You bet your ass they didn't!

I've seen more than my share of discrimination in basketball, you can be sure of that. About the time I broke in, the NBA actually had a quota, an unwritten rule—no more than three blacks per team. And those had to be good blacks—starters, stars, not bench-warmers. Then Boston started winning all those championships with Bill Russell and K. C. Jones, and before long, the whole starting team was occasionally black—Russell, K. C., Sam Jones, Satch Sanders and Willie Naulls. Winning meant money to the team-owners, and if they had to choose between being rich and being bigoted, why, they'd just magnanimously take the green road, rather than the white one.

Now blacks compose about 65 percent of the NBA, and we've even had several black head coaches (Al Attles, Chink Scott, Bill Russell) and black assistant coaches (K. C. Jones, John Barnhill, Draff Young), as well as black front-office people— Wayne Embry, the general manager in Milwaukee; Herman Russell on the Atlanta board of directors, and Simon Gourdine, the vice president for administration of the whole NBA.

There still aren't enough blacks in top positions, but we're way ahead of all the other pro sports. There still hasn't been a black pro quarterback in football or a black head coach in pro or big-time college football. And baseball, the big civil rights pioneer, hasn't had a single black manager yet.

It's still much tougher for blacks to get endorsement and advertising opportunities than whites, too. I've done pretty well— Volkswagen, Brut, Miranda cameras, Aamco, BOAC, a cough medicine, a paint company, a few others—but not nearly as well as I would've done if I were white. Like, isn't it amazing that I haven't been asked to do commercials for 7 Up? I'd be a natural. I'm seven feet tall, and I drink it all the time—make a big deal out of it, too, if the trainer only has Coke.

Hell, look at Mark Spitz. He must be doing a dozen TV commercials a day. They say those seven Olympic gold medals will mean $5 million to him. And swimming isn't even that big a sport in this country. I can just imagine what would have happened to him if he'd been black, like some of our other multiple-event Olympic champions—say, Jesse Owens and Wilma Rudolph. Then he would've been lucky to get even one TV commercial—and that one probably would've been for chocolate milk!

If a white athlete has one or two great years, he's practically set for life. Guys like Joe Namath and Tom Seaver get endorsements, business opportunities, the works. When they're through with sports, they'll still make good money. But most blacks are just used. When they're no longer able to perform in sports, it's all over; no one is setting up annuities and automobile dealerships and franchise operations for them. A Willie Mays gets traded after giving the Giants 20 years, but a Stan Musial is given the Cardinals' vice president's job.

A black athlete has to take all these things into consideration when he's negotiating a contract with his team; I always tell Jack Kent Cooke, or whoever my boss is, that he's going to have to pay me more than he would pay a white star of equal ability and drawing power because of that. A black athlete better get a good playing contract; that's about the only source of income he's going to have.

The NBA may be predominantly black now, but the USA isn't, and I guess that's the reason these things happen. It's really funny—in a sad sort of way—to watch the press and the owners build up new "white hopes" coming into the NBA. They know a good, flashy white player can usually bring the fans in better than almost any black player of equal ability, simply because there are more white fans—actual and potential—than black fans. (That's one big reason why the Boston Bruins always outdrew the Boston Celtics during all those years the Celtics were winning one NBA championship after another, and the Bruins weren't winning anything. The Bruins sold out every home game; the Celtics averaged fewer than 8,000 fans per game most of their championship seasons—just about 50 percent of the Boston Garden capacity. But hockey was—and is—a white man's sport.) Back in 1960, when Jerry West first joined the Lakers, blacks were just beginning to take over (in quality, though not quantity yet). In Jerry's first year, me, Oscar Robertson, and Elgin Baylor —all blacks—ran 1-2-3 in the scoring race. Me and Bill Russell ran 1-2 in rebounds. Oscar and Guy Rodgers ran 1-2 in assists. Boston, with Russell and the two Jones boys, won the NBA championship. The whites really needed a hero, and Jerry was elected.

Now I'm not saying Jerry wasn't good. He was—and is—one of the best. And I'm not saying he's prejudiced himself. I've played against him for eight years and with him for five years, and I think he's one of the most unprejudiced guys I've ever

54

known, particularly when you realize that he comes from a small, unsophisticated town in West Virginia. But the owners need white hopes, and what they did with Jerry, they did again with Rick Barry and Pete Maravich when they came into the league—and they'll do in spades (no pun intended) when Bill Walton turns pro.

These things bother me, and I've always supported the civil rights leaders who worked to right the wrongs in our society. I was deeply saddened by the death of Martin Luther King, and I've had much the same affection and respect for black leaders like the Rev. Jesse Jackson and Julian Bond and Dick Gregory. But I do not support the militant black power "hate whitey" types like Stokely Carmichael and Rap Brown and some of the early Black Panthers. I realize they serve a valuable function: however unwittingly, with all their threats and angry rhetoric, they make the demands of more moderate blacks seem as reasonable as they actually are. I just can't take their hate and their determination to drive a wedge between blacks and whites. Black pride is a good idea—but not as good as human pride—and I'm afraid that what they're doing is a kind of reverse racism.

It can be a hard thing to avoid, though. I remember when I first saw a black distance-runner. Blacks had always been sprinters until then, and this was the first time I'd ever seen a black run over a half-mile, and I found myself really rooting for him. Then I got ashamed and wondered why. I might have had more in common with one of the white runners in the race than with him, but I was rooting for him just because he was black. That was wrong. Besides, I'm not really black myself. I'm kind of brown or bronze or copper-colored. And whites aren't really white. So why get all hung up in the color thing? It's just a lazy habit. It's easier to pin labels on people—whether the label is "black" or "seven-foot freak" or "loser"—than it is to dig down beneath that superficial level and try to understand people. The trouble is, laziness like this just makes the invidious connotations to such phrases as "black day" and "black mark" and "white hat" and "white knight" that much harder to expel from our language.

That black power salute—the raised, clenched fist—might have the same effect. Black dudes will pass me on the freeway or see me in an airport and flash me that sign like we're supposed to be long-lost brothers or something. I usually acknowledge just about anyone I make eye contact with, black or white—I'm just naturally a garrulous guy—so I'll raise my fist back. But I do it as a greeting, not a political symbol. I think it's a more forceful, positive greeting than just waving, and I give it to all my friends now—black and white.

Despite those early bad experiences at Kansas, I think I have basketball to thank for not turning me into a bitter, vengeful black. I've had so many white coaches and teammates who became as close to me as brothers that it would be impossible for me to look on all whites as evil. When I was playing at Kansas, my best friend was Bob Billings, a white guy on the team. We're still close. Calvin Vanderwerf, a chemistry professor at K.U., was probably my closest advisor and a good friend as well. Guys like Eddie Gottlieb and Abe Saperstein, both white, gave me my start in pro basketball, and Frank McGuire—a white man from a Southern school—was the best and most human coach I ever had. Ike Richman, a white man who was Eddie's attorney and later mine, was a dear friend; few events in my life have saddened me as much as his death a few years ago. When I played with the Philadelphia 76ers, my best friend was Billy Cunningham, a white man from North Carolina. Al Domenico, the 76ers trainer, has been a great friend since I was in high school. He's white, too. I've even got some friends who aren't white *or* black. The one friend I'm always sure to see when I go to Europe is Bill Dhrumbi, a Pakistani who now lives in Copenhagen. Don Ho (not the entertainer) is a Japanese I've been very close to for several years. In San Francisco, my closest friend for about ten years now has been a Persian insurance salesman named Jim Bryant. In fact, I remember how pissed I got one day when I was getting my hair cut in the Fillmore District, a black neighborhood in San Francisco, and this black barber kept saying how "the only good whites are those in Forest Lawn." Finally, I jumped out of his god damn chair, paid him his money and stormed out of the shop, with my hair still half-cut. There's absolutely no excuse for his kind of attitude. It doesn't help solve the problem; it aggravates it.

Just this last season, in Chicago, a black sportswriter from the *Sun-Times* interviewed me before our game with the Bulls, and he kept asking me if I thought there should be more black sportswriters covering the NBA for big-city newspapers. I told him I'd be happy to comment on the need for more black basketball officials and coaches and front-office men, but I just didn't know enough about the requirements of newspapers and the availability of competent black writers to give him an intelligent answer. But he wouldn't let it go at that. He kept hammering away, with the same stupid question. When I kept giving him the same answer, he changed his approach slightly, and said, "I understand you're writing your autobiography. Is your co-author black or white?" The way he asked it, it was more an accusation than a question —like he already knew the answer and was just daring me to tell him. Well, I just glared down on the little prick and said, "He's Jewish."

I suppose I could've added that my attorney in Los Angeles and my accountant and my doctor in Philadelphia are all Jewish, too—and all very dear friends—but I didn't want to give the poor guy apoplexy. Besides, I have plenty of close black friends—Vince Miller, the guy I grew up with in Philadelphia; Carl Green, whom I've known since my college days; Charlie Polk, who works in my nightclub in Harlem; Benjamin Sneed, my attorney in New York. My three closest friends in the NBA are probably Al Attles, Chet Walker, and Nate Thurmond. My closest friend in Los Angeles is Steve Claiborne. They're all black. But I pick my friends by their character, not their color, and I haven't found that any one race has a monopoly on good *or* evil. I want good friends, warm friends, caring, loving, human friends—not black or white or purple friends. I felt that way before my experiences in Kansas, and I feel that way now, and I don't think I have to apologize to anyone for that!

5

WHEN I SAW WHAT HAPPENED in the restaurants during my first few days at Kansas, I went to Dr. Allen and a couple of other people and let them know I had no intention whatsoever of playing basketball for K.U. if they were going to let that kind of thing happen when the team went on the road. I intended to eat where the team ate and sleep where the team slept, I said, and if they couldn't guarantee me that, they might as well tell me now and I'd go to college somewhere else.

Well, the freshman team was supposed to play an exhibition tour at Rice, Southern Methodist, and Louisiana State that year, and Kansas canceled out of those in a hurry. The varsity usually played Texas Christian, too, and they took that off the schedule for the next year.

With those problems apparently straightened out, it was time to play basketball—but without my Overbrook buddy, Doug Leamon; he got homesick and split after three or four days.

(Dumbshit Kansas! I told 'em they should've recruited Vince Miller instead.)

My first game at Kansas was as a freshman, against the varsity. It was a game they'd played every year since 1923, and the varsity had always won. We thought we had a pretty good freshman team, and all of us were really looking forward to the game, but then I got some kind of stomach flu and a high fever, and we weren't sure I could play. I was disgusted, man. There had been all this advance publicity on how great I was going to be at Kansas, and this was going to be my first chance to show people what I could do, and here I was sick. So, sick or not, I had to play —and I did.

They had about 14,000 people there—the biggest crowd in Kansas basketball history (which goes back to about 1899)—and we beat the varsity by 10 points, 81-71. I got 42 points (including 10 of 13 free throws) and 29 rebounds, even though the varsity was double- and triple-teaming me the whole game.

There were a lot of coaches and scouts from other colleges in the stands that night, and I was later told I had quite an effect on them—particularly this one guy, Jerry Bush, the coach at Nebraska, one of our Big Eight opponents. I was hitting jump shots and one-handers and set shots all over the place, and on one play, I drove to the top of the key, went up for what looked like another one-hander and just kept floating in the air, toward the basket. By the time I got there, I'd twisted my body around so that my back was to the basket, and I rotated my right arm like a helicopter rotor and dunked the ball in backwards as I went by. The guy sitting next to Bush told me later that Bush got real pale and said, "I feel sick."

Freshman teams at Kansas didn't play a regular schedule in those days, so after the game against the varsity, we just played intra-squad games and a few exhibition tours around the state. Even so, we always had more people come to see us than the varsity did—and the varsity had a winning season that year.

Coach Allen tried to work out with me once or twice a week, and he was always giving me advice. One of the first things he did was give me a copy of Helen Keller's autobiography. He said if I could really get into it, it might help me develop my sensitivity

59

and my feel and touch with a basketball. He even tried to implement that theory by teaching me finger manipulation and how to put English on the ball and how to spin it into the basket from any angle. (He called the technique "pronation.")

When I wasn't playing basketball my freshman year, I was running track. In fact, it's always been a secret source of pleasure to me that I lettered in track before I lettered in basketball. I triple-jumped and put the shot as a freshman, and I set a Big Eight freshman indoor record in the high jump. I also tied for first place in the freshman high jump at the Big Eight conference meet.

But neither track nor basketball brought me my greatest fame—or should I say notoriety?—as a freshman; money did. The NCAA was really digging into my scholarship arrangements, and it seemed like every time I bought a 7 Up for a friend, there would be an NCAA investigator lurking behind the vending machine, ready to pounce on us and say, "Ah hah! I gotcha. Where'd you get the money to buy that?"

The first big stink came in April when a sportswriter back in Cumberland, Maryland, wrote a column saying I'd played there under an assumed name in a pro game before I even got to Kansas. By NCAA rules, he said, that would make me a professional, and I should be ruled ineligible and expelled from Kansas.

Well, I had played in Cumberland—and in Quakertown, Pennsylvania, and a few other cities as well. And I had played under an assumed name. But you could hardly call them "pro" games. We got expense money and maybe a few bucks extra. It was a way for us good young guys from different parts of the East who weren't really getting much competition in high school to play against each other and develop our skills.

We all used assumed names because we knew what the NCAA would say if they found out who we were, and I've always been ashamed of having done that—not ashamed of having played but ashamed of having given in to the hypocrisy of the NCAA, rather than fighting it. I can understand the need for the distinction between amateurs and professionals, and I'm not one of those who says, for example, that we should pay all our Olympic athletes and make them pros, the way the Russians do. The United States is a rich country, so that wouldn't be fair to most of the other countries in the world. Same thing with the amateur-level competition within our own country; making everyone a pro would create a harmful imbalance in competition. But the fine lines the NCAA and the AAU are always trying to draw is pure bullshit.

If I get paid to play before I go to college, what difference should that make when I go to college? Or if I'm a paid, professional basketball player, like I am now, and I want to play amateur volleyball in the Olympics, why shouldn't I be able to? As long as I'm not getting paid now for the amateur sport I want to play now, why should I be ruled ineligible?

Well, needless to say, the NCAA didn't quite see it that way; so they had another big investigation.

Then rumors started circulating that I was getting special treatment in my classes—taking basket-weaving and finger-painting and that kind of stuff. Another investigation. Hah! My first year, I was taking psychology, literature, algebra, statistics, government, geography, and accounting, in addition to the two required physical education classes, and I was getting a little better than a "C" average, with no special treatment whatsoever.

With all the investigations going on, I decided to get out of Kansas for a few weeks during the summer after my freshman year. I headed back to Philadelphia, by way of North Carolina, where I picked up my friend Vince Miller at his college. I guess I was still pretty naive about racial matters then, even after my recruiting experiences and all those hours I spent sitting in Kansas restaurants, and the afternoon I picked Vince up, we went to a soda fountain for a drink, and the guy wouldn't serve us.

"I know you two guys are basketball players," he said, "but we can't serve you here; we're still practicing."

I thought he meant he was a basketball player, too, and he had to close up early to go to practice, so I just shrugged and we left. When we got outside, Vince explained what he'd meant: "practicing" is a Southern euphemism for "practicing segregation."

After that, Vince and I and another friend from Philly, Joe Howe, decided to split. I was so pissed, Vince volunteered to drive. He drove the first 150 miles or so, and then I took over. About 10 minutes after I got behind the wheel, a cop pulled us over for speeding. We were in Bowling Green, Virginia, and he told us we were going five miles over the speed limit.

61

"Gonna have to take you in, unless you got the $40 fine," he said.

I had about $30 on me and Vince had $4 and Joe had about 80 cents. That left us more than $5 short—and there was a Western Union strike on, so we couldn't send a telegram home, collect, to get the money right away. That meant I'd have to spend the night in jail. We gave the cops about $30 of our money, and I kept the rest, figuring I might be able to get a card game up in my cell and win enough to get out in a couple of hours. I've always been a good card player, but it took me a few hours just to get the other guys in my cell interested in playing. They all played conservatively, too, and it was the next morning before I had enough bread to get out.

I kept laughing to myself about the situation all night. According to all those slush-fund rumors at Kansas, I was supposed to be practically a millionaire—and here I was spending the night in some rathole Virginia jail because I didn't have $5.20.

I did a lot of that kind of laughing that summer. Remember, I said I didn't start getting spending money at Kansas until my sophomore year, so when I brought Vince back to Kansas City with me for a month before my sophomore year began, we really had to scratch for our bread. We rented a room from an old woman, and we used to sneak downstairs and drink some of her milk and orange juice and all.

The only time we ate real well was when I got into another poker game, with some doctors and lawyers and other big wheels in Kansas City. I won $35 or $40, and we ate like kings for a week. Then we were broke again. I had one job the school got me that summer—selling tires. I kept the job for a year or two, and I think I only sold two or three sets of tires the whole time —one of them to myself.

Of course, I didn't try very hard. I used to report for work in the morning, then go play cards or basketball all day. No wonder I didn't make much in commissions. (Not that the guy who ran the store helped much; his favorite sales gimmick was to have me show prospective customers a movie about a gory car wreck, and tell them that's what could happen to them if they had bad tires. Hell, after they saw that movie, they not only didn't buy new tires, they were so scared, they didn't even want to think about driving again for two days.)

It was a great summer, though, our abject poverty notwithstanding; we had one wild trip to Chicago that I'll never forget. Me and a couple of friends drove up to the college all-star game, and a cop stopped us for speeding about ten seconds after we got to Chicago. He looks at us—three young black dudes, all pretty casually dressed—and he says, "Well, now, you look like businessmen to me. Let's discuss this situation like a business proposition."

I knew what he meant, so I got out of the car. He wanted $20 to forget about our speeding; I offered him $10. He said, "Just put it on the seat."

That took care of the cop, but it also took care of our ticket money for the all-star game. So I, being the biggest, posed as a YMCA counselor. I bought my own ticket, and said the other two guys were "underprivileged students" and got them in free.

Then, on the way back from Chicago, we had car trouble. I called Skipper Williams, one of the alums I'd met in Lawrence. He said he'd get help to us right away. What I didn't know was that when he called his contact in Chicago to help us, he also told the guy to try to keep things quiet. He figured Kansas had enough trouble over me without any extra attention. But we had some time to kill while we were waiting for the garage to send someone out, so we just took our basketball out of the trunk and went through some Harlem Globetrotter–type routines on the highway. By the time Skip's friend got there, we had a crowd of about 300 people watching us, and traffic was backed up for miles. Good old Uncle Wiltie scores again!

We got the car fixed, but with the delay, we got hungry before we made it back to Kansas City—and we still didn't have any money. I devised an ingenious little plan when we came to small grocery store on Route 66:

"Look," I told the other guys, "I'll go in and walk around some. Everyone'll start looking at me, and while they're busy gawking, one of you grab a couple of loaves of bread and one of you grab some salami and mustard."

It worked like a charm. When we got outside, in the car,

we made sandwiches—and I provided the milk; even with all those fools staring right at me, I'd copped a couple of quarts!

All too soon, the summer was over and it was time for school —and my varsity basketball debut. But I wasn't going to get to play for Phog Allen. He'd turned 70, and the university had forced him to retire. We'd all known that 70 was the compulsory retirement age, but everyone figured old Phog would figure out a way to get them to extend it. He'd given them so much of his life, he thought he deserved it, and with me coming in, he really wanted to stay around a few more years. He couldn't make them change their minds, though, and his assistant, Dick Harp, got the job.

Our first game my sophomore year was against Northwestern. The day of the game, the Lawrence *Journal-World* ran a picture of me two columns wide down the full length of the front page. It showed me dunking, with my elbow way above the rim. But the picture didn't show the bottom of my feet, and none of the Northwestern guys wanted to believe it. When they saw me before the game, in the lobby of the hotel where they stayed, they laughed and joked about the "trick photography." They had this center, Joe Rucklick, who was later on the Warriors with me and became a close friend, and he was supposed to be a real hotshot. He came over to me and said, "C'mon, Wilt, you can tell us. That picture's bullshit, right? No one can jump that high. They just put you on top of a stool, right?"

I think I made a believer out of Joe and his teammates that night, even before the game started. I must've dunked ten times in practice, and that crowd of 17,000 just went crazy. The poor Northwestern guys were all just standing around with their mouths open by the time we were through warming up. When I hit four outside jump shots in the first ten minutes of the game, and we jumped ahead, 11-2, it was all over. We won, 87-69, and I hit 20 of 29 shots and got 52 points and 31 rebounds—both all-time Kansas records.

In our next game, against Marquette, we won, 78-61, and I got 39 points and 22 rebounds. I blocked 14 shots, and held the other center, Mike Moran, to four points; he fouled out about halfway through the second half trying to guard me.

Things went pretty well for us the rest of that year. We won our first 12 games in a breeze, even though the other teams started double- and triple-teaming me and stalling like crazy.

Finally, in our thirteenth game, we got beat. Iowa State froze the ball damn near the whole game, and surrounded me with so many guys I felt like the last survivor of an Indian raid. I scored 17 points, including two free throws to tie the score with nine seconds left, but they won, 39-37, on a 15-foot jump shot at the final buzzer.

We won our next five games by an average of almost 20 points, even though I played the worst game of my college career in one of them. We won that one, 76-56, over Oklahoma; I hit only three field goals all night, scored a measly 11 points and fouled out—for the first time all year—midway through the second half. We lost our very next game, 56-54, to Oklahoma State, in another stall game. I got 32 of our 54 points, but the rest of the team hit only seven field goals all night, and we lost on another long shot at the buzzer. Then we won four more to end the regular season with a 21-2 record (Kansas' best in 20 years) and the Big Eight championship.

When we went to Dallas for the Western regionals, we stayed in a motel in Grand Prairie, about 30 miles away. The coach said he did it to keep us together in a quiet spot, away from the big city, and we believed him . . . until someone burned a cross in the vacant lot across from our motel. Then we realized Dallas had made the decision, not Coach Harp; they just weren't about to let any blacks in their fancy downtown hotels. In fact, when I tried to go to a drive-in movie, in my own car, they wouldn't even let me do that!

The crowd at the game that night was plenty hostile, too. They booed and jeered and called me "nigger" and "jigaboo" and "spook" and a lot of other things that weren't nearly that nice. I tried not to let it bother me too much; I figured I'd answer them on the basketball court.

That's exactly what I did. We played Southern Methodist in the first round, and they hadn't ever been beaten in the first 36 games in their new fieldhouse. We beat them, 73-65, in overtime. I got 36 points and 22 rebounds, and held their all-American center, Jim Krebs, to 18 points and six rebounds before he fouled out.

65

The next night, we played Oklahoma City for the regional championship and flattened them, 81-61. I got some racial abuse in that game, too—and not just from the stands. One of the Oklahoma players kept calling me a "nigger" and a "black son-of-a-bitch," and he jabbed me and tried to trip me every time he went by. But one of his teammates, Hub Reed, who was also white, came over and apologized to me for him and the fans several times, and that more than offset all the abuse. Of course, the fact that we won and that I had a good night also helped make me feel better. With all the roughing-up that one guy gave me, I wound up going to the free-throw line 22 times. I hit 14 of them, and wound up with 30 points. I figured I was better off shoving the ball through the basket than shoving my fist down the cat's throat—tempting though that may have been.

The next week, we played the University of San Francisco in the NCAA semi-finals. We won easily, 80-56, on 8-0 and 16-0 bursts early in the second half.

That same night, North Carolina, the No. 1 rated team in the country, beat Michigan in a triple overtime. North Carolina was undefeated, but Michigan should've won. Johnny Green, who later became a star in the NBA, blew two free throws late in the game to give North Carolina the victory; Frank McGuire, the North Carolina coach, always said he was sure his team was fated to win the championship after that game.

So it was No. 1 North Carolina, 31-0, against No. 2 Kansas, 24-2, for the 1957 NCAA championship. McGuire, a shrewd strategist and psychologist, had his smallest player, 5 foot 11 Tommy Kearns, jump center against me for the opening tipoff. Tommy and I have since become such good friends that we always try to have dinner together at least once anytime I'm in New York, but we didn't know each other at all then, and a lot of people said McGuire made the surprise move to confuse me and throw me and my teammates off stride, wondering what the hell he was up to. But that was only part of it. Coach McGuire knew he didn't have anyone who could outjump me, so why waste a tall guy in the jump? Why not stick a little guy in there, and have all your tall guys outside the center circle where they could grab the tip when I hit it? We got the tip, but North Carolina immediately put their 6-9 center Joe Quigg in front of me and damn near

66

everyone else on their team behind me and alongside me. Coach McGuire, who later coached me on the Warriors, said he told his team, "We're playing Wilt, not Kansas; just stop him and don't worry about those other guys on his team; they're not all that good."

I didn't get many shots off against that kind of defense, and I didn't hit my first field goal until about five minutes into the game. By that time, North Carolina was ahead, 9-2. They hit their first nine shots, and jumped ahead 19-7 before we knew what hit us. It seemed like everything they threw up there went in. They didn't miss a shot for the first ten minutes of the game!

My teammates, meanwhile, couldn't put a pea in the ocean. With North Carolina surrounding me, they were all wide open, but they just couldn't buy a basket. At halftime, North Carolina was hitting 64.5 percent from the field, and we were hitting 27.3 percent.

North Carolina stalled in the second half, but we came back and actually went ahead, 40-37, with about ten minutes left in the game. Then *we* stalled. With 1:43 left, we were ahead 46-43 —and North Carolina's big star, Lennie Rosenbluth, committed his fifth foul. It looked like we had the championship in the bag. This was in Kansas City, and I remember looking up in the stands at some friends and thinking how groovy it was going to be to celebrate with them later. I mean, one of our best free-throwers, Gene Elstun, was at the line, and if he made it, we'd be ahead by four points; even if they scored again, we'd get the ball back with a two-point lead and less than a minute to go. I was sure we could stall the game out.

Well, Elstun misses the free throw, and the ball bounces damn near all the way to midcourt where they have a guy standing. They get a layup, and a few seconds later one of our other guys blows an in-bounds play and they get a free throw, and the game goes into overtime.

The first overtime is scoreless. We each get a basket in the second overtime. Now it's 48-all, and we're going into triple overtime.

We go ahead, 53-52, with just a few seconds left when their center hits a jump shot from the corner to put them ahead, 54-53. We call time, and Coach Harp gives us the obvious play: "Pass it in high to Wilt right under the basket, and let him dunk it."

Good idea—except that the guy who takes the ball out, Ron Loneski, throws the damn thing right into a North Carolina player's hands while I'm standing there under the basket, completely helpless, and we lose the national championship.

I've always been more bitter about that loss than almost any other single game in my whole college and professional career. I guess it's because that's the game that started the whole "Wilt's a loser" thing that's been thrown at me for more than 15 years now.

For most of those years, people have been writing that Kansas was the preseason favorite to win everything my sophomore year —and my junior year, as well—and that we, *I,* blew it both times. That just isn't true. But people only remember what Phog Allen said when I enrolled at Kansas. He told everyone:

"Wilt Chamberlain's the greatest basketball player I ever saw. With him, we'll never lose a game; we could win the national championship with Wilt, two sorority girls and two Phi Beta Kappas."

That was ridiculous, of course, but it gave the public an image of me that has endured to this day—the image of Wilt Chamberlain as Superman, a guy who should never lose. So when my team does lose, it must be my fault, right? I'm not performing up to expectations. Or I'm choking. Or I'm blowing free throws. Or I'm letting Bill Russell psych me out. Or I'm being selfish. You certainly can't blame my teammates. After all, Phog Allen said I didn't really need teammates.

But basketball, more than any other sport (except, perhaps, hockey) is a team sport. A great passer like Joe Namath can damn near take a defensively inadequate, injury-crippled team like last year's New York Jets into the NFL playoffs; a great pitcher like Steve Carlton can win 27 games for a last-place Philadelphia Phillies team that only wins 32 other games in all of 1972.

You can't do that in basketball. Winning basketball depends upon teamwork—coordination, unity, switching off, setting screens, passing off, knowing where your teammates are and what they can do at any given moment.

Maybe if Phog Allen hadn't retired and he'd been our coach, he could've made his predictions of a national championship come true. He was a helluva coach, I know, and, in my opinion, Dick Harp wasn't. Harp was just too nice a guy to be a successful coach. Take that North Carolina game. Ron Loneski, the guy who threw the last pass away, had a terrible game. He choked. He didn't make a field goal all night. The coach should've pulled him early in the game. He admitted that to me later. But he said he was afraid of hurting Ron's feelings. Well, shit! What's better, to hurt one guy's feelings or deprive your whole team of a championship?

Coach Harp is working with the Fellowship of Christian Athletes now, and that's the ideal place for him. He's a good, decent, moral man. But I sure as hell don't think he was much of a basketball coach. (I've never said any of this before, but I think he must know how I feel. In all the years since I left Kansas, he's never once sent me a card or a letter, asking how I am or wishing me good luck in a big game or congratulating me for anything. He's never even sent me a Christmas card. But Ted Owens, the coach at Kansas now, writes me all the time. And he wasn't even there when I was! Of course, I've never written Coach Harp either, so maybe it's not all his fault.)

Anyway, the myth is that Kansas was supposed to win the national championship that year, and *I* lost it for us. Never mind that I got 23 points against North Carolina—high for the game. Never mind that I was named most valuable player in the tournament. Never mind that I had three or four men guarding me all night. Never mind that the rest of the team couldn't hit when they were left wide open. Never mind that Ron Loneski threw that pass away in the third overtime. Never mind that North Carolina—No. 1, undefeated, with a great coach and great players—was actually favored going into the championship game. The people who were there know what happened, but by the time I'd been a pro a few years, and we'd lost to Boston a few times, everyone was pointing back to that North Carolina game as proof that I was a loser.

Bullshit!

As you can imagine, I was in a rotten frame of mind when the basketball season was over my sophomore year at Kansas. And I shouldn't have been. After all, playing against an undefeated, veteran team, we'd come within one point of the national championship—and I personally had averaged 30 points, 19 rebounds and nine blocked shots a game throughout the season (that's right —nine blocked shots! not bad for a guy who was "just a scorer" and didn't even "learn" to play defense until 1971, huh?). But that loss to North Carolina had left me with a bad taste in my mouth.

Fortunately, I was still interested in my classes (I was taking some more of those "snap" courses—economics, history of Western civilization, German, literature, etc.) I was also working part-time my sophomore year. That caused some more NCAA investigations. I was really into music then, and I carried my portable stereo when the team went on the road, and I had a disc jockey show on the campus radio station KANU. I also did a show for KLWN in Lawrence and KPRS in Kansas City, and the shows were picked up on five or six other stations in the area. I called my show "Flippin' with the Dipper," and I played all the top records of the day and had different guests on. Sometimes I'd play my bongos on the air and have one of my basketball teammates, Monte Johnson, come on and play the spoons. We made a helluva sound.

The NCAA never believed me, but I really didn't get paid for the radio shows. I did them because I liked music and liked the work, and was taking some classes in radio and television speaking and I thought the shows would be good, practical, on-the-job experience.

I did get paid, though, when I'd make an appearance at some of the nightclubs in Kansas City. Between basketball and my radio shows, I had a pretty big name there, so clubowners would pay me $50 or $100 or $200 to stop by. They figured it would help them draw bigger crowds, and I liked to go to the clubs anyway to see singers like Gloria Lynne or James Brown, so things worked out fine for both of us. But the NCAA made a big deal out of that, too. And they made an even bigger deal out of a 1956 Olds I got. I've always been a freak for cars, and I'd bought my first one, a '49 Olds, when I was a junior in high school in 1953, with $700 I'd made as a bellhop at Kutsher's. The next year, I bought a '51 Buick for about $600. When I was first at Kansas, I had a '53 Olds I'd bought for $900 (plus my trade-in), and then I saw the '56 Olds, and I really dug it. The student it belonged to wanted to sell it, but I didn't have the

70

$2,800 he was asking for it. I went to one of those alums I'd been told to ask for any help I needed, and he bought the car for me. You should've seen the furor the NCAA kicked up over that one! (Three years later, they put Kansas on two years' probation because of the car.)

I tried not to let it bother me, though. I just went around town in my new Olds, racing anything that moved. I even raced on the Kansas Turnpike before it was finished and open to the public. After they opened it officially, I used to get a kick out of getting on, taking my time-stamped ticket, then roaring off to the Kansas City exit, 29 miles away, in, like, 14 minutes. I'd do 120, 130 miles an hour, and when I'd pull up to the ticket booth at the Kansas City exit, I'd give the guy my ticket, and he'd look at it and say "35 cents" or whatever and, whooosh! I'd take off again before he could check the time and see how fast I'd gone and call some cop on me for reckless driving.

After a while, they got to know me and my car, and as soon as I'd get on, they'd telephone ahead and radio some cops to be waiting and hiding for me. But I drove that turnpike so often, there wasn't a crevice between Lawrence and Kansas City that I didn't know. They couldn't hide from me. I'd see them turn off their lights on the side of the road, and I'd think, "Man, there's some slick old son-of-a-bitch waiting for me," and I'd slow down and cruise on by at 60, 65, and when I'd go by, I'd toot my horn and wave. When I'd get about a mile down the turnpike, I'd see the lights come back on and I'd laugh and—whoosh!—I'd take off again.

The only time I ever lost a race on the Kansas Turnpike was when my engine was starting to burn up and two sailors in a Chrysler 300 took me on. I knew they had more power than I did, so I just straddled the center line, and figured I'd stay there all the way, at about 90. They were about two feet behind me all the way, when, all of a sudden, my hood flew up and I couldn't see anything. I don't know how I did it, but I got off to the side of the road without them rear-ending me. They went right on by, honking and giving me the finger.

I did some fast running, as well as fast driving, my sophomore

71

year. I was still out for track—I won the Big Eight outdoor high-jump championship—and I liked to go around challenging all the fast track guys to race me.

I usually beat everyone—except my roommate, Charley Tidwell. I've always felt that Charley and Jim Brown and Bill Sharman are about the three best all-round athletes I've ever seen. Charley could've made a big name and a million bucks if he hadn't been so shy and lacking in confidence and so, well, so ignorant and unwilling to really dedicate himself to being the best. Charley had some severe emotional problems his whole life, and when I heard a few years ago that he had killed himself, it hit me pretty damn hard. I'd tried to help Charley several times, but I always wondered if maybe there wasn't something more I could have done for him. It's a tragic waste for such a great guy—and a great talent—to die so young, under such horrible circumstances. Charley could run and jump and play football and baseball and basketball, and he was great at all of them. I remember watching him run in ten track events at a big meet one time; he won nine of them.

'Course I always thought I was pretty fast, too, so one night when we were leaving a movie, I waited till we were about 300 yards from the car, and said, "Charley, I'll race you to the car for Cokes and donuts." I got a great start, but after about ten yards, he passed me like I was standing still. By the time I got to the car, he'd opened his door, opened my door, gotten in, started the engine and damn near driven away. I couldn't believe it. A few weeks later, we were walking back from the Student Union to our room, and I challenged him again. We were both carrying books, so I figured that gave me a little edge, being stronger and all. But I didn't take any chances; I took off at top speed almost before I challenged him.

He still beat me by ten yards.

I think the only other race I ever lost at Kansas was to Wes Santee, the miler. Wes was always hanging around the track, and one day I challenged him to run in my specialty—the quarter mile. I knew these distance runners weren't much good under a half mile. At least, I thought I knew that. He must've beat me by 30 yards.

I was still pretty damn skinny for my height at this time,

and some of the guys on the track team suggested I take a shot at weightlifting to build my weight and strength. I'd fooled around a little with weights before, and I decided that was a good idea. Like everything else I try, I went all the way; I pressed and jerked and lifted all hours of the day. I started getting muscles, and my muscles started getting muscles, and even my muscles' muscles started getting muscles.

We had two big, strong Olympic champions at Kansas then —Bill Nieder (the shot putter) and Al Oerter (the discus thrower)—and I used to arm-wrestle them all the time. I'd either win or we'd have a standoff. Nieder said I was the only guy he'd ever arm-wrestled that he couldn't beat.

When I got back to Philadelphia that summer, I couldn't wait to show off my weightlifting to this one guy, John Clad, the guy from my old neighborhood who'd given me the nickname "Dippy." He was a big, powerful guy, with a 45-inch chest; he'd been lifting weights in the service for three years, so me and another friend, Sonny—a real puny guy I'd taught to lift weights— took him up on the roof to have a contest.

I had big John lift against Sonny first, and Sonny beat him. John was shattered. It was easy for me to beat him after that. I'd just let him lift whatever weight he wanted, and then I'd lift the same thing with one hand. I don't think the poor son-of-a-bitch ever recovered from the embarrassment.

I spent a lot of time that summer playing basketball. I played in the Big Nine (now the Eastern Professional Basketball League) around Philadelphia, and I traveled all over the East and Midwest, looking for games. I'd go up to New York and play in the school-yards against other college and pro stars, men like Satch Sanders and Walter Dukes, and I'd go to Indianapolis and play guys like Oscar Robertson, and I'd go to Chicago and Detroit and Kansas City and St. Louis and play the same kind of high-caliber, rough-and-tumble pickup games. Like the games at Kutsher's, this competition did far more to develop my skills than the formal interscholastic basketball I played.

When I returned to Kansas for my junior year, I'd gotten over most of the disappointment of the North Carolina loss, and I was ready to play another season. We'd lost three starters from our 1956-57 team, but we still won our first four games against

73

pretty tough opposition—Oklahoma State, Canisius, Northwestern, and Marquette. In our fifth game, we beat St. Joseph's, 66-54. It was the only college game I ever got to play in Philadelphia, and they had a sellout crowd to see me. I hit 11 of 15 from the field and nine of 15 free throws for 31 points.

We beat Washington, California and Oklahoma in our next three games, and that made us No. 1 in the nation.

We won two more games before disaster struck.

I got kneed in the groin—accidentally—in our 79-65 win over arch-rival Kansas State in the annual Big Eight Tournament championship game. My balls swelled up like watermelons, and they hurt something fierce. You couldn't talk about that kind of injury very specifically in Kansas—or anywhere else—in 1957, so the school just announced that I had "a glandular infection." As usual, when you try to hush something up, a grain of truth seeps out, and then all sorts of wild stories start circulating. Sure enough, in a matter of days, it seemed like everyone on campus knew the precise anatomical location of my problem . . . and the rumor that I had the clap swept the campus. Kids started snickering and referring to me as "The Big Dripper."

But it wasn't so funny to our basketball team. We'd won ten straight, and were ranked No. 1; with me on the sidelines, we lost our first two Big Eight conference games, to Oklahoma State (52-50) and Oklahoma (64-62). I made it back for our next game, against Colorado, and scored 32 points. We won, 67-46. We also beat Missouri, 68-54, and the box score might make it look like I had fully recovered—I scored 35 points. But I didn't score at all in the first ten minutes of the game, and I fouled out in the second half—the second time I'd done that in college, and the last time it's ever happened to me.

I wasn't really recovered, the 35 points notwithstanding, and when we played Kansas State again, we lost, 79-75, in double overtime. I scored 25 points, and my friend Bob Billings got 19, but it wasn't enough. That just about ended the season for us before it was even half over. We had three conference losses—too many with a team as good as Kansas State in our conference.

With me still hurting, we got down on ourselves. Then Bob Billings got injured, too. He missed three conference games, and we lost two of them. I played pretty poorly in those games, but

74

to show you what kind of season it was, one of those losses came when Nebraska beat us, 43-41, on a last-second shot by Jim Kubacki, a little guy who had a bad knee, and had been sitting on the bench in street clothes for most of the game. Late in the game, one of the other Nebraska guys twisted an ankle, and their coach told Kubacki to go put his uniform on.

He got back out on the floor just in time to take the final shot that beat us.

After Kansas State clinched the Big Eight championship, about our only consolation was that in the last conference game of the season, with me and Bob Billings finally healthy again, we showed Kansas State who really was the best team. We mashed them, 61-44, and I got 23 points and Bob got 16. Their star, Bob Boozer, scored only two points off me all night and fouled out. But it was too late. We'd beaten Kansas State two of three times that season, but it wasn't enough. They were going to the NCAA playoffs; we could sit home in Lawrence, and watch the game on television.

I finished out my junior year at Kansas—winning the Big Eight indoor high-jump championship with a school record jump of 6-6¾—but I was pretty sure I wouldn't be coming back for my senior year. I practically stopped going to classes and let my grades slide and got on academic probation. I just didn't care any more.

Even though I wanted an education, the main reason I'd come to Kansas was to play basketball, and we just weren't playing serious basketball.

I know the losses and the injuries helped make me unhappy, and I probably wasn't mature and sophisticated enough to handle all the disappointment and constant pressure, but the style of ball we were forced to play was my main gripe. Other teams would double- and triple-team me, and I'd have to run up and down the court carrying half the other team on my back. It was more like an earthquake evacuation than a basketball game, except that the guys I was carrying were trying to knock me down and beat me up. I've never been very aggressive by nature—that's why I've never fouled out of a pro game in 14 years (and only fouled out of two college games)—so I never dished out nearly as much as I took. I figured I was in there to play basketball,

75

not brawl. Besides, one of my first schoolyard coaches had psyched me out; he'd told me there would always be guys on opposing teams trying to make me lose my cool and either foul or get thrown out of the game.

"You'll always be more valuable to your team than those guys will be to their teams," the coach said, "so don't fall for it. It's a sucker play. Keep your cool."

I followed his advice, but things got so bad at Kansas sometimes that when we'd get a big lead and I'd leave the game, my back-up center, Monte Johnson, would damn near kill two or three guys on the other team. He got the reputation of being the dirtiest player in the league, but he was just so mad about what the other guys did to me, he was trying to get back at them and show them they couldn't get away with it.

Teams didn't just clobber me, though. They also froze the ball. People used to ask me why I never led the nation in scoring or rebounding when I was at Kansas. Hell, I averaged 30 points a game, and hit almost 50 percent of my shots, but with the other teams freezing the ball, I couldn't get enough shots to score more. I averaged about 16 rebounds a game, too, but how do you get rebounds when the other team won't shoot? We had one game against Oklahoma State where they passed the ball 160 times before taking a shot! That's not basketball; that's a farce!

A lot of good teams wouldn't even play us. Adolph Rupp, the coach at Kentucky, was a K.U. alum, and he was talking about starting a home-and-home series with Kansas until I got there. Then he changed his mind. Other teams did the same thing. We wanted to play in the East and the West and everywhere, but hardly anyone would take us on. Elgin Baylor was at Seattle then, and he told me that his coach, Johnny Castellani, came to him and said, "Hey, Elg, Kansas wants to play us. What do you think? They've got Wilt and all. They might beat us." Elg told him, "Go ahead and make the game. Let's play them."

They never did.

Chicken-hearted coaches and schedule-makers weren't the only ones who robbed me of a lot of pleasure from intercollegiate basketball. The rules-makers jumped in, too.

We had an in-bounds play at Kansas where one of our guards would take the ball out right behind the basket and pass it in over the top of the backboard, and I'd jump up and stuff it in. They changed the rule so you had to pass the ball in from the side of the basket; you couldn't throw it in from behind.

They also put in the offensive goal-tending rule about the same time; you couldn't touch the ball when it was on the rim or in the imaginary cone above the basket. That was to keep me from guiding my teammates' shots in.

Another rules change: it used to be that when teams lined up along the key for a free throw, there was one player from each team next to the basket—one on each side. When I got to college, they changed it; the nonshooting team would have both positions next to the basket.

But the wildest rules change was the one about where you could shoot your free throws from. In practice my freshman year, I'd fool around sometimes and stand about midcourt, run to the free-throw line, broadjump, and dunk the ball before I landed. That was legal then because the rule only said you couldn't set foot in the key until the ball had hit the rim or backboard. I had no intention of actually doing that in a game, but some of the coaches in our league—particularly Tex Winter at Kansas State— got scared. They could see me making 100 percent of my free throws that way. So they pushed a new rule through; it said you couldn't break the imaginary vertical plane of the free-throw line until the ball had hit the rim or the backboard; you had to shoot from—or behind—the free-throw line. In other words, no running-jumping dunks.

The rule changes were really more a minor nuisance than a real hindrance, but they helped contribute to my general feeling of dissatisfaction, my feeling that everyone was ganging up on me. I mean, when I was just a sophomore, a big national magazine—I think it was *Saturday Evening Post*—ran a story by Jimmy Breslin titled, "Can Basketball Survive Chamberlain?" Isn't that stupid? No one guy is going to take over any sport—not me or Joe Namath or Willie Mays or anyone. But the way the coaches and athletic directors and rules-makers acted, you would've thought I was a monster from the deep, out to destroy their game, rape their wives, and eat their children alive.

I not only wasn't having fun, I wasn't learning anything about basketball either. With the lanes so clogged up against us, we didn't get to work many plays, and I didn't get to run much or do any of the other things you have to practice and polish to be a good pro. I knew guys like Bill Russell and Bob Pettit would kill me in the NBA if I didn't learn those things. I figured once I got to the NBA, I wouldn't have those kinds of problems any more. With the 24-second clock, more good players, better officiating, and a rule against zone defenses, I thought I'd get to play serious basketball. That isn't altogether the way things turned out, as I learned in my rookie year, but that's what I thought then. Besides, basketball had become such drudgery at Kansas that I was afraid another year there might leave me so disillusioned with the game, I'd quit playing completely and never try the NBA. Deep inside, I knew I didn't want to miss that opportunity. So I quit Kansas instead.

As bitter as some of this might sound now, I didn't leave Kansas on bad terms. I had a pleasant talk with the chancellor, Franklin Murphy, and he said he thought I was making the right decision. So did Bob Billings. Bob was just about a straight-A student, a real mature kind of guy, and he used to help shield me from some of the hassle and the pressure; he said he would have quit, too, if he'd been in my shoes. Even some of the big businessmen in town, like the Vickers Petroleum people, agreed with my decision; Vickers offered me a job and a chance to play for their AAU basketball team (which was then coached by Alex Hannum, who later coached me in both San Francisco and Philadelphia). The deal included an executive position with the company, deferred salary benefits—damn near enough to make me comfortable for the rest of my life . . . another lovely example of the kind of hypocrisy and double standards that so permeate the whole amateur sports scene.

Vickers wasn't offering me a job because they thought I'd make a great sales manager, right? I mean, if they had any such ideas, my miserable performance as a tire salesman should have disabused them of it. They were going to hire me—*pay* me—to play basketball. But because they could channel the money through the company, and give me some figurehead job, the AAU says it's a perfectly proper kind of arrangement. Not that I object, you understand. The Vickers people were damn decent folks, good friends to this day, and I can't see anything wrong with the deal they proposed; it's no different than using an athlete or a celebrity in any other kind of testimonial venture. What I *did* object to was the bullshit reasoning that said this was OK, but other, very similar arrangements were not. In effect, the AAU and NCAA say you can use a ruse that's so transparent a blind baby could see through it, but you can't be honest up front and say, "Look, this guy's a great basketball player; he'll be a big benefit to our school, and we want to pay him to come here."

An even better example: the thing I regret most about quitting Kansas and turning pro was missing out on the 1960 Olympics. I didn't want to go as a basketball player so much, but as a high-jumper or—what I really wanted—as a decathlon man. I've always thought my speed and strength and endurance would make me a good decathlon man. To go to the Olympics, though, I would've had to play my senior year at Kansas, then wait around another year as well. Why? Why couldn't I be a professional basketball player and an amateur track man? Because the AAU and NCAA says that's illegal, that's why. Talk about bullshit reasoning!

Anyway, I didn't stay at Kansas and I didn't go to the Olympics and I didn't play with the Vickers. I played with the Harlem Globetrotters instead.

Goose Tatum, the clown prince of the Globies for 15 years or so, lived in Kansas City while I was going to college, and since there weren't any girls worth blinking at in Lawrence, I usually went into K.C. for my, uh, rest and recreation. I met Goose there in my sophomore year, and we talked basketball some and went up to his hometown, Detroit, a few times. I idolized him when I was growing up, and here we were friends; he even let me drive his new car.

Goose had left the Globies and formed his own barnstorming basketball team by the time I met him, and he wanted me to quit Kansas and come with him after my sophomore year—for $100,-000! I still wanted to play college ball then, but when I decided to leave Kansas, I got to thinking about his offer. We met again, and talked about scheduling and about how I should quit at midterm in my junior year and join him. Then I got a call from Eddie Gottlieb, the owner of the Philadelphia Warriors. They'd drafted me when I was still in high school, I told you, and Eddie wanted to talk to me about joining the Warriors right then.

We met in a hotel room in Detroit to talk about Eddie's proposition. He said he was willing to pay me more than the $25,000 Bob Cousy and Bob Pettit, the highest-paid players in the league, were then getting. But first, he said, he'd have to get an OK from the league to sign me. Technically, I couldn't play in the NBA until my college class graduated. That would've been 1959; this was 1958. Eddie said he'd try to get me into the NBA as a financial hardship case, the only possible loophole. He couldn't get the league to go along with him, though. At least that's the story I got.

Abe Saperstein ran the Globies then and also owned a piece of the Warriors, and I always thought Abe and Eddie made an agreement that had nothing to do with what I wanted or what anyone in the NBA said: Eddie would tell me I couldn't play for the NBA for a year, and Abe would sign me to play with the Globies for that year, with the understanding that I'd join the Warriors the next year.

I considered Abe a dear friend until the day he died, and Eddie is still a dear friend, so I don't want to go around making any accusations. All I know is that's exactly the way things worked out. When the NBA "turned me down," as Eddie put it, and Goose Tatum's financial backers couldn't come up with the money he'd offered me, Abe stepped into the picture and I agreed to play with the Globies during what would've been my senior year in college.

A month or so later, in a press conference at Toots Shor's in New York, Abe would announce that I'd signed a contract for $65,000—almost twice what he'd paid Goose Tatum. Actually, the contract was for $46,000. But with various side agreements we made on bonuses, I was assured of at least $65,000.

Once I made the decision to leave Kansas and join the Globies, only one onerous chore remained: telling everyone.

Fortunately, a couple of months earlier, in March, I'd met a writer from *Look* at an NBA playoff game between Boston and St. Louis. His name was "Iggy" McVay, and he told me he'd heard I might be leaving Kansas soon.

"If you have anything to say, get in touch with me," he said.

I did just that. We worked out a deal for me to do two pieces for *Look*—the exclusive story on my decision to leave Kansas, as well as some other story, to be determined later.

But there was a problem—a time lag of about two or three weeks between the time me and "Iggy" and Tim Cohane, the *Look* sports editor, got the piece done, and the time the story would hit the newsstands in the June 10 issue. Under the terms of my contract with *Look*, I wasn't permitted to tell anyone anything about my decision before then. So here I was, a guy who's always prided himself on being, if nothing else, candid and outspoken, and with the rumors flying hot and heavy, and everyone asking me if I was leaving or staying, I had to go around saying "no comment"—or just plain lying.

Finally, it got to be too much for me; I called *Look*. They told me to come to New York, and said they'd put me and a friend up in a hotel, to hide from the press and everyone else, until they were ready to call their own press conference and release the story.

I left Kansas as quickly as I could after that, and headed for New York with Elzie Lewis, one of the guys who'd taken that wild trip to Chicago with me after my freshman year. We spent about ten days in New York, as I recall, playing basketball in the schoolyards almost the whole time. Every night, we'd come dragging back to this nice hotel, me and Elzie and six or eight of the guys we'd been playing with, and we'd order about six tons of food from room service, and sign *Look* on the tab.

After a while, one of the hotel executives came up to see us. He didn't quite know what to say, but we could see he thought we were eating in my room because we were afraid the hotel wouldn't serve blacks in their restaurants. He wanted us to know that wasn't so. We thanked him, and explained that we were only eating in the room because we were always hot and tired and sweaty from playing, and it was easier that way; we didn't have to shower and shave and dress and all.

Then, at long last, came the *Look* press conference, and the publication of my story, "Why I Am Quitting College."

With that out of the way, we were free to leave New York. I decided to take Elzie by my home in Philadelphia and visit there awhile—not realizing that I was about to play cupid again.

81

I think I already told you about my sister Selina, marrying my Philadelphia YMCA basketball buddy Claude Gross. Well, I'd met Elzie playing basketball at the "Y" in Kansas City, and one day while we were at my house that summer, after the New York trip, I was inside and he was outside, and all of a sudden he starts calling, "Hey, Dippy, come on out here. There's two fine-looking women out here."

I've always liked fine-looking women, so I raced outside. Shit, man, he was talking about my sister Barbara and her girl friend! It didn't take long before Elzie didn't want to go run or play basketball with me after dinner any more. He always had an excuse—"I'm tired"; "I don't feel so good"; "I've got a headache." I finally found out he was helping Barbara wash the dishes and trying to bullshit and score with her. A few years later, they got married.

While I was in Philadelphia that summer, before joining the Globetrotters in Europe, everyone kept asking me the same question: Don't you wish you'd never gone to Kansas? I guess I've been asked that question 5,000 times since then. Knowing what I know now about the life style in Southern California, I'd probably go to UCLA if I had it to do all over. But I couldn't have known that then, so, no, I don't regret having gone to Kansas. I regret not having won any NCAA championships there; I regret not having had the opportunity to play under Phog Allen; I regret missing the Olympics, and leaving so many friends so prematurely. But the decision to go to Kansas? No, I don't regret it, and I never have.

6

WHEN I ANNOUNCED I WAS leaving Kansas and joining the Globetrotters so that I could start playing serious basketball again, most people thought I was crazy. It was like a nun announcing she was leaving the Church and going to work in a whorehouse so she could protect her virginity.

But I knew exactly what I was doing. I desperately needed the kind of relaxed, stress-free, who-gives-a-shit atmosphere the Globies played in. For six years, I'd been living in a pressure cooker—hounded by college recruiters and NCAA investigators, besieged by fans and alumni and sportswriters, pushed and shoved and plotted against by opposing players and coaches. Remember, I was just 21 years old when I left Kansas; if I'd gone straight into the NBA then, feeling as I did, I might never have made it. I might have cracked up under the rigors of an 82-game schedule and all the physical pummeling I'd have to take until I learned how to use my body and my elbows like the rest of the big men I'd be facing.

I wasn't kidding about playing "serious" basketball with the Globies, though. The Globies are about 95 percent clown stuff now, but they started out as a serious basketball team, and even though the transition to comedy had already started when I joined them, they still played good basketball. They'd just finished a ten-year series with the college all-stars throughout the 1950s, and the Globies had won about two-thirds of the 200 or so games they played. The college all-stars weren't any humpty-dumpties either. They had guys like Bob Cousy, Paul Arizin, Cliff Hagan, Tommy Heinsohn, K. C. Jones, Walt Bellamy, Guy Rodgers, Tom Meschery, Larry Siegfried, Johnny Kerr, Jack Twyman, Tom Gola, Frank Ramsey, Larry Costello, Frank Selvy, Gene Shue. . . .

Over the years, the Globies had some fine ballplayers themselves. I always thought Marques Haynes was a much better ball handler than Cousy, for example, and Globies like Curly Neal and Roman Turmon probably could have made the NBA if they'd been white. Other Globies, men like Sweetwater Clifton and Connie Hawkins and Andy Johnson and Woody Sauldsberry, ultimately did play in the NBA. Actually, only a few Globies really clowned around. Meadowlark Lemon and Showboat Hall and Tex Harrison and J. C. Gipson were the clowns, and everyone else played serious basketball. But the clowns got all the laughs—and all the attention —and, in time, when the Globies had to choose between basketball and comedy, they chose comedy.

When I joined the team, the first move Abe Saperstein made was to have me play guard. The move had great comic potential, of course. Just the idea of a 7 foot 1 guard would freak out most fans. But for me, it was a good basketball decision. It gave me a chance to handle the ball and shoot from outside, and practice all those skills I'd need in the NBA but had been denied in college. Just as important, playing guard relieved me of any pressure I might otherwise have felt. I mean, no one could expect me to be a Cousy in the backcourt, right?

I wasn't actually supposed to join the Globies until October 18, when they'd begin their season in Madison Square Garden. But after all the hassle of college, I was anxious to get started— and Abe wasn't exactly indifferent to the crowds I could draw in Europe. So, on July 12, I joined the Globies in Milan, Italy. I played almost a month, and poor Abe was torn the whole time betwcen exulting in the fantastic attendance we had and worrying himself sick that I'd somehow hurt myself. You see, the contract we'd signed didn't go into effect until October, so his insurance on me didn't apply either. With the Globies playing in every imaginable arena—bullfight rings, wheatfields, cow pastures, tennis courts, you name it—Abe could just see me falling down and breaking a leg on some slippery ground, and there goes his investment. It got so he'd go out before every game and inspect every square inch of the playing surface himself. He'd walk over it and test it with his fingers and even get down on his hands and knees to eyeball it.

Until I joined them, I didn't know too much about the Globies individually, except that they were good basketball players and great clowns. Outside of that, most of them were just names to me. I soon learned that basketball and comedy were only the second and third most important things in their lives. The first, by far, was girls. The Globies, individually and collectively, were the greatest girl hounds I've ever seen. They spent almost very waking moment trying to figure out how to cop good-looking girls they'd meet on tour—and they damn near always succeeded, despite language barriers that would've stymied most men. They could even pick up girls in the middle of the game!

Globies speak their own language—blacks are "rocks," for example, and whites are "you-alls"—and one of their favorite phrases was "bomb" . . . as in "Did you drop the bomb on that girl yet?" (meaning, "Did you get her phone number?" or "Did you give her your phone number?") A Globie might see a girl in the stands that he really liked, so, during halftime, he'd write his name and hotel and room number on a slip of paper, and stick it in his jock or in his mouth, and sometime during the second half, he'd come up with a "ream"—that's what they called a basketball comedy routine—that would enable him to go galloping into the stands, near the girl. He'd drop the "bomb" on her so smoothly, no one would even notice it. And that night, you can bet, he'd cop her.

My introduction to the Globies-as-lovers came on my very first day with them in Europe. I got to Milan about 10 o'clock in the morning, and as I was walking into the Albergo Cavaleri Hotel, I bumped into Tom "Tarzan" Spencer, a 6 foot 7, 250-pound dude who'd been playing with them for about three years. We introduced ourselves, and when he told me he was going to be my roommate, I asked him where the hell he was going so early.

"Got a hot date," he said.

Being a night person, I normally have trouble talking, no less screwing, at that hour, so I just shook my head, and walked off, thinking, "Wow! Those Italian girls must really be something." That night, about six o'clock, "Ripper"—we called him "Ripper," as well as "Tarzan"—comes into the locker room, and I ask him how the girl was, and he says, "Fine, man, fine."

"I didn't know you could speak Italian," I told him.

"I can't."

"Oh, she speaks English then?"

"No."

"So how do you communicate? How'd you even meet?"

Well, it turns out they hadn't actually met at all—yet. She was a governess, and "Ripper" had seen her in the park with her babies, two days ago, and she'd really turned him on. So he'd gone back again, convinced that neither language nor her position nor her country's tradition could stop him.

"We just kind of sat there all day," he said. "I'd wave at her, and she'd wave at me. I think I'm going to cop her tomorrow."

I cracked up. "Cop her? How can you cop her if you can't even talk to her?"

"Ripper" said he was going to give her a ticket to the game.

"Man, after she sees me in action, it'll be a cinch."

He did give her a ticket. She did come to the game. And "Ripper" did cop her.

We played three games in Milan in three days, and before we left, a group of Italian businessmen came to me with a proposition: they wanted me to come back to Italy after my year with the Globies, and play pro basketball there. We'd drawn tremendous crowds in Milan, and basketball was just starting to get popular, and they figured I'd really make the sport a financial windfall for them. They made me a helluvan offer, about $35,000 a year— $10,000 more than Cousy was making in Boston—and I'd get it tax free, plus expenses to travel all over the continent. But I was determined to go into the NBA the next year and prove I could play with the best, so I turned them down.

That's one of the few decisions I've made in my life that I've subsequently regretted. I go to Europe almost every summer now, and I've come to really love it. It would've been great to play there for a couple of years, and get in on the ground floor of European basketball.

After Milan, the Globies went to Lugano, Switzerland, then back to Italy—Turino—for three days. That's where I learned another of the Globies' tricks—putting people on.

A couple of them would pick up a small foreign sportscar, set it down on the sidewalk and walk away, whistling, while the natives just looked at them like they were crazy.

Another trick, one I started doing with "Ripper" and "Boat" —Bob "Showboat" Hall—was to walk down the street until we had a small crowd following us (which, given our size, didn't usually take too long). Then one of us would point at something eight or ten feet off the ground—maybe a mark on a building or a leaf on a tree—and "Boat," who was about 6 foot 2, would start shaking his head "no" and me and "Ripper" would nod our heads "yes."

We'd do this for a few minutes, and, finally, "Boat" would shrug, and walk over to what we'd been pointing at, and jump up in the air and try to touch it. On the first jump, he'd always miss. We'd point at it again and nod our heads vigorously, and he'd jump again, and this time he'd touch it. By the second jump, the crowd would've caught on, and when he touched it, they'd cheer. So we'd walk down the street a bit till we saw something else, just a little higher up, and we'd go through the whole routine again—me and "Ripper" pointing and nodding our heads, "Boat" shaking his head, jumping, missing, jumping again and touching it. Every time he missed, the crowd would groan. When he'd touch it, they'd cheer.

After five or six rounds of this, we'd cross the street—"changing the crowd," we called it—and sure enough, the crowd would follow us. Finally we'd find something that looked impossible for "Boat" to touch. He'd try and try, and on his fourth or fifth jump, he'd really get up there and touch it, and the crowd would let out this huge gasp. Then we'd find something that really was beyound his reach. We'd go through our elaborate pantomime, and "Boat" would refuse to even try. He'd point at "Ripper," who was about five inches taller than he was, and then we'd start all over with "Ripper," picking a higher mark each time, drawing out the can-he-or-can't-he? agony longer each time—and drawing a bigger and bigger crowd as we marched through the city. Sometimes, we'd even involve the crowd. "Boat" or "Ripper," whoever was jumping, would pick out someone in the crowd and turn to him for moral support—shrugging his shoulders and shaking his head and looking sad, pretty much saying, "Why are these guys picking on me? You and I can see that's an impossible jump."

After "Boat" and "Ripper" finished their routines, we'd be up to marks maybe twelve, thirteen feet in the air, and then it would be my turn. For my first touch, we always picked something that looked impossibly high to the average European, but that I could actually touch rather easily. I'd be really casual about it, and when I got through, they'd be figuring I could probably touch the top of the Statue of Liberty. We'd always keep building until we got to one last really high mark, and I'd jump as high as I could and touch it, and the crowd would burst into frenzied applause and we'd all bow and walk away.

We had fun doing that in Italy on my first trip, but it was more than just a means of passing idle time and drawing attention to ourselves to build up the gate for the Globies' game that night. As soon as we finished, we'd run around the block and come up behind the crowd and sort of filter through it, looking for the best-looking girls.

Me and "Ripper" did the same thing from our hotel balcony. We'd go out on the balcony without our shirts, and start flexing our muscles. "Ripper" had a magnificent build, and before long, there'd be a big crowd down below. I'd pretend I was measuring his chest or his biceps or whatever, with exaggerated exclamations over how big he was, and when the crowd got large enough, one of us would leave the balcony, race down the stairs and circulate through the crowd, picking out the best-looking women and making arrangements to have them come to our hotel room later. If there were no good-looking girls in the crowd, I'd go back up to the room, tell "Ripper" and he'd leave the balcony for an hour or two. Then we'd start all over.

One night in Torino, we got back to the hotel after a game and some partying about 3 o'clock in the morning. I walked out on the balcony, where we'd done our little show earlier in the day, without much success, and I saw this absolutely gorgeous girl standing on the balcony outside the next room, wearing nothing but a nightgown. I go tearing back into our room to tell "Ripper" about it, but he won't believe me.

"Look, Wilt, we been looking for girls all day, and ain't found one, and here you want me to believe there's one standing on the balcony at 3 o'clock in the morning?"

He had a point. Maybe I was seeing things. I walked back out on the balcony. She was still there. I'd picked up a few words of Italian, so I tried *"Buona Sera!"* (Good evening) on her. She said *"Buona Sera"* back, and asked me if I spoke Italian. I said I didn't. She asked if I spoke Spanish. I said I didn't. I asked her if she spoke English. She said she didn't. Well, "Ripper" hears me talking, and figures I'm really putting him on, so he comes running out on the balcony in his shorts. As soon as he sees the girl, he stops dead in his tracks, turns around, runs back into the room, pulls his Globie warmup suit on and comes strolling back out, super-cool.

We all introduce ourselves, as best we can, and with smiles and gestures, she lets us know she'd like us to come over to her room for a drink. Well, me and "Ripper" are both so excited, we don't even bother to go back through our room, into the corridor, into her room. We just jump from our balcony to hers.

We get into her room, and she pours us some Pernod and water. I'd never heard of it, and it looked like dishwater, but by then I would've drunk from a cesspool if I thought it would help me cop her. The three of us sat there for about an hour, drinking and trying to understand each other, and it turned out she was an acrobat in the circus. When we asked her for a demonstration, she started doing handstands and backflips and some absolutely fantastic stuff right there in the room. "Ripper" was really putting the Pernod away, and by the time she was through with her little show, "Ripper" was ripped.

"Hey, I can do that," he tells her.

Before we can stop him, he jumps on the bed and tries a back-flip. Italian hotel rooms just aren't made for 6 foot 7 guys to do back-flips in, and "Ripper's" feet go crashing into the wall. In fact, they go through the wall; I guess it was plasterboard or whatever they use for walls in second-class hotels. When "Ripper" extricates himself, he says he's going to use the bathroom and go back to our room, so I kind of forget about him, and sit on the bed with the girl, trying to cop her.

All of a sudden, just as I'm getting ready to kiss her for the first time, I hear this horrendous crash coming from the bathroom. "Ripper" had gotten into the bathtub by mistake, fell asleep standing up—and fell down and banged his head when he woke up ten minutes later. We decided it was time to leave. But, since we'd come by way of the balcony, we didn't have the key to our room. The balcony had been an easy jump when we'd come over because we were sober then, and we'd only had to jump out and down. It was a distance of maybe ten or twelve feet and we just jumped out that far, and then dropped onto her balcony. But now we had to jump ten or twelve feet and reach *up* slightly to grab our balcony. Being the nice, thoughtful, considerate guy I am, I let "Ripper" go first. He made it—barely. Then I went back into the room with the girl and screwed her before I made the jump myself.

That was Torino, Italy.

We went from Torino to Naples to Bologna to Pesaro, and in Pesaro, I meet this sensational looking girl named Chi Chi who even speaks English. I get tickets for the Globies game for her and her little brother, and after the game, they get on her scooter and she tells me to grab a cab and follow her to their house. Italian cab-drivers make New York cabbies look like winners of the National Safety Council safe-driving award, and about seven accidents and five near-accidents later, we pull up in front of her house. Her father is there, and he pours me a drink and we all visit, and by then, I can see I'm not going to cop her—not right then anyway. So I make an appointment to see her on the beach at 10 o'clock the next morning and I leave. Only I don't know where the hell I am or how to get back to my hotel. It's after midnight. It's pitch-black outside. I can't see my hand in front of my face. I'm in the middle of nowhere, and I'm too embarrassed to go back and ask the girl for directions. I flipped a coin to see if I should walk to my right or my left, but it was so damn dark, I couldn't even see which side came up. I just started walking—and walking and walking and walking. I finally got back to my hotel about 9 o'clock in the morning—just in time to change clothes and meet Chi Chi on the beach. I told her what had happened, and she told me I'd walked in the wrong direction. If I'd gone the other way, I would've

90

passed a cab stand about ten minutes from her house. But everything turned out well. I copped her, and we became good friends and we corresponded for about five years—until she got married.

From Italy that first summer, the Globies moved on to Vienna. First day there, just before the game, me and "Boat" spot another gorgeous girl. She had coal-black hair and a great tan, and she was wearing a stunning, candy-apple red dress. But by the time me and "Boat" stopped staring and started chasing, she was already inside the arena. We tried to find her, but we didn't have much time because the game was about to start. We were already in uniform, and we started wandering through the stands, looking for her. Before we know it, the Globies are on the floor, the record player's playing "Sweet Georgia Brown," and me and "Boat" are still in the stands. Well, we turned it into a "ream." We made a big production of stomping out of the stands onto the court, and we join the team, and we spend the whole game looking up at the stands, one section at a time, trying to find the girl.

We never did find her, and I don't remember the score of the game. But I know we won. I know that because we won every game I played in that year with the Globies. People thought the Laker's 33-game win streak was a big deal a couple of seasons ago. Hell, the Globies won 224 in a row that year. I didn't even have to concentrate sometimes. I not only searched the stands for girls, I practiced counting the crowd while the game was in progress. I got pretty adept at it, too. Abe Saperstein kept attendance records for every city we'd played in the previous year, and my agreement with him was that I'd get a percentage of the gate any time the Globies drew more people with me than they had without me. I knew Abe wasn't anxious to give away any more money than he had to, so I tried to keep a close watch on the house, just to be sure he didn't suddenly forget how to count.

Abe was a funny guy in many ways. Like all the Globies, he was very competitive—competitive to the point of cheating. We all played cards a lot, in hotel rooms and on the bus, and Abe always wanted to win. When he didn't, he'd get so grumpy, the guys would let him win the next time. But they didn't like losing either. So they'd cheat each other. My first few weeks with the Globies, a couple of the better-known players cheated me like crazy at "Tonk" and "bid whist" and poker and all the other games we played. They'd stack the deck, deal "seconds," deal off the bottom—anything they could get away with. I'd have great poker hands, but they'd always have just a little better—three of a kind to my two high pair, a straight to my three aces, a full house to my straight. Finally, when I caught them, I got mad, and told them they'd better give me my money back or I'd go to Abe and have them bounced off the team. They were veterans, but they knew I was the big drawing card that year, so they gave me my money back, and went looking for new fish. Abe never caught on when they let him win, though. At least, he never said anything. He just kept raking in the money.

It's fashionable now for some people, particularly blacks, to criticize Abe for exploiting blacks and using the Globies to perpetuate the Stepin' Fetchit image of the black man, but I don't go along with that. In the first place, exploitation can be a two-way street. Sure, Abe "used" us to get rich. But we "used" the Globies to make money, too. Not as much as Abe, of course, but better than most of us could have made elsewhere. Abe started the Globies in 1927, and the NBA didn't integrate until 1950, so for all those years, he gave blacks a chance to play. Otherwise, given the structure of American society, many of them might have become janitors or gone on welfare.

As for the Stepin' Fetchit stereotype, well, there's all kinds of stereotypes, and I don't like any of them. I'm not exactly thrilled by the image of the black man you see in all these "Shaft"/"Super Fly"/"Hit Man" movies either. That's exploiting the blacks, too, and the image of the black-man-as-Superman, who can't say anything except "mother-fucker," is just as dangerously misleading a stereotype as the black-man-as-stumblebum, who can't say anything except "yassah, boss." But I'm not sure I agree that the Globies were Stepin' Fetchits. They had—and have—a highly developed skill for comedy, for making people laugh at them. It's the same skill that guys like Jerry Lewis and Charlie Chaplin and Jackie Gleason have. They're clowns, actors playing a role Jews would call a "shlemiel" or a "shlimazl." Even today, I enjoy making fun of that stereotype—and all black stereotypes. I'll pick up someone's baggage coming out of the airport and pretend to be a skycap, or I'll stand in front of a hotel and pretend to be a doorman. My first few years in the NBA, before I became so well known, I got a big kick out of walking into a busy department store, standing in front of the elevator and saying things like, "Ladies' lingerie, third floor. Hardware, fifth floor. Home furnishings, seventh floor. Watch your step, please."

I think one of the best ways to disprove a stereotype is to make fun of it—not to pretend it doesn't exist—and I think Abe saw that, too. Contrary to what some critics say, I truly believe he and the Globies have helped destroy the stereotype, not perpetuate it. Abe deserves much of the credit for that. He also deserves credit for making the Globetrotters into the best goodwill ambassadors this country ever had. The Globies have played in 85 or 90 countries now, before more than 70 million people, and a lot of those people have never seen any Americans other than the Globies—except maybe for some big-mouth, big-spending "ugly Americans."

Not that I think Abe was any kind of saint. He was out, first and foremost, to make money, and he wouldn't tolerate anything that might jeopardize the Globies' box-office popularity. He didn't want us to date white girls, for example, because he was sure the predominantly white fans would resent that. And he didn't want the NBA to start signing black players because he wanted them all for the Globies. For years, Abe and the Globies kept the NBA afloat. For the first ten or twelve years after the NBA was formed, the Globies would play the first games of doubleheaders. Fans would flock in to the Globies, and leave before the NBA game started. As NBA ball got better, fans began staying longer. But the Globies got them there in the first place, and Abe knew it. He also knew the Globies' lure would be diminished if they couldn't continue signing the best black players. He was really proud of his players, the good ones, and he wanted everyone to know he had great athletes as well as great clowns. Like the year I was with the Globies, Abe was always coming into the dressing room at halftime, and complaining that the other guys weren't letting me shoot enough.

"You gotta shoot more, Wilt. You gotta score," he'd scream.

I didn't see why. I mean, we'd be ahead by 35 points; why should I score? But Abe wanted everyone to know he had the greatest basketball player in the world on his team, and he thought scoring was one way to do that. Abe was never altogether comfortable as the promoter/producer of a clown show; he was a

93

basketball man first and an entertainer second, and players like me helped him maintain that image—to himself and to the public.

Abe wasn't very happy when the NBA first started to integrate. Walter Brown, one of the founders of the NBA, was the owner of the Boston Celtics, and he was going to sign Chuck Cooper as the first black man in the league. Abe went crazy. He threatened to boycott Boston Garden. Fortunately, Brown wasn't intimidated. He signed Cooper, then other blacks, and the other NBA owners gradually followed suit—without the Globies losing any of their formidable drawing power. In fact, I'd guess that's when the transition from serious basketball to comedy became irreversible; with the Globies no longer assured of getting the best black players, they had to build their show on something they knew would always be there. That something was laughs, and since Abe owned a piece of the Philadelphia Warriors anyway, he wound up making money on both sides of the fence. But after all he did for the NBA in its early years, when it came time for the owners to do something for him, they screwed him. He wanted the first West Coast NBA franchise, and he said the league promised him he could have it. Then, in 1960, the NBA moved the Lakers from Minneapolis to Los Angeles and shut Abe out. He got so pissed, he started his own league—the American Basketball League (ABL). The league only lasted about a year, and it must have cost Abe a few million bucks, but that's the way he was. He had this power complex, a Napoleon complex really. He'd even stand around with his hand stuck in his jacket all the time.

I remember that first summer I was with the Globies, and we were in Vienna, and I left this girl about 5:30 one morning, and started walking around the city. I've always liked to do that in a strange city early in the morning, and this time, I see a guy who looks like Abe, standing on the street corner, his fingers hooked into his suspenders and his chest puffed out as far as his belly. I walked up to him, and asked him what he was doing out at that hour—before he could ask me the same question. He said:

"Wilt, I'm so excited I can't sleep. I just had to come outside and look at this gorgeous city and reflect on its history. Do you realize I'm staying in the very same hotel Napoleon Bonaparte once stayed in?"

94

I shook my head. "You mean the Napoleon that got his ass blown off in Russia? What's so fantastic about that?"

"I'm staying in the very same suite he stayed in."

"No shit."

"I'm sleeping in the same bed, the actual bed that Napoleon slept in."

"You're kidding."

"No, honest."

I cocked my head, and leaned over a little. "Tell me, Abe. Have they changed the sheets since then?"

I'm not sure Abe ever fully forgave me for making fun of him like that, and he tried to get back at me by making fun of my preoccupation with pretty girls. He'd come rushing over to me before a game, and point to some fine-looking girl, and say, "See her? That's Esther Williams (or Ava Gardner or whoever). She's here to see you." I knew better, but some of the other guys fell for it, and Abe would pull the same stunt on them, time and time again.

J. C. Gipson was one of the guys Abe could put on the easiest. "Gipper"—as in "Gipper," "Dipper," and "Ripper"—was about 6 foot 8, 230 pounds, and he wasn't exactly what you'd call a genius. One time we were in Marseilles, in a restaurant, and the menu's in French, and "Gipper" can't decide what to order. Finally, he says, "I'll have some of this *potage de jour*." I said, "How do you know you'll like it? Why don't you ask what it is first?" He said, "Oh, I know what it is. I had some yesterday, and it was great."

The Globies had just come to France from Germany and Switzerland, and the next day, "Gipper" decided he was going to impress our waitress with his knowledge of French. So he orders "*ein* Coca Cola *bien cuit*." *Ein* is German, not French, for "one"; *bien cuit* is French, all right . . . for "well-done."

(I have to admit I wasn't always the suave, sophisticated world traveler either. I remember the first time this fine French broad had me over to her house, and her father poured me some rare old cognac. I didn't know what it was, and I poured Coke in with it.)

"Gipper" was one of the Globies you could always count on

95

to get in trouble. One time, he didn't like the way a French cab driver was looking at him in the rear-view mirror, so he pulled his switchblade out, just in case the cabbie was thinking of rolling him. When the cabbie saw the knife, *he* thought "Gipper" was going to rob *him.* So the cabbie starts going around corners, looking for a cop, getting more frightened all the time, and "Gipper" doesn't know where he's being taken, so he gets scared, thinking the cabbie is going to take him for a ride and dump him in an alley some place. Suddenly, the cabbie hits the brakes, jumps out and starts screaming for a cop in French. "Gipper" thinks he's calling for some other cabbies to help jump him, so he hops out of the cab and starts waving his knife around. The next thing we knew, they were both surrounded by cops.

We didn't see "Gipper" again for two days.

Another time, "Gipper" was trying to cop a girl in a Paris bar, and a little French dude, about 5 foot 6, comes up and says something to the girl in French, and she turns to "Gipper" and says, "I gotta go now." "Gipper" turns around and picks the guy up and pushes him against the wall and starts to shake the hell out of him and tells him to "quit cutting in on my girl, you cocksucker." The guy starts screaming, and the girl starts banging "Gipper" on the back and we damn near have a riot. It turns out the guy is the girl's father, and he's just come to take her home after work.

The Globies were characters, all right. The same trip "Gipper" showed off his linguistic prowess, my first summer with the Globies, we're in Geneva, and it's about 2:30 in the morning, and me and Meadowlark and "Boat" and "Tex" Harrison are just getting back to the hotel when here comes "Ripper" with an ugly, short little broad—what the Globies call a "mullion." The worst sin a Globie could be guilty of was to be seen with a "mullion." If a guy got horny and couldn't find anything but a "mullion," he might cop her, but if he spotted another Globie, he'd just take off and leave her standing there. If you said you'd seen him with a "mullion," he'd have 101 excuses—"That wasn't me" or "She was beggin' me for it and I couldn't get away" or "You should've seen the fine fox I copped before you got there; this one was her friend, and I was just being nice."

Well, this sure was a "mullion"—the ugliest girl I'd ever seen—

and it sure was "Ripper," and the minute he saw us, he realized he couldn't run for it, so he started stumbling and staggering like he was drunk, and all the time he kept pushing on the girl and walking by us. As soon as they got around the corner, he grabbed her hand and they ran like hell. Next day, when we asked him about her, he pretended he didn't remember anything. "Man, I was falling down drunk last night," he said. "What mullion you talking about?"

"Ripper" had more than his share of "mullions," and one night, one of them stood out on the street, beneath our hotel window, calling "Ripper." To this day, when any of the Globies meet him, we imitate her falsetto voice and start calling, " 'Ripper,' yoo hoo, 'Ripper.' "

A few nights after "Ripper's" Geneva triumph, the Globies were in France, and he bought a case of beer, and took it back to our hotel. He could drink beer by the keg, and it was something he often did when we got to a new city. But there was no ice available. So he put the case in the bathtub, and filled the tub with cold water. This was in Nice, on the Riviera, in the Hotel Negresco, one of the few first-class hotels we ever stayed in (I think all the second-class hotels were full or something). Anyway, when we got back after the game that night, the hotel was surrounded by police and firemen. It seems that one of the beer cans got stuck in the drain hole and the tub overflowed and water inundated half the hotel.

Of course, the biggest clown on the Globies was—and is— Meadowlark Lemon. "Lark" is not much of a basketball player, but he is one helluva funny clown. Trouble is, he didn't like any competition as a clown. The Globies' games are like Broadway plays—with rehearsals and fall-guys and timing and all—and "Lark" was the star. We'd do so many "reams" a game, with some improvisation, and he always got the most laughs. That's how it was planned. If anyone else stole the limelight, either deliberately or just because some routine happened to work out that way on the spur of the moment, "Lark" sulked and bitched and threatened to clobber the guy.

One time, I was having a lot of fun on the court, with one "ream" after another, and "Lark" got pissed. After the game, he tried to jump me in the locker room. But I saw him out of the corner of my eye, and I grabbed him in mid-air, and held him over my head like a barbell until he stopped screaming.

Actually, it was amazing that there wasn't more friction on the team than there was. After all, we were performers, with the sensitive egos you expect in performers, and we were thrust together constantly. You'd think the pressure of traveling all the time and being together all the time would have led to one blowup after another. But it didn't.

The Globies' grind was staggering. We hopscotched back and forth across Europe—and the United States—by plane and train and bus and car. We'd travel 300 miles in one day, play that night, ride 150 miles the next day, play again, ride 80 miles after dinner and play again. We played almost every day, and sometimes twice or three times a day.

Abe would usually slip us an extra $5 or $10 or $20 when we doubled up like that, but that didn't compensate for the lack of sleep and the bad eating habits and nonexistent personal hygiene that resulted from playing 300 or 400 games a year and traveling God knows how many millions of miles.

We rarely had time to wash our uniforms between games, so we'd wear the same smelly, sweaty uniforms night after night, until it rubbed our skin raw. I've always perspired a lot anyway, so it was really tough on me. That's when I started putting a Band-Aid over my nipples before each game, to keep them from getting rubbed raw by the jersey; I still do that now, even though I'm probably the only player in the NBA who changes his uniform top at halftime every game. I usually lose anywhere from eight to twelve pounds a game in perspiration, so I'll drink two or three gallons of liquid after a game—mostly milk, orange juice, and 7 Up. We all drank a lot of that stuff on the Globies, generally straight out of the can or carton. Room service, even in second-rate European hotels, has always seemed ridiculously expensive to me, and I just couldn't see paying $1 for a thimble-size glass of orange juice, so I'd stop in the grocery store and buy it by the gallon and take it back to the room or on the bus.

We were on the road so much, we ate on the run most of the time, and until I came along, most of the Globies existed on greasy-spoon hamburgers. They'd have the bus stop every once in a while and load up on them. Well, I started having the bus stop at grocery stores, so I could buy my orange juice, and I'd buy a lot of food, too—Vienna sausages and bread and salami and cold cuts and potato chips. I'd set up a regular delicatessen in the back of the bus. That's another habit I carried with me into the NBA. I still stop at grocery stores, particularly these 7-11 markets they have in most cities, and buy a couple of shopping bags full of stuff to take back to my hotel room when we're on the road.

For all the missed meals and missed sleep, though, I thoroughly enjoyed my month in Europe with the Globies. When I left them in August, I'd seen Italy, Switzerland, France, Austria, and Germany, and I had only one regret: For several years I'd wanted to buy a red Mercedes 300 SL. In Basel, Switzerland, right next to the Excelsior Hotel, where we stayed, there was a Mercedes dealer, and he had my car in the window. I went right to Abe and said, "I got to have it." He just smiled and said, "You want it? It's yours."

I was like a little boy whose father had just told him he could have his first toy fire truck. I raced out of Abe's room and down the stairs and into the showroom and up to the salesman and pointed to the car and said, "That one. I want it." He gave me a little speech about all its features, and put me in the passenger's seat and took me out for a ride in the countryside. God, it was fantastic. Then he got out and said, "Your turn. You drive back."

I couldn't do it.

No matter how hard I tried, I just could not fit into that driver's seat, under the steering wheel. It was too small for me, and the seat frame was welded to the body; it couldn't be moved back. I was heartbroken. I don't think I said a word the whole ride back. But that was really my only disappointment of the whole European tour, and I soon got over it.

After my month in Europe with the Globies, I left them and went off to Paris by myself, and then came home to await the start of the American tour in New York on October 18. I have to admit I didn't enjoy the six months of play in America as much as I enjoyed the four weeks in Europe, but I'm sure that's partially because I'd already seen most of the big American cities on my recruiting trips and my summer wanderings for schoolyard games. Of course, we didn't only play in big cities. We played in places like Niles, Illinois; Connersville, Indiana; Abington, Pennsylvania;

Prestonburg, Kentucky; Minot, North Dakota; Ironwood, Michigan; Yakima, Washington—any place that was big enough to have a basketball court (plus a few that weren't; we carried our own portable floor around with us, just in case).

Still, it was a great year—the happiest of my life. I made enough money to pay cash for a new car for my father and a new home in a nice section of Philadelphia for him and my mother, and I traveled abroad for the first time and fell in love with Europe. Hardly a summer would pass after that without my returning to Europe. I was a young, naive, unsophisticated boy during my year with the Globies, but in time, I'd come to know the best restaurants and the best hotels; I'd learn my way around cities like Paris and Rome and Milan and Copenhagen; I'd learn to speak Italian pretty fluently and French, German, and Spanish well enough to get by in most situations; I'd even pick up a smattering of Persian, Arabic, Swedish, Danish, and Russian. I played with the Globies almost every summer until I got myself traded to the Lakers and really got into the Southern California lifestyle, with the beach and volleyball and all. I'd go to Europe after the NBA season was over, and I'd call the Globies office to find out their schedule, and whenever our paths crossed—usually in Italy—I'd play six or eight or ten games with them, sometimes more.

But when that first season ended, in the spring of 1959, I was ready to play in the NBA, ready to join the Philadelphia Warriors and go up against Bill Russell and Bob Pettit and all those other guys I'd been hearing and reading so much about.

Abe didn't want me to go. He made me one great offer after another to play another season with the Globies. He and Eddie Gottlieb, the Warriors owner, had a falling-out over that. When I'd signed with the Globies, Abe had promised Eddie he wouldn't try to keep me more than the one year. But with me, the Globies' attendance had increased 20 percent over the previous year. That was money in Abe's pocket, and he wanted more of it. They fought bitterly about it, and they never did completely patch things up; they were never again as close as they had been, and I've always been sorry that I was the cause of that, even though it wasn't really my fault.

When I signed with the Warriors, we announced my salary as $35,000—more than anyone else in the NBA was getting. Actually,

100

with bonuses and side deals and all, I probably got more than twice that much. In fact I got close enough to $100,000 that I called Haskell Cohen, the NBA publicity man, to remind him of a prediction I'd made the previous year. Haskell was the guy who first got me a job at Kutsher's, in the Catskills, and he'd always taken a fatherly sort of interest in my career. When I joined the Globies, he recommended against it—until I told him how much Abe was paying me. Then he said, "Well, you might as well go head; you're sure never going to get that kind of money in the NBA."

I disagreed. "I figure I can play a year with the Globies, and come into the NBA with a six-figure contract," I told him.

"You're nuts," he told me.

When I signed with Eddie, I just picked up the phone, called Haskell and said, "Remember what I told you about my first NBA contract? Well, I just did it."

Actually, although money was important, it wasn't the most important thing Eddie and I talked about at the first contract signing. I'd heard that blacks in the NBA were still having trouble when their teams played in the South—Elgin Baylor had gone to West Virginia with the Lakers, and had had to stay in a different hotel from the rest of the team; the same thing had happened with Bill Russell and the Celtics in several Southern cities. In later years, when Bill got the reputation of being something of a militant—or, at least, a black man who fought for his race—and I was supposed to be an "Uncle Tom," I always remembered that he'd played in all those places that humiliated him. Not me. Before I even signed my first contract, I told Eddie the same thing I'd told Phog Allen at Kansas:

"Don't schedule any games where I can't eat with the team and sleep with the team, or you can bet your ass I won't play with the team."

He agreed.

During the summer after I signed with the Warriors, I continued to play schoolyard games and benefit games, and in August I got my first real taste of pro ball. Maurice Stokes, the great Cincinnati forward, had had a stroke in March, 1957, and there was a benefit game for him every year after that at Kutsher's in the Catskills, where I'd worked in high school. I'd made good friends with Milt Kutsher, the owner, and I was about to start

101

my own summer basketball camp up there, so I got up to Kutsher's quite a bit anyway. Also, I knew Maurice and really liked him, and in later years, I'd fly all the way home from Europe just to get there in time to play. This year, I just drove up from Philadelphia. All the big stars were there—Bob Cousy, Dolph Schayes, Frank Ramsey, Johnny Kerr, Tommy Heinsohn, Jack Twyman, Richie Guerin, Larry Costello . . . all of them among the top 20 scorers in the NBA the previous year.

I scored 20 points and got 15 rebounds and blocked 14 shots, even though I only played half the game.

I decided I was ready for the NBA.

7

I MADE MY NBA DEBUT IN AN
exhibition game in Los Angeles on September 30, 1959, against
the St. Louis Hawks. There were 12,443 fans in the Sports Arena
that night—the biggest basketball crowd they'd ever had in Los
Angeles—and we won, 106-102. I scored 28 points, but I was
real nervous, and I didn't think I played very well. We played
the Hawks a total of nine times in an exhibition series throughout
the West that first year, and we won six of them. I averaged about
30 points a game, outscoring Bob Pettit almost every night, but I
was still feeling my way along.

Part of the problem, I imagine, was that I had picked up a
few bad habits with the Globies, and it was taking me a few games
to get rid of them. Walking with the ball was probably the worst
of the bad habits, but I was also prone to clowning around occasionally. I remember one exhibition game where the official, a little
guy named Sid Borgia, called a foul on me for blocking when a
guy on the other team charged right into me. I couldn't believe the
call, and I went stomping over to Borgia, and got nose-to-nose.

"What did you call that?" I screamed.

"Blocking."

"What?"

"Blocking."

With that, I picked him up by the arms, lifted him about two feet off the ground and repeated my question:

"What did you call that?"

"Charging."

After our exhibition season, we opened league play Oct. 24 in Madison Square Garden against the New York Knicks. Fuzzy Levane was the Knicks coach then, and he and some of his players were quoted before the game as saying they'd stop me by blocking me out on the boards and making me shoot from the outside. That's not quite the way things worked out. It was almost like my first college game all over again—I hit four jump shots from the top of the key in the first few minutes. Then I got into a battle for a rebound with Kenny Sears, one of the Knicks' veteran forwards. We both grabbed the ball at the same time, and I just stuffed it through the basket, with Kenny still hanging on. I think his arm went through the basket, too—up to the elbow. Kenny was always a smooth player, but he wasn't exactly famous around the league for his courage or his determination, and I don't think he ever tried to get in my way again the rest of his career.

I wound up that first game with 17 of 27 shots from the floor and 43 points. I also got 28 rebounds. We won, 118-109.

You can imagine how much publicity I was getting in Philadelphia then, and a week later, on a Saturday night, the Warriors had their biggest crowd ever for our home opener against Detroit. I got 36 points and 34 rebounds, and we won, 120-112.

We were 3-0 when we went to Boston for the first time on November 7. The newspapers were building the game up as the match of the century—the first meeting between me and Bill Russell . . . the unstoppable offensive force versus the immovable defensive object. I don't mind saying I was a little nervous at the time, and I guess it showed in the game. Still, I thought I played pretty well for a rookie going against a guy who was supposed to be the greatest defensive player in history—and playing in a madhouse like Boston Garden at that.

Boston beat us, 115-106. I outscored Bill, 30-22, but he

outrebounded me, 35-28—hardly a disgrace, particularly when you realize that Russell would've had more rebounds than God in Boston Garden. In the NBA, the home team provides the statisticians, so the home team players tend to get the benefit of the doubt on things like rebounds. For some reason, I seem to be about the only exception to that. Russell always had far more rebounds at home than on the road. Same with Bob Cousy on assists. But I've always had just about the same stats at home as on the road. The only explanation I've been able to come up with for that is the old "Wilt is superman" idea everyone has always had—the feeling, at least subconsciously, that I'm so good, I don't need help from the statisticians (or from anyone else).

Anyway, some of the newspaper and magazine reports of that first game against Boston were hilarious. Like *Sports Illustrated* said it was "a shocking experience for Wilt Chamberlain" when Russell blocked one of my shots. They made it sound like I'd never had one of my shots blocked before. One newspaper even said just that. Bullshit! I'd been playing against guys older and more experienced than me for years, and I'd had more shots blocked than I could count. So I was hardly "shocked" when Russell did it. Besides, this was my rookie season, my first game against Russell—and only my third NBA game ever; if the great Bill Russell could only block *one* of my shots, I imagine *he* was the one who was shocked, not me.

In my second game against Russell, I just plain destroyed him. I outscored him, 45-15, and outrebounded him, 35-13, and he fouled out trying to guard me. The Warriors won, 123-113.

There was another early-season game my rookie year that should be mentioned—our second meeting with the New York Knicks. It was one of the most bizarre experiences I've ever had on a basketball court, but you have to understand a little of the background to fully appreciate it.

Back when I was in junior high, just starting to play basketball with those four friends—Vince, Tommy, Marty, and Howard—we all wore red-white-and-blue lumberjack socks that came almost up to the knee. After we played a while, they'd start to slip, so we got in the habit of putting rubber bands around the tops and folding the socks over. To be sure we always had enough rubber bands, we picked them up off the street, and took them off the neighbors' newspapers, and walked into grocery stores and dime stores and took them off merchandise there. We always wore at least one extra rubber band on our right wrists at all times, whether we were playing, studying, sleeping, or showering. That way, if one of the rubber bands on our socks broke during a game, we knew we'd have one handy.

On the night of my first college game at Kansas, when the trainer, Dean Nesmith, came over and put tape around the tops of my socks, I looked down at that rubber band on my right wrist, and thought, "Wow, I don't need my rubber band any more." But just looking at it, I flashed on all the stuff we used to do to get them and how much fun we had together and how that was when basketball really started for me. I decided to keep the rubber band, as kind of a reminder of those good times, back when I didn't have much in the way of material posessions.

To this day, I wear a rubber band on my right wrist at all times. It's not a superstition or anything because I'm not superstitious. If I were, I sure as hell wouldn't have become the first professional athlete to wear No. 13. But, like I said, it's a nice reminder. I still pick rubber bands up off the street when I see them, and people are always sending me extras, so I have plenty around when one breaks or gets weak or dirty or smelly. I've had girls pull on my rubber band in bed, in the heat of passion, and I've had a lot of people kid me about wearing it, but I usually just say, "We have some pretty complicated plays in basketball, and I only wear it so I'll know which hand is my right hand when I start to move on the court."

Anyway, that night against the Knicks in my rookie year, Willie Naulls, who's about 6 foot 6 and 225 pounds, gets the bright idea that I probably wear the rubber band as a good-luck charm, and since I'd killed the Knicks in our first game, he decides he'll try to upset me by pulling it off. Well, for the first five minutes of the game, me and Willie are running up and down the court, and he's grabbing and pulling and yanking at me like some kind of madman. It must have looked crazy from the stands, these two great big guys playing some kind of kids' tag game or something. Finally, he gets the rubber band off—and I miss my next seven shots. They're easy ones, but I miss them. For six minutes, I don't get a basket. The ball goes in and pops back

106

out almost every time. Then the ball starts dropping for me again, and I wind up with 35 points and we win, 109-108.

I had one other amusing experience my rookie season; I cut a rock 'n' roll record, and was a guest on Dick Clark's "American Bandstand" TV show. Everyone in my family always sang in the church choir, and they always kidded me about having the worst voice in the family. Finally, I just said, "OK, I'll show you guys. I'll make a record." And I did. The side I liked best, "That's Easy to Say," never got any radio play at all, but the other side—"By the River"—actually made the charts in Philadelphia. Hell, it made No. 14 in Boston! The critics weren't too tough on it either. They said things like "it's generally pleasing" and "his voice displays flashes of timbre."

I thought my voice was just awful, to tell you the truth. And the lyrics didn't exactly pack the cosmic significance of Bob Dylan's best. As I recall, it started something like this (you'll have to provide your own musical accompaniment):

By the river 'neath the shady tree,
Just my baby, just my baby and me.
We hugged, kissed, huddled close
By the river 'neath the shady tree.
Every Sunday by the bright sunshine.
Chicken in the basket all the time.
Then in the evening, when the sun goes down,
We hold tight, strolling back to town.*

Sensational, huh?

About the same time I was dazzling music-lovers from coast-to-coast with that aria, I got hurt bad playing basketball. It was a nationally televised game on a Sunday in St. Louis, and Clyde Lovellette, one of the roughest—make that "dirtiest"—players in the league, deliberately hit me in the mouth with his elbow. Lovellette was a big stud from Kansas—about 6 foot 9, 245 pounds or so—and he really slammed me. He knocked two of my front teeth clear up into the roof of my mouth, and by the next day, I had a helluva headache and a serious infection. The pus

107

and poison were building up inside, and my face was so swollen out of shape, you literally couldn't recognize me. But our coach, Neil Johnston, didn't seem to be concerned about my pain *or* my appearance. He left me in to finish the game against St. Louis (we got creamed, 130-108), and he played me again two days later against Detroit. The press said I played in Detroit because I had a chance to break George Yardley's all-time record for the most points in one season. Bullshit! The season was only two-thirds over; I had about 25 more games to do that, and I only needed 15 or 20 points. I didn't want to play at all. My face hurt so much I couldn't eat or sleep. But we'd lost two of our last three games, and I guess Neil didn't want to take a chance on our falling too far behind Boston or getting into a long losing streak. So, I played—wearing this hideously grotesque mask to protect my face—and we lost, 122-113. I went over the 2,000-point mark in that game, and broke Yardley's record, but I wasn't really thinking much about records *or* losing. I was in real agony.

The next night, we were in New York, and Neil played me again. When Willie Naulls accidentally elbowed me in the mouth, I *had* to come out; the team doctor told Neil the infection was so bad, I could actually die if I didn't have surgery right away. Neil grumbled about losing me, but he finally agreed to let me go to the hospital. I missed three games recovering from the operation (the Warriors lost two of the three), and I didn't miss another game for more than four years.

The rest of my rookie season was pretty successful. I scored 58 points against the Knicks two weeks after I was hurt, and I got more than 50 points four other times that year—the first time anyone ever did it that often. After breaking Yardley's record of 2,001 points, I went on to score 2,707 points for the season. I broke nine league records in all, including highest average (37.6), most rebounds (1,941) and most rebounds per game (26.9)—both better than Bill Russell had ever done. Despite having missed those three games when I was hurt, I also tied Gene Shue of Detroit for most minutes ever played in one season—3,338.

I was named rookie of the year *and* most valuable player—the first time anyone ever won both awards the same year. I was also the starting center in the NBA all-star game—in Philadelphia.

We won, 125-115, and I scored 23 points and got 25 rebounds and was named most valuable player in the game.

But for all these records and accomplishments, my rookie season in the NBA was not a happy one. For one thing, I had the feeling that Neil Johnston hadn't liked me since I'd shown him up in the Catskills, when I was still in high school. He seemed to resent my making more money and getting more publicity than he ever got, too, so we just didn't get along very well. My rookie year was also the beginning of my battles with Bill Russell, battles I always seemed destined to lose—at least that's how the sportswriters and most fans came to look at it. We lost to Boston in six games that year in the Eastern Division playoffs, and they went on to beat St. Louis for the championship. We might have beaten Boston in that series if I hadn't been injured again. After they beat us, 111-105, in the first game, we won the second one, 115-110, to get a split in Boston. But it was a costly victory. The Celtics kept roughing me up, particularly Tommy Heinsohn, and the officials wouldn't call anything. Finally, I got mad and threw a punch at Tommy. But I missed and hit Tom Gola, one of my teammates, on the forearm. We damn near had a riot in Boston Garden, and the police had to come out on the court to restore order. The doctors packed my hand in ice and ordered me not to play in the third playoff game, but I played anyway. The coach wanted me to, my teammates wanted me to, and I wanted to. I figured if we could beat Boston that third game, in Philadelphia, we'd have a helluva shot at the title, and I wanted to do everything I could to help. Unfortunately, I couldn't do much. My hand was sore and swollen, and I only got 12 points, and Russell got 26 and outrebounded me something awful. After we jumped out to a 33-22 first quarter lead, they ran away and hid. In the second quarter alone, they outrebounded us 31-9! They won, 120-90, and they beat us again the next night, 112-104. My hand was a little better by the time we got back to Boston for the fifth game, and I scored 50 points, and we won, 128-107. Two nights later, Boston eliminated us, 119-117, on a tip-in by Heinsohn at the buzzer. We should've won that game. We had Guy Rodgers at the free throw line with the score tied and 11 seconds left, and he missed both shots.

That was typical of what often happened when my teams played Boston. I'd play my heart out against Russell, and someone else on my team would blow the game. I averaged 30 points a game in that first playoff series against Boston, and outscored and outrebounded Russell. My teammates? Guy had one game where he didn't score at all and another where he got just one point. He fouled out of two games, and played two others with five fouls on him. He was just trying too hard, I guess, and he choked. He wasn't the only one. Gola fouled out twice. Woody Sauldsberry fouled out twice. Paul Arizin was the only guy on our team besides me who played up to his potential. He averaged about 20 points a game in the playoffs, just a couple of points less than his regular-season average.

In later years, though, people would say the series was Chamberlain against Russell—not Philadelphia against Boston—and Boston won because Russell beat Chamberlain.

The press started the Russell versus Chamberlain thing the very first time we played against each other in my rookie year. Curiously, they didn't do the same thing with me and Bob Pettit. He'd led the league in scoring the year before I turned pro, and with Philadelphia playing St. Louis those nine exhibition games at the beginning of the year, you would have thought it would be natural to build up the games as Pettit versus Chamberlain. But they never did.

Even though Russell, being a center, was a more natural rival for me, I think there was more to it than that. The white media was always building up blacks to go against each other—a sort of "OK, niggers, let's you and him fight." That was particularly true then in boxing, where they would match all the good black fighters in one division against each other, and let the white guy wait to fight the winner—or should I say the survivor? In basketball and other sports in those days, they did much the same thing; they set it up so that one of the blacks constantly had to demonstrate his superiority against the other, and that left only one black superstar to challenge the white superstars.

But Russell didn't demonstrate his superiority over me. I scored better against Boston than almost any other team in the league, and I outscored him in head-to-head meetings my first year, 440 to 212—better than two to one. I outrebounded him, too—333

110

to 161, also better than two to one. I even blocked more of his shots than he did of mine!

I guess sportswriters are human, and they have their favorites, like everyone else. Their favorite, especially after I came into the league, was Bill Russell. Why? I've asked myself that question a thousand times, and I'm not very happy with any of the answers. One explanation is that Bill's lifestyle has never been as ostentatious as mine; he was married and had children, and that made him a respectable family man. For some reason, Americans view husbands and fathers as being more "respectable" than swinging bachelors with a variety of girl friends—even though it's not exactly unheard of for some husbands to cheat on their wives. I guess that's why it's so hard for a bachelor to be elected to high political office— or even to go to the moon. But it wasn't just that Bill was married; the fact that his wife was black helped, too—particularly since my dates were white (as well as black and Oriental and Spanish and Italian and . . .). Back when I was getting started in the NBA, most sportswriters—like most other whites—didn't like that interracial sex one bit. They were terrified that their own daughters might be next, and we all know how terrible that would be; some of my color might even rub off on them.

Another thing that operated to Russell's advantage was our respective heights. He missed the freak stigma of being a sevenfooter—and, being three or four inches shorter than me, the press made him the underdog: I had the great natural physical asset, and he had to work hard to outsmart me and outmaneuver me. Or so the sportswriters said. They helped create a climate in which it was easy for many fans to dismiss my accomplishments as an accident of height and race—"He's so big; he should be great" or "All those niggers are good at sports; they can't earn an honest living at anything else."

But Russell *was* tall and he *was* black, so whatever our differences on those counts, there had to be more to it than that. Unfortunately, the only other explanation I've ever been able to come up with sounds so egotistical, I'm almost afraid to suggest it: I think most fans and sportswriters subconsciously resented my ability to do so many things so well; I could shoot, rebound, pass, run, and block shots. That made me seem almost inhuman. There was no way anyone could identify with me. They couldn't envision

111

my suffering the normal human frustrations. Russell, on the other hand, was a great rebounder and shot-blocker, but he was a horrible shooter. Early in his career, everyone acknowledged that he was a horrible shooter, but as his legend grew, people started saying he probably could score more, but he "chose" to concentrate on defense. That was bullshit and Bill knew it was bullshit. That's why he worked so hard on defense and rebounding; he knew he couldn't score. Hell, even though I've taken four times as many shots as Bill in my NBA career, my lifetime field goal percentage is still way ahead of his—54 percent to 44 percent! Bill Russell couldn't score as well as I could if he had a stepladder, three basketballs, and a cannon with a range-finder. And that, ironically, made him seem more human. He was not the awesome, omnipotent presence I was on the court. People could identify with him —so they liked him. The only real shortcoming I had on the basketball court was my foul shooting, and at this early point in our careers, I was actually better than Bill at that, too. I hit 58.2 percent of my foul shots as a rookie, compared to his 50.8 percent. Even after five years, I was ahead, 56.5 percent to 55.7 percent. But Bill wasn't supposed to be a shooter, so no one laughed at him. Me? Anyone who can do everything I could do should certainly be able to shoot free throws. So people were more likely to ridicule me than feel sorry for me or identify with me.

I realize all my reasoning may sound both tortured and self-serving, but I think my explanations make far more sense than the one most people offer—that Russell was popular because he was a selfless team player who always won, and I was unpopular because I was a selfish gunner who always lost. Russell *was* a "selfless team player,"—and a great one—but he couldn't have been anything else; like I said, he couldn't score, and scoring a lot of points is most people's definition of being selfish. But I think most of my teammates on every team I've played would tell you I was far from being a "selfish gunner." I scored because I had to—and because my coaches told me to; we didn't have a Cousy or Sam Jones or Tommy Heinsohn or John Havlicek to score for us like Boston did. Besides, Russell played one way, for one team and one coach, his entire career; he was always a defensive specialist. I played for three different teams and eight different coaches, and I had to change my whole game at least twice. I came into the league as a scorer; then, with the 76ers, in the middle and late 1960s, I became an assist man; then, with the Lakers, I became a defensive specialist. I always tried to do as much as I could in every phase of the game for every team, but I've had to change the emphasis, depending on what my coach wanted and what was required to mesh with the skills and short-comings of my various teammates. That's being "selfish?"

As for the "Russell's a winner, Wilt's a loser" thing, I guess that goes back to Kansas' loss in the NCAA finals my sophomore year. Just like everyone now says we had the better team and we were favored to beat North Carolina, so they say my NBA teams were better than Russell's and we were always favored to win. I was Superman, remember; my teams weren't supposed to lose. But Boston, like North Carolina, was almost invariably the favorite against us—the 3-1 favorite my rookie year, in fact. They were supposed to be the greatest team of all time. They had Russell, supposedly the best defensive player and rebounder of all time. They had Cousy, who was voted the best basketball player of the first 50 years of the 20th century—supposedly the best ball-handler of all time. They had K. C. Jones, the best defensive guard of all time. They had Bill Sharman, probably the greatest pure shooter of all time. They had Frank Ramsey, the greatest sixth man of all time. They had Red Auerbach, one of the two or three greatest coaches of all time. Plus they had Sam Jones and Tommy Heinsohn both NBA all-stars—and Jim Loscutoff, a strong, tough forward, one of the best hatchet-men of all time; he'd come in and literally beat the shit out of you if you let him. Who was supposed to beat that team? The Phila-delphia Warriors? A team with a rookie center? A team that finished last the year before?

The Warriors did have some good players. I always thought Guy Rodgers, for example, was the best ball-handler I ever saw —better than Cousy or Jerry West or Oscar Robertson or Walt Frazier or Pete Maravich or anyone. And Paul Arizin was a genuine all-pro. But that was about it. Sportswriters and other knowledgeable basketball fans knew that then. After my first game against Boston, *Sports Illustrated* even wrote:

Aside from the fine shooting of Paul Arizin and the excellent playmaking of Guy Rodgers, the Warriors cannot support him [me] in the style to which Russell is accustomed. If Philadelphia is to beat the better teams in the pro league, he must do both of Russell's jobs, on defense and rebounding, and also score a great many points himself.

So, there it is. As a rookie, I was supposed to do everything Russell did—and more. I think I did just that. But Boston beat us in the playoffs, so Bill was the winner and I was the loser. When that continued to happen—particularly after my 76er and Laker teams each lost a playoff series to Boston that we should have won—people tended to run all the playoff losses together in their minds and say Bill always beat me, even though I was always on the better team. That, they said, made him the better player. Somehow I was supposed to do the impossible; I was Superman. As a rookie, I took a last-place team all the way to the playoffs and got beat, and I was "a loser." But exactly ten years later, a rookie named Lew Alcindor would take a last-place team all the way to the playoffs, and get beat—and everyone would hail him as the savior of the Milwaukee franchise. You figure it out; I can't.

The playoff loss to Boston was not the only thing that marred my rookie year, though. It wasn't even the most disturbing or disappointing thing. After all, I'd been playing basketball for awhile; I knew you can't win them all. At that time, I had no way of knowing that this would happen again and again, of course, and I figured we'd have other opportunities to beat Boston in the years ahead.

What bothered me the most my rookie year was the physical pounding I took around the league. The incidents with Lovellette and Heinsohn were typical. I got pushed and shoved even more than I had in college, and the officials let the other guys get away with it. I guess they figured I was big enough to take care of myself and good enough that the handicap would just help equalize things. But that's like saying Larry Brown is such a great runner, it's OK to grab his face mask to stop him. My coach and my teammates kept hounding me to fight back, but except for that incident

114

with Heinsohn, I never did. Like I said earlier, I'm just not basically an aggressive person.

Fortunately, Andy Johnson was on our team. Andy was the roughest player I ever saw—maybe the only guy I know whom I'd be afraid to get into an alley fight with—and he acted as our policeman at times. He'd rip up a few opposing players who nailed me. Andy had been on the Globies, and when I'd get particularly down on myself as a rookie, he'd always come along with a few Globies stories to get me laughing again. That helped, too. The only trouble with Andy was that he was absolutely terrified of airplanes. When we flew between cities, I had more fun looking out the window and telling him one of the engines was on fire. Once that actually happened. In fact, two engines caught fire. I told Andy about it, and he damn near had a stroke on the spot. If you've never seen a black man turn white with fear, you can't imagine how funny it was.

When I joined the NBA, I had not only expected to get away from the roughhouse tactics of college ball; I also thought I'd get away from the zone defenses and the two-on-one and three-on-one gang defenses that had made basketball at K.U. so unpleasant. Well, the zone was—and is—illegal in the NBA, but clever pros can simulate man-for-man guarding and still drop off to play what amounts to a zone against a certain player. Even Bill Russell didn't play me one-on-one. His guards and forwards were always collapsing back to help him handle me.

The NBA, like the NCAA when I was at Kansas, also changed some rules to stop me. They prohibited offensive goal-tending and widened the free-throw lane from twelve to sixteen feet and adopted the "three-second rule"—prohibiting an offensive player from remaining in the free-throw lane for more than three seconds without trying to shoot.

Although friends like Andy Johnson helped me to maintain my emotional equilibrium as an NBA rookie, I found myself increasingly upset by the animosities that seemed to build up between opposing teams—and between players on the same team. In college, you played each team on your schedule only once, maybe twice. You didn't see each other often enough to hold grudges and look for revenge. But in the NBA, you played each team ten or twelve times, and the big, nasty guys like Lovellette or Loscutoff or Charlie Share would get pissed at you for beating them or making them look bad, and next time, they'd be waiting for you with their favorite trick—tripping you or spearing you with a forearm or jabbing a finger into your breastbone when you shot. A guy like Zelmo Beaty, who was 6 foot 9, 240 pounds, would stand on your toes when you tried to run or jump; he'd hold your arms when you tried to pass or shoot; he'd even try to yank your shorts off to slow you down or throw you off balance. I remember one time when he tried to do that to me, and I gave him a gentle push back. He went flying across the floor like he'd been shot out of a cannon. The official ran over, and told him not to get up: "Don't even twitch a muscle. Wilt's mad, and if he thinks you're already dead, he might not come over to look."

The NBA was much tougher in those days, and the officiating was much looser, and you had some real butchers playing. There were no black officials then either, so blacks often took the brunt of the dirty play.

There was also more friction within most teams then because you traveled so much together by bus and train, not just plane. The travel itself, which bothers most rookies, was no strain at all for me. It was a picnic compared to the travel the Globies did. But tempers could get hot in such quarters on long trips. On the Hawks, for example, the two stars—Bob Pettit and Cliff Hagan—didn't like each other at all. Sometimes they wouldn't even speak. On the Knicks, Johnny Green and Richie Guerin had a couple of really brutal locker room fights. Johnny was a great leaper, and he had this habit of jumping up and grabbing his teammates' shots in midair and putting them in the basket himself. He'd get credit for the basket, and they'd get pissed. Richie was a natural-born street fighter, so he went after Johnny a few times—once in the showers, when they were both all lathered up and slipping all over the place on the soap and grime. I don't know how they managed to avoid busting their skulls open.

The Warriors were never a real close team either, and we had clear racial cliques—the blacks in one clique, the whites in another. I remember being in an elevator once that season with Tom Gola and Joe Graboski, and this absolutely gorgeous black girl got on,

116

and Gola—who was pretty liberal for those days—turned to me and grinned and said, "Go get her, big fella." I said, "Why don't you go get her, Tom, if you think she's all that fine?" But he couldn't accept that. He was white and she was black, and that ended it in his mind. Guy Rodgers, who was supposed to be the team leader, didn't help matters any either. I don't want to detract from Guy's basketball ability—I know I couldn't have broken all those scoring records without his great passing and penetration—but, unfortunately, Guy was a light-skinned, straight-haired black man who seemed to wish he was white instead. He deliberately hung around with the white players, not the blacks, and he'd go out of his way to avoid using ghetto phrases and mannerisms, and that pissed the other blacks off. There wasn't any real racial dissension on the team, just a sort of vaguely tense atmosphere at times, and that contributed to my general feeling of disenchantment with the NBA.

Late in my rookie year, I decided I'd had enough. I was going to quit. I even wrote a story about it for *Look*. The story fulfilled the commitment I'd made to *Look* when I quit Kansas, and it caused an even greater furor than the first story had.

No big sports star had ever retired after just one year, and no one knew quite how to react. Most sportswriters and fans said I was making a mistake. So did most club owners. They were appalled by my decision; attendance had been up 23 percent —about 500,000 fans—my rookie year, and Haskell Cohen, the NBA publicist, attributed 19 or 20 of the 23 percent to my presence. That was money in the owners' pockets. Not surprisingly, though, many players were happy to see me go. They figured they could manage just nicely without having to worry about me on the court. Bob Cousy even said, "Now we can all go back to playing basketball again." Of course Bob had been *the* big name in the league until I came along. I guess he didn't like relinquishing that role—or thinking about Philadelphia maybe beating Boston in the playoffs the next time.

I didn't worry much about what guys like Cousy said. I never have. I figured I'd come into the NBA to prove I could play with the best, and I'd done just that. I'd broken nine records, led the league in scoring (and damn near everything else) and taken a last-place team all the way to the playoffs. Now it was time to look for new fields to conquer. I could've gone back to the Globies or formed my own barnstorming team—both of which I considered—but what I really wanted to do was organize a world decathlon tour. I would have a group of great all-round athletes, and we'd compete in a different decathlon event in every country. Only there was no money in it.

I was really serious about quitting the NBA. In fact, in my own mind, I did quit. I retired. Eddie Gottlieb finally talked me into returning by appealing to both my pride and my pocketbook. He came up with a $100,000 contract (although the announced figure was $75,000), and he kept telling me I could break every record in the book if I'd keep playing. But Abe Saperstein probably had more to do with my returning the next season than Eddie did. I was in much the same frame of mind after my rookie year in the NBA as I had been after my junior year in college, and—once again—the Globies came to the rescue. I'd planned to go to Europe after the season anyway, and when Abe called me to say he'd gotten an OK to take the Globies to Russia for the first time, I jumped at the chance to go with them. It was an utterly fantastic trip—un-fucking-believable!—and by the time I got back, I was ready to play in the NBA again.

In Russia, a tremendous crowd greeted us at the airport with flowers and formal welcoming speeches. We were scheduled to play nine games in seven days, and they'd sold out all 14,000 seats in Lenin Central Staduim for every game. Another 40 million people watched on television. We even had 5,000 people show up for our first practice.

Before we could play, though, we had to perform for a huge group of state censors. The censors made us take out all our "reams" that made fun of the officials. I guess you can't take jibes at any authorities in Russia, not even basketball referees. At our first game, the place was often deathly quiet. The Russian fans would cheer good straight plays, but they wouldn't laugh at the "reams." We had a hurried conference after the game, and found out that the Russians took their basketball very seriously. Before our next game, the public address announcer had to explain that we were not only great basketball players but great comedians, too, and it was OK for them to laugh. From that time on, it was a riot; they really loved us. After every game, they'd come down along the court, and we'd have to shake hands with thousands of them on our way to the dressing room. Apparently the only thing the Russians love more than basketball is shaking hands; they gave a real hard grip, men and women alike. We had to soak our hands in hot water after every game, and we were lucky we could still hold the ball and carry our uniform bags by the end of seven days. (Fortunately, Abe had a few people there to help us carry our luggage around. One of his helpers was J. Walter Kennedy, who's now the commissioner of the NBA. In Russia, Walter was Abe's Man Friday, and his duties occasionally included carrying my bags for me.)

One of the highlights of our trip to Russia was meeting Nikita Khrushchev. Me and "Boat" were taking a walk around Red Square, by Lenin's Tomb, one day, when we saw this entourage of dark limousines come by, and as soon as Khrushchev got out, every window and rooftop for a mile around sprouted guards with machine guns at the ready. "Boat" looked at me and said, "That must be the man himself." Eddie and Abe spotted Khrushchev about the same time we did, and they raced over to see who could be the first to say hello to him. Me and "Boat" weren't running no place—not with all them machine guns out. We sauntered over, casual as can be, and when we were introduced, Khruschev pantomimed a little dribble and we all started laughing.

We saw quite a bit of the Red guards during our week in Russia. Anytime someone bothered us or tried to give us a big pro-Communist pitch, two of them would suddenly materialize out of nowhere and hustle them off. I guess they wanted us to have a good impression of their country, but after a couple of days, we started feeling like we were probably being followed—and bugged. We started watching what we said, just in case they were listening. Naturally, being Globies, we had some fun with that. If, say, "Boat" tried this horrible Russian soft drink, and said, "God, this stuff tastes like piss," one of the other guys would say, "You shouldn't say things like that, 'Lark.' " Then "Lark" would get all panicky, and think he might get sent off to Siberia.

The Russians weren't too happy about our music either. We played rock music on our record players, and we had a small band playing with us at halftime, and the Russians thought rock 'n' roll was decadent—an evil influence on young minds. The

119

Russian musicians really dug rock, though, and they'd have a jam session with our guys before every game. By the night of our last game, we had them playing "Sweet Georgia Brown" for us, and the crowd ate it up.

We played our games in Russia against one of the traveling all-star teams we brought with us—the San Francisco National Chinese Team—but we had hoped to play at least one serious game against a Russian all-star team. No dice. They had about 23,000 excuses why that game couldn't be played.

Our only other disappointment in Russia was that there wasn't one good-looking girl in the whole god damn country—just 100 million "mullions."

On the whole, the Russians were very warm and hospitable, and the farewell party they gave us after our last game is one of my fondest memories.

We had a big state dinner, and when the speeches started, the three Russians sitting across the table from us started proposing toasts. Except for an occasional glass of wine, I don't drink at all now, and I only drank a little then, but it would've been rude to turn them down, so I joined them in a champagne toast.

"Lark" is on one side of me, and "Boat" is on the other, and the next thing I know, my glass is full again, and the three Russians are proposing another toast. When I drained that one, too, the Russian sitting directly across from me filled it up again—this time with vodka. I'd heard stories about that bad-news stuff, so I kind of looked over at "Boat," and he just says, "Go ahead on, big fella. Have some Russian vodka." I told him, "I'm drinking champagne. Why don't you have some vodka?" Well, "Boat" knew that Abe was a teetotaler who didn't want any of his players drinking, so he shook his head. The Russian looked disappointed. I couldn't let the night end like that. I picked the glass up. Even before I started drinking, you could see the Russians' eyes light up. I proposed a toast and touched glasses with them and drank the vodka. Shit, man, the first sip knocked me down to about 4 foot 8. My head was throbbing like a dinner bell, and my eyeballs felt like they were going to pop out of my head, and my throat felt like it was on fire. By the time I could see straight again, the three Russians were laughing their asses off.

"Boat" looks over at me, and says, "Hang in there, Wilt—you can handle it."

I look at the Russians, and they're just draining their glasses and setting them down hard on the table.

"That's the nastiest shit I've ever tasted in my life," I tell them.

But they don't speak much English, and they fill my glass with vodka again, and the next time I look up, they have their glasses full, too, ready for another toast.

"Toast?" I say. "These guys are crazy."

But "Boat" and "Lark" and "Tex" see what's happening. It's a contest, and Globies love competition of any kind. My head is still woozy, and my stomach is sick, but these guys are cheering me on—"Go on, big fella, you can do it, you can do it."

I drain the glass again. Now I'm really in bad shape. I feel like the last survivor of a nuclear attack. But the Russians are still swilling the vodka, and it's toast time again. I don't stall around this time. Down the hatch. Then, the minute they're through, *I* pick up the vodka bottle and fill *their* glasses.

"Toast," I say, clinking the glasses together hard enough to break them. No such luck. Well, to make a long story at least a little shorter, we do that seven more times! I'm taking the lead now, though, and after about the sixth time, I notice they aren't raising their glasses quite as quickly as they had been. The Russian on the left, in particular, looks rocky, almost glassy-eyed. "Boat" nudges me. "You got 'em, big fella. They're about to fall." *They're* about to fall? Hell, I feel like I already fell. But now *my* competitive instinct is aroused. I always like to beat a man at his game. Maybe I can beat the Russians at drinking vodka.

"Boat" really starts pushing me. "Couple of more drinks, big fella, and they'll be under the table."

About that time, Abe is making his formal speech. I haven't heard a word of it, and when he says, "Isn't that right, Wilt?" I just yell, "You tell 'em, Abe."

Then I pour another round. We down that, and I reach for the bottle again. But the Russians are through. They're shaking their heads, and covering their glasses with their hands.

I hold my right index finger up. "One more," I say. "One more." One of the Russians, the guy on the left, tries to stand. His legs get tangled, and he falls over. The other two guys are leaning on each other, and when I pour another round, one of them slides off his chair on to the floor. The third one tries to drink his vodka, but winds up pouring it all over himself.

I stand up and say, "Spas'i be" (thank you), and "Boat" and "Lark" and "Tex" are clapping me on the back like I just won the heavyweight championship. "You got 'em, Wilton, you done got 'em," they say.

I strode off triumphantly, got in the elevator, and went to my room. Or, at least, I thought that's what I did. The next day, "Lark" told me I took seven unopened bottles of vodka and three unopened bottles of champagne off the table and stuffed them in my travel bag, which was sitting against the wall. Then, he said, I staggered over to the elevator, got in, and rode up and down eight or ten times.

All I remember is going to my room and lying down on my bed and feeling like the whole world was spinning around at about a million miles an hour. My doctor from Philadelphia, Dr. Stanley Lorber, was on the trip with us, and I knew he always liked to get up before dawn and walk around the city, taking pictures, so I went out after him. I must have stumbled around Moscow for four hours, but I never did find him.

After the headache and hangover I had the next day, it's no wonder I came back to the United States ready to play in the NBA again. Bill Russell, Bob Pettit, and Willie Naulls combined couldn't give me as much trouble as all that vodka.

But my second year with the Warriors turned out to be an extremely unpleasant one.

Statistically, it was even more successful than my rookie year. I broke all nine records I'd set in my first season, and broke another one as well—for highest field goal percentage (50.5 percent); I was the first NBA player ever to make more than half his shots. I scored more than 50 points in eight games that year and led the league in almost everything—including scoring and rebounding; no one had ever done that twice before either. Statistics don't make basketball, though. It's a team sport, and —primarily because of our coach—our team didn't perform up to its potential.

When Eddie Gottlieb signed me to play my rookie year with

122

the Warriors, he had wanted to hire either Red Holzman (then a Knicks' scout) or Harry Litwack (the coach at Temple) to coach the team. Neither would come, and Eddie hired Neil Johnston instead. Neil had been a great center for the Warriors, and he had injured his knee and couldn't play any more, so Eddie—being the good man that he was—felt a certain obligation to Neil. He made him the coach, figuring Neil might be able to help me learn how to play center in the NBA.

Well, Neil had a great hook shot, but, in my opinion, he didn't know shit about basketball strategy or tactics or how to work with our players—or anything else a coach needs. The team had no respect for him, and neither did our opponents, and he just lost all control over us. We finished second to Boston in our division again that year, but our record was worse than my rookie year. In the first round of the playoffs, Syracuse beat us three straight, then lost four out of five to Boston, and Boston went on to beat St. Louis again for the championship. We'd finished twelve games ahead of Syracuse in the standings, and there's no way they should have beaten us—even though we had no home court for the playoffs. (Our court was being used for something else, and we had to play one "home" game in the Palestra and one in the Philadelphia Arena.) It didn't help matters any that some of my teammates didn't play too spectacularly against Syracuse in those three games. Tom Gola, our No. 3 scorer all year, got only seven field goals in the three games, and fouled out when we really needed him in the third game. Paul Arizin, our No. 2 scorer, played with five fouls in the first game and fouled out of the last two. Guy Rodgers fouled out of the first two. I averaged 37 points a game, just about my regular-season average, but I have to admit I didn't play too inspired either. All of us were grumbling and bitching about Neil, and he didn't know how to handle it.

I probably would have quit for good if Eddie hadn't called me into his office before the season was over, and told me he was going to fire Neil.

"I made a big mistake hiring him in the first place," he told me. "He's too weak. He's just not a coach. If we'd had someone like Red Auerbach these first two years, and Boston had Neil, we would have won two world championships, not them."

Eddie seemed generally contrite about having hired Neil

123

—contrite for me, for the rest of the team, for himself and for our fans. He'd hired Neil against his own better judgment, and for two years, he'd had to pay the price. Of course, I realized it was tough for Neil to coach the Warriors. He'd played for years with guys like Paul Arizin and Guy Rodgers and Woody Sauldsberry, and it's always difficult for anyone to suddenly go from being a peer to being the boss. But Neil bungled the job so badly, the other players—some of whom were once his friends, as well as his teammates—openly shunned him. They'd even sneak out of a bar to avoid drinking with him if they saw him coming.

Neil just wasn't a good coach. His idea of strategy was to come into the locker room at halftime when we were ten points behind, and say, "All right, guys, get eight of these points back this quarter, and you'll only be two behind going into the fourth quarter. OK, that's it. Let's go get 'em."

But Neil had other problems, too. For one, he seemed to resent blacks. For another, he seemed to think sex was the number between five and seven. He was always telling us not to "mess around with girls"—so much so that I got to wondering if he thought *he* had been the product of an immaculate conception.

As you might imagine, I had a few disagreements with Mr. Johnston. I was young and sensitive then, and he really rode me. He'd say things like, "With the money you're making, you should be able to do better than that," or "Come on, quit playing like you're carrying all your money around with you."

One of the running disagreements I had with Neil was over how much time I would play each game. I've always had the stamina to play a full 48 minutes, and—since it takes me a while to get warmed up again after I'm taken out—I wanted to play the full 48, or as close to it as possible. He didn't want me to, but he never said why.

After Neil was fired, he went around bad-mouthing me, and saying how uncooperative I'd been. His own record since then isn't all that sparkling, though. He hooked on as the head coach of the Pittsburgh Rens in the ABL, and was an absolute disaster there. The players grumbled, the team floundered, and the league folded. The last time I looked, Neil was the assistant coach for the Portland Trailblazers, the last-place team in the Lakers' division.

My second year in the NBA was memorable—or rather, eminently forgettable—for another reason besides my ongoing conflict with Neil Johnston: It was also the first time I really had any trouble with any aspect of my game. The problem, as you might have guessed, was with my foul shooting.

In high school, I'd been an 85 percent foul shooter. In college, with the opposition preventing us from playing the run-and-gun basketball I was accustomed to, I didn't have the same opportunities to shoot from the outside that I had had at Overbrook, and my outside shooting proficiency suffered; so did my free-throw shooting. But I still hit 65.1 percent of my free throws my sophomore year. That's not great, but it's better than either Bill Russell or Kareem Abdul-Jabbar did as college sophomores, and no one jeers at their foul shooting. I shot my free throws with one hand back then, taking a deep knee bend kind of motion, and it was something of a strain on my knees; like many men who grow too quickly in their youth, I had arthritic knees from childhood on, and at Kansas, that problem was exacerbated by an exercise Coach Harp had us do—duck-waddling around the court for ten minutes every day.

Then, during track after my sophomore season, I injured my knee. That did it. By the time my junior year rolled around, I had to change my free-throw style; it was just too awkward and painful for me to use my natural style. My free-throw percentage dropped to 60.8 percent—still not disgraceful, but well on its way there.

My first year with the Warriors, it got even closer—58.2 percent. My second year, it was down to 50.4 percent. From that time on, the problem became almost completely psychological. I'd try a new stance and a new grip and a new style every few games, and I never again felt comfortable at the free-throw line. I shouldn't have let it bother me so much, but I wanted to excel at everything, and the harder I tried—the more different ways I tried to shoot—the worse I got. By my ninth year I was down to 38 percent, and I've only been over 50 percent in four of the last ten years. My lifetime NBA percentage is now 51.1 percent—*lower* than my field goal percentage, for Christ sake!—and no one else among the top 100 all-time scorers is any lower. In fact only two guys are close to me—Russell (56.1 percent) and Johnny Green (54.9 percent). Everyone else is over 60 percent, and most of them are over 70 percent; 25 of them are over 80 percent!

125

I know the problem is in my head now because I shoot free throws well in practice. I'll hit 15 or 20 in a row, and win bets from Gail Goodrich and Jerry West all the time. Ironically, I also seem to hit free throws well in the clutch—including two that clinched the Western Division championship for us in 1972. Every once in a while, I'll get hot at the line in regular-season games, too; I'll have good rhythm, and hit most of my free throws. Then I'll go back to being a one-man disaster area out there. It happens every season. Just this past February, I had a stretch where I hit 22 of 28, and another where I hit eight of ten. For about the first third of the month or so, I was shooting almost 75 percent. But I missed 50 percent of my next 40 free throws. In the next ten games after that, I hit 28 of 42—67 percent. But I wound up the season hitting only 11 of my last 22—exactly 50 percent.

In my second year with the Warriors, when things were just beginning to get desperate at the foul line, and I was shooting down around the 40 percent mark, Eddie Gottlieb hired a guy named Cy Kaselman to coach me in underhand free throws. Kaselman had been a star with the Philadelphia Spahs in the old American Basketball League in the 1920s, and he'd been a great foul shooter; one season, he hit 247 of 261 free throws. That's 95 percent! He even gave exhibitions shooting blindfolded! Cy was 51 in 1960, but he was still a great foul shooter, and with his help, I improved tremendously; I could hit 65 percent, sometimes 70 percent of my free throws. But I felt silly—like a sissy—shooting underhanded. I know I was wrong. I know some of the best foul shooters in history shot that way. Even now, the best one in the NBA, Rick Barry, shoots underhanded. But I just couldn't do it. I'd start out shooting that way some years, and shoot pretty well, up around 65 percent or so, and then I'd get cocky and figure I could do just as well—and feel a lot better—shooting one-handers; as soon as I did that, my percentage would drop like it had an anchor tied to it. Sometimes, I'd start the season with one-handers and switch to the underhanded style later, out of desperation. I always shot better that way, but I never kept at it.

There are several possible explanations for my horrendous foul shooting, other than the ones I've mentioned, and I suspect the real answer may lie in taking a little from each of them.

One theory is that most tall men don't shoot free throws well

126

because their height prevents them from putting the kind of arc and trajectory on the ball that makes most good shots go in.

Neil Johnston always said I had trouble shooting fouls because my natural outside shot had so much English on it—a trick Phog Allen had taught me in Kansas. For once in his life, Neil may have been right. English is helpful in banking the ball off the backboard at an angle, but it can be disastrous when you're trying to put the ball straight in, without banking it—as you do in free throws.

My brother-in-law, Elzie, says he thinks my foul-shooting prowess began to diminish when I started lifting weights. He says the strength I got from that destroyed my touch, and I started "overpowering" the ball. That may be right, too, and I've tried to compensate by standing two or three feet behind the foul line when I shoot.

Other people say I shoot fouls poorly because my hand is so big, it's not a natural grip—like an average-sized guy handling a cantaloupe.

Whatever the explanation, I no longer feel quite the paranoia and humiliation I once did on the line, with everyone laughing and booing and all, but I still must get a dozen letters a week from well-meaning fans who want to help me shoot fouls. They'll suggest I shoot backwards or with my eyes closed or with my left hand, and they'll send me every imaginable prayer and good-luck charm and magic cure. Unfortunately, the one guy who probably could have helped me the most was Neil Johnston. Neil had been a fine foul shooter himself—a lifetime record of 76.8 percent—and he was my coach during my first two years in the NBA, when I first started having trouble and got mad and embarrassed and tried everything I could think of to improve. He might have been able to show me a good, comfortable, efficient technique—or at the very least, he might have tried to take the pressure off me and rebuild my confidence at the line by telling me not to worry about it. But Neil was neither a teacher nor a psychologist. And a good coach, in any sport, must be a little of both.

8

IBEGAN MY THIRD SEASON WITH
the Warriors in a far better frame of mind than I'd ended my
second one. I'd been to Europe again that summer, and I'd played
with the Globies, and that always seems to make basketball seem
like fun. I'd also fulfilled a lifelong dream by visiting the Moulin
Rouge in Paris—and copping the two best-looking girls in the
show. For some reason, growing up in Philadelphia and going to
college in Kansas, I'd always had an idealized view of the Moulin
Rouge showgirls. They were the epitome of beautiful women for
me, and I'd always said I'd cop one some day. Copping two, well,
that made for a helluva summer.

But what excited me the most about the upcoming basketball
season was that I knew I'd be playing for a real coach for the first
time. After firing Neil Johnston, Eddie Gottlieb had searched and
thought very carefully, and he'd hired Frank McGuire, the man
who coached North Carolina to that NCAA championship victory
over my Kansas team. I'd heard nothing but good things about
Coach McGuire, as a coach and as a man, and I was anxious to

see if they were true. They were—and then some! He was the finest man and the best coach I've ever played for, before or since. He was a brilliant strategist, a master psychologist, a warm, selfless human being, and a guy who always looked out for his players' best interests. Unlike Johnston, he didn't give a damn how much money his players made or how much publicity they got. He figured if he could keep them happy and make them winners, he'd get his share, too—and he was right, of course.

I even had a pretty good year shooting free throws under Coach McGuire—good for me, anyway. I hit 61.3 percent—my best year ever in the NBA. He just told me to relax and not worry about it. One day when I was grousing about going two for ten or something like that, he came over and said, "Look, Wilt, if you were a 90 percent free-thrower, we might never lose. That would take all the fun out of basketball, right?" It was bullshit, but it made things easier for me.

Coach McGuire used the same approach with the other guys on the team. Like, some of them might get in pretty late at night. Neil Johnston would have gone out of his mind telling them how important sleep was to a professional athlete. Coach McGuire figured we were adults and treated us accordingly. If we wanted to go with less than eight hours sleep, that was up to us. If our play suffered because of it, well, he figured we were pros; we'd shape up. Besides, it's like he told one sportswriter, "Sleep is over-rated. My mother, rest her soul, used to say she'd be a long time sleeping when she was dead."

With an attitude like that, it was no wonder all the Warriors liked and respected him. We didn't even bitch much when he made us do the most agonizing, muscle-straining calisthenics you've ever seen. We figured he knew what was best.

I can still remember my first meeting with Coach McGuire after he got the job. It was at training camp, in Hershey, Pennsylvania, and he came to my hotel room at the Coco Inn, and he had this huge box of file folders with him. He told me he'd spent about $400 calling all over the country to ask other coaches and players and friends about me, and he'd read everything about me he could find, and he felt he knew me pretty well. He said, "You're supposed to be tough to coach. I don't believe it. I just don't think

129

you've had a coach who treated you like a man yet. You're smart, you're the greatest basketball player who ever lived and you want to win. That's enough for me. If I'm wrong, either you'll beat me down and ruin my reputation, or I'll beat you down and ruin your career. If I'm right, we'll work together and beat Boston."

I told Coach McGuire I didn't think we could beat Boston. I thought they just had too many good players. But I said I'd try my damnedest to do things his way.

"OK," he said. "I've been through all the scouting reports, and you're right. We aren't as good as Boston—not with you scoring 37, 38 points a game like you did your first two years. We can't get enough scoring out of the rest of our guys to equal them. But if you can score 50, I think the rest of the guys can make up the difference to get us even with Boston."

"Fifty?" I yelped. "Impossible."

But Coach McGuire said he knew I could do it—and he said I had to do it if we wanted a shot at the championship.

I told him I thought the other players might be unhappy about that.

"No they won't," he said. "They're pros. They want to win, and they know you're their meal ticket."

So, Coach McGuire starts out by telling Guy Rodgers, "You have one job on this team and one job only—get the ball to Wilt." Guy asks him, "When I sit down to negotiate my contract next year with Mr. Gottlieb, and he says he won't give me a raise because I didn't score enough points, will you be sitting there with me to tell him why?"

"You bet your ass I will," Coach McGuire told him.

Well, Guy's scoring average dropped from 12 points a game to about eight—but I understand he got a raise the next season.

McGuire was always looking out for his players that way. Like, we stayed in crummy, second-class hotels until he became the coach. The first time we checked into one of them with him, he took a look around and said, "No team of mine is staying in this flophouse. We'll stay in a decent place if I have to pay the tab myself." He didn't have to, though. Eddie Gottlieb was a first-class owner—the only real basketball man who's ever owned a club I played for—and he gave the coach what he wanted. Coach McGuire also saw to it that we didn't ride around in rickety old

130

buses any more—or have to crowd five guys into a cab for short trips.

"We want you to play first-class basketball," he said, "and the only way you can be expected to do that is if we give you first-class treatment."

Not that he was a snob. I remember one time we were on our way back to Philadelphia after a game in New York and we stopped in this little coffee shop to get something to eat. There were about 15 of us, and the place was already crowded, and there was only one waitress there. Eddie Gottlieb and his attorney, Ike Richman, were on the trip, too, and they and Coach McGuire just took their jackets off, rolled up their sleeves, and went to work behind the counter, making hamburgers and french fries and mixing malts.

But Coach McGuire was not a pushy know-it-all or a tyrant who demanded everything his own way either. From the very beginning, he told us he was just a rookie in the league, and he wanted us to feel free to make suggestions and give him advice. Before the season started, he called us together and said we should decide among ourselves which of us would guard which opposing players.

"After we've been around the league once, I'll know individual strengths and weaknesses better, and I can decide the match-ups myself," he said, "but you guys know more about yourselves and your teammates and your opponents right now than I do, so you do it."

That worked out well in most games, although I remember—before our first game in Cincinnati—we went around the locker room deciding who would guard who, and no one volunteered to take Oscar Robertson. Coach McGuire smiled and said he thought someone ought to be assigned to Oscar "just to make it look good." Tom Gola said he'd do it, "but Oscar's probably gonna get 36 points off me." Gola guarded Oscar that night, and that's exactly what Oscar got—36. But we won, 145-133.

For all his willingness to listen to his players, Coach McGuire was no pushover. We had this one reserve, Ed Conlin, and he got to second-guessing the coach a bit too loudly on the bench one night, and the coach's Irish temper exploded in the locker room at halftime. I've never seen a player so thoroughly chewed out. Another time, the coach got exasperated by Guy's refusal to stop

131

dribbling so much when he should have been passing. So, at practice, he snuck a new ball in the game just as Guy was going to take it. The new ball didn't have any air in it.

"OK, Guy, play with that one a while," Coach McGuire told him.

Guy got the point. He didn't dribble so much after that.

I had a few run-ins with the coach, too. Some people have said the only reason I liked Coach McGuire so much was because he let me do whatever I wanted. They said I loved scoring 50 points a game and playing damn near every minute and practically running the team myself—even dictating substitutions and all. Well, anyone who knows Frank McGuire knows that's absolute bullshit. Just because a coach is open-minded enough to listen to suggestions from his players and not act like Almighty God doesn't mean he's soft. Frank's a tough, strong-minded coach, and no one's about to tell him how to run his team. In fact, one of the first things he did as coach was cut Carl Green from the squad—and Carl was (and is) one of my closest friends. He was also a much better basketball player than the guy Coach McGuire kept—York Larese. York lasted one year, and averaged about five points a game, but he'd played for the coach at North Carolina, and coach wanted to give him a chance. So he cut Carl. I never quite forgave him for that, but it sure was proof that I didn't tell McGuire what to do.

About the only thing I did give him "instructions" on was dress. Coach dressed real smartly, but he was into the gray flannel look, and I got him to wear some flashier clothes and classy shoes, and he got a real kick out of that. So did his wife. She kept thanking me for turning Frank into such a jazzy dresser.

With Coach McGuire around, we were a much closer, more easy-going team than we had been under Neil Johnston, and that made for a most enjoyable season. In my case, it also helped that I had made a close friend on the team in Al Attles, who's now the coach of the Golden State Warriors and still one of the closest friends I have. Al had come to the Warriors as a fifth-round draft choice in my second year, and no one thought he'd make the team. We had a mostly veteran roster, and only one rookie figured to make it. Everyone thought that would be our No. 1 draft pick, Bill "Pickles" Kennedy, who'd gone to college in Philadelphia—at Temple, I think. He was supposed to be a damn good player, as well as a big favorite with the local fans. Al was only a little over 6 feet, and he wasn't a very good shooter; it didn't seem like much of a contest. It wasn't. Al wiped "Pickles" out. He ran and hustled and went crashing into the scorer's table after loose balls, and "Pickles" got cut after seven games. I liked Al immediately, and he and Guy and Andy Johnson and I used to pack a big suitcase full of sandwiches and go to the drive-in movies together all the time. By my third year, Al and I were real tight, and he was playing as much as our other guards, Guy and Tom Gola.

That season wasn't all sweetness and light, though. The coach did his best to break down the racial cliques, but you can't change human nature overnight. I remember meeting this beautiful white stewardess on a flight back from St. Louis or some such place that year, and making a date to see her that night. She really seemed hot for me, but when I called later to confirm the time, she hemmed and hawed and said she had to go somewhere else. I didn't much like the sound of that, so I drove over to her place, and got there just in time to see her and her girl friend and two guys going out. I didn't recognize the guy she was with, but her girl friend was with one of my teammates, Tom Meschery.

Later that night, I called her again and told her what I'd seen. She said she'd wanted to go out with me, but when Tom asked her girl friend out and she suggested we all double, Tom had said he didn't want to socialize with me because I was black.

Well, the next night, before the game, I walked into the locker room and invited Tom outside for a brief chat. I told him he'd always seemed like a bright, liberal guy to me, and I was surprised to find out he was such an ignorant prick. I also told him I didn't much care what he thought about blacks in general or me in particular, but if he ever fucked up one of my dates like that again, I'd fuck him up so bad, it would be hard to tell his face from a 20-year-old basketball.

Tom started crying and apologizing all over the place. He said he *was* liberal and had a lot of black friends, and had never been involved in anything like this before. He said he'd only made the comment he had to the girl because other white guys on the team had told him he shouldn't associate with me off the court. Tom was a rookie that year, and I guess he thought he was doing the only thing he could do to avoid friction, and I told

133

him I understood that. We talked a little more about it that night, and I don't think either of us ever mentioned it again. We became good friends.

Tom teamed with Paul Arizin as our starting forwards that year, and with Al and Guy and Tom Gola in the backcourt, we were a stronger team than in either of my first two years. But Paul was the only guy besides me who could score with any consistency, so—as Coach McGuire had told me before the season started—it was up to me to do most of the scoring.

In our season opener, against the Lakers, I scored 48 points. The next night, against the Lakers again, I scored 57. In our third game, against New York, I scored 53. In our fourth game, against Syracuse, I scored 55. That's the way it went the whole season. I scored more than 50 points 44 times. I averaged 50.4 points a game. I broke nine of the ten records I'd set the previous year. Of the 43 highest individual scoring games that year, Jerry West and Cliff Hagan had one each, Elgin Baylor had two, and I had the other 39. I scored more than 60 points 15 times, in the 70s twice and 100 once.

I also set one other personal record that year. People always say I've never fouled out of a pro game, and they're right. But I have been thrown out three times. The first time was that third season, in Los Angeles—on January 3. Referee Norm Drucker called a foul on me. I argued. He gave me a technical. I kept arguing. He gave me a second technical. In the NBA, that means automatic expulsion—and in this case, it cost the Warriors the game. I had 36 points and 18 rebounds at the time, and there was 8:33 left to play; we were ahead, but after I left, we lost, 124-123.

That 8:33, incidentally, was the only time all season I wasn't in the Warrior lineup. I played every other minute of every other game—a record that still stands.

Two months, almost to the day, after that ejection in Los Angeles, I had my 100-point game.

Most basketball fans know all about that game, but hardly anyone knows about the events that led up to it. I was living in New York part-time then, and commuting to Philadelphia, and I had a date with a fine young lady in New York the night before the game. It took me a little longer to cop her than I thought it would—and she was better than I thought she'd be—and by the time we were through enjoying ourselves, it was 6 o'clock in the morning. I drove her back to her place in Queens, then caught an 8 A.M. train for Philadelphia—eating and talking the whole way, instead of sleeping. When I got to Philly, I met some friends who wanted to go to lunch. By the time we finished, it was almost time to catch the team bus to Hershey for the game that night.

Before I could stumble off to my room in Hershey for a few winks, I came across Eddie Gottlieb and Ike Richman, playing a pinball-type machine where you shoot a rifle at targets that light up. Ike, who later became one of the closest friends I've ever had, asked me if I was any good at the game. Naturally, I said I was. He gave me the rifle. Well, Ike and Eddie had been shooting about 300 or 400 points, and right away, I hit 900. Ike says, "Wilt, I bet you $2 you can't get 1,100." I took the bet, hit 1,125 and offered to double the bet on 1,300. Ike agreed. I hit 1,430.

What I didn't know was that Ike had already asked the doorman, who'd been there 15 or 20 years, what the highest score ever was, and he'd said 1,800. Ike was just setting me up and sucking me in—sandbagging me. When I won the second bet, he offered to bet me dinner and a good bottle of wine that I couldn't hit 1,700. I said, "Ike, I'll go you one better. The loser has to pay for the winner *and* the winner's date—and I'll get 1,800." Old Ike could barely conceal his smile. He thought he had me dead.

I got 2,040.

I guess that should've tipped me off about what to expect in the game that night. The first thing that happens is Coach McGuire comes over to me in the dressing room, and shows me two New York newspapers with quotes from some of the Knicks about how they're going to run me ragged because they "know" I'm pretty slow and don't have much stamina. Coach McGuire knows that's ridiculous, but he doesn't know I haven't had any sleep yet, so he just grins slyly and says, "Let's run 'em tonight, Wilt."

We ran, all right—and ran and ran and ran. I hit my first six jump shots from the outside, and at the end of the first quarter, we were ahead, 42-26, and I had 23 points—including nine straight free throws. At the half, I was 14 of 26 from the field and 13 of 14 from the line, and I had 41 points. The record was 78—I'd set it in December—and it looked like I had a good chance to break it. When I got 28 more points in the third quarter, the fans really started screaming. I broke the record early in the fourth quarter, and now the fans were going crazy. They were chanting "100! 100! 100!" I thought they were nuts. Whoever heard of scoring 100 points in an NBA game? But my teammates wanted me to do it, too. They started feeding me the ball even when they were wide open. The Knicks did everything they could to stop me—including holding the ball almost the full 24 seconds every time they got it late in the game. One of the Knicks, Willie Naulls, later told me their coach, Eddie Donovan, had called time out, and given them explicit orders to freeze the ball and pass up good shots so I couldn't rebound and score and embarrass them. I finally got my 100 points, on a dunk, with just 42 seconds left in the game, and the fans came pouring out of the stands and mobbed me.

There wasn't a very big crowd there that night—only 4,124—but in the 11 years since then, I'll bet I've had at least 20,000 fans tell me they saw me score the 100. I've also heard a lot of them use that game as "the ideal example of why Wilt's a loser; he got 100 points and his team lost, as usual." But we didn't lose. We won easily, 169-147.

A lot of people ask me if that 100-point game was my biggest thrill in sports. Frankly, it isn't even close to the top—for several reasons. In the first place, I've always thought field goal percentage was more important than total points; anyone can get hot and have a big game if he shoots often enough. Hell, I'm the world's worst foul-shooter, and I hit 28 of 32 free throws that night—87.5 percent. That shows that anyone can get lucky. Just check the box scores over a few months; some really weak players will have fantastic games. Walt Wesley got 50 points in one game a couple of seasons ago, and he's got to be one of the worst centers in the history of the NBA. I really think I shot too often in that 100-point game—particularly in the fourth quarter, when everyone was egging me on toward 100. I took 63 shots, and even though I made 36 of them (57 percent), I think I took too many bad shots. Besides, I've always thought rebounding was more important than scoring. In the NBA, a lot of guys can score. But someone has to get the ball for them first, and there's not nearly as many great rebounders as there are great scorers. That's why I'm a lot prouder of my NBA record of 55 rebounds in one game than I am of the

100 points. I'm also prouder of being the all-time NBA rebound leader than of being the all-time top scorer.

But I'd be lying if I didn't say I enjoyed scoring a lot of points. It was tremendously satisfying to the ego, and in that context, I'd have to say my greatest personal satisfaction was averaging 50.4 points a game that third year. Scoring 100 points in one game is a freak, but averaging 50 for a whole year is something else again. That's incredible consistency. I mean, no one had ever averaged over 30 until I came into the league. Fifty? That meant any time I hit 30 points in a game, it was a "bad" night; I'd have to get 70 the next night just to make up for it and stay even.

Late in the season, I realized I was creating a monster. I was averaging almost 55 points a game then, and I realized if I did it for one season, everyone would expect me to do it every season. I started passing off more, and let my average drop to just above 50. I was right about the monster thing, of course. No matter what I've done since then, people always measure me against that third season. I set *ten* records that year that still stand today. No one could ever come close to that again—not Kareem Abdul-Jabbar, not Bill Russell, not Elgin Baylor, not Jerry West, not Oscar Robertson . . . and not Wilt Chamberlain.

Kareem is smart enough to realize that. I remember seeing him seven or eight years later, at the all-star game in Philadelphia during his rookie year, and he hold me:

"I'm not going to make the same mistake you did, Wilt. I'm not going to average 40 or 50 points a game, and get people expecting more and more every year. I'll get my 25 or 30, and let my teammates score the rest. You built a Frankenstein, and you'll never get away from it. Not me."

A lot of other players resented my scoring all those points and breaking all those records, too. I didn't even make the all-NBA team that year, if you can imagine that. Here I was, breaking every record in sight and leading the league in everything but ingrown toenails, and the other players in the NBA voted for Walt Bellamy —*Walt Bellamy* for Christ sake!—as the best center in the league. Maybe he did more for his team than I did for mine, you say? My team, the Warriors, went to the seventh game of the playoffs; his team, Chicago, finished in last place, with the worst record in the NBA.

137

But for all my misgivings, I truly enjoyed my third year with the Warriors. It was almost as great a year for the team as it was for me individually. After losing our season opener to the Lakers, 118-113, we won six of our next eight games, and had several similar streaks throughout the year—five of six in late November, ten of twelve in mid-December, seven straight in January, seven of eight early in February. We still finished 11 games behind Boston, and they beat us eight times in twelve regular-season games, but six of their victories came early in the season, when we were still adjusting to Coach McGuire's style of play. We beat them four straight late in the season, and we thought we had a good chance to knock them out of the playoffs—particularly after we smashed Syracuse four out of five games in the first round.

Unfortunately, we had to play virtually the entire Boston series without Tom Gola, our No. 3 man in scoring, rebounds, assists, and free throws. He hurt his back against Syracuse, played only briefly against Boston in the first two playoff games, and missed the third game altogether. Then he hurt his ankle in the fourth game and didn't get back on the floor until the seventh game.

In the first playoff game, Boston bombed us, 117-89. Newspaper reports on the game were typical Chamberlain-Russell stories. I outscored him, 33-16, and outrebounded him 31-30—even though the game was in Boston Garden—but the United Press International story the next day said Russell had "scored a clear-cut decision over Chamberlain."

I outscored Russell 42-9, in the next game, and we won, 113-106. We split the next two games, and then had another near-riot in the fifth game when Sam Jones and I collided, and he ran over to the sidelines, picked up a ball boy's wooden stool and came charging at me with it. The cops quieted everyone down, but before anyone could even score another point, Boston's Carl Braun made a menacing gesture toward Guy Rodgers, and Guy punched him in the mouth. More cops. Then, about 45 seconds later, my old Celtic friend Jim Loscutoff started picking on Guy—who was about five inches shorter and 50 pounds lighter—and Guy went diving for the same stool Jones had tried to use on me. A few Boston fans came charging out of the stands to "protect" Loscutoff. I wasn't even in this fight, but—as always happened with the fights in Boston—a big group of fans came running at me, screaming for blood. More cops. Later that same quarter, Tommy Heinsohn threw a vicious shoulder at the Warriors' Ted Luckenbill. This time, the officials stepped in quickly and kicked Heinsohn out of the game. But not once, in all these brawls, did the officials call a foul.

Boston won that game, 119-104, and we won the next one, 109-99, so it was 3-3 going into the final game.

The seventh game was tight all the way. We led, 56-52, at the half and 81-80 after three quarters. Tom Meschery was great for us in that game. He got 32 points. Paul Arizin got 19. Tom Gola, hobbling around on his bad ankle, got 16. I passed off and rebounded and played defense most of the game, and got 22. But Guy fouled out for the *third* time in the series, and Boston rallied in the fourth quarter to go ahead by three points with less than ten seconds left. I dunked the ball over Russell, and when he fouled me, I hit the free throw to tie the score at 107-all. Then Sam Jones got loose, and hit a jumper with two seconds left to win it, 109-107. But I'll always remember that series as the one Mendy Rudolph beat us in, not Sam. Mendy officiated the seventh game, and he made two critical calls, both against us. First he said I was out of bounds when I was at least three inches in bounds. Then, late in the fourth quarter, he called me for goaltending when I blocked a Tommy Heinsohn jump shot deep in the corner, at least 15 feet from the basket. In that spot, there was just no way it could have been goaltending. But Mendy always did like Boston—and Bill Russell. Other people have noticed that, too. Alex Hannum told me Mendy made some calls you wouldn't believe when Alex was coaching St. Louis, and they were playing Boston in the finals. Hell, Mendy even told *me* Boston and Russell were his favorites. He made the comment several years later, when I was with the 76ers and we were all snowbound between games in Detroit, and a group of us went to the movies. Mendy just kind of blurted out how he "always loved" watching Russell and Boston play, and how Russell "always seems to have what it takes in the clutch."

That kind of attitude just can't help but affect a man's judgment, at least subconsciously, and I remember thinking back to that seventh game in Boston my third year—and to all those other games in Boston that Mendy had officiated—and I really got pissed. What really bothered me, though, was not that Mendy had his favorites. He may have gone a little overboard at times, but,

139

aside from that, he's one of the very best officials in the league. Officials are only human, and you can't expect them to watch the same players and the same teams night after night and not have their favorites, and even subconsciously lean in their direction on occasion. They just shouldn't deny they do it; they shouldn't insist they're all paragons of impartiality, and start dishing out technical fouls at the drop of a "Shit!" when a player protests one of their calls. Officials are not omniscient and infallible, and they shouldn't pretend they are. Their judgment calls are just that—judgments, not papal decrees—and they should be treated accordingly. That's why I'm in favor of using instant replay to confirm all officials' decisions in every sport. It would take an impossible burden off the officials' backs, and it would make things fairer for all participants. As long as we have the technical capacity to do it for the TV viewer at home, why not do it for the officials and players and coaches and fans in the arena?

Even though Mendy Rudolph helped screw us out of that seventh game in Boston, I wasn't nearly as bitter as I had been when Boston beat us in my rookie year. I wasn't even mad at the press for the way they wrote about me and Bill Russell. This was the end of the third year of our personal duel, and it was obvious that our head-to-head confrontations had caught the public fancy; thanks to us, pro basketball was finally about to become a big-time sport, and that meant more money—and glory—for both of us. Besides, just one little break in that series, and we would've won. If we'd had a different official, or if Tom Gola hadn't been hurt, or if Guy hadn't fouled out three times, or if Sam Jones' last-second basket hadn't gone in—any one of those things could've won the world championship for us. In fact, as soon as the seventh game ended, I ran over to the bench and told Coach McGuire:

"You remember, at the beginning of the season, when you said we could beat Boston, and I said we couldn't? Well, you were right, and I was wrong. We *can* beat them—and next year, we will!

9

THE SUMMER AFTER MY THIRD
year with the Warriors was the first time I was able to go to Europe
without feeling like I was running away from something. The
1961–62 season had been fun, and the next season looked like it
could be even better, and playing with the Globetrotters this time
was just going to be like a big, fluffy mound of whipped cream on
top of those two scoops of basketball-flavored ice cream. The
cherry on the sundae—if you and Baskin-Robbins don't mind the
metaphor—was a new car I had waiting for me in London.

For more than a year after I'd been unable to fit into that
Mercedes 300SL in Basel during my first summer with the Globies,
I'd had a vague yearning for some other high-class car, something
better and more exclusive than the new Eldorado I was driving.
Then, on the Hollywood Freeway in Los Angeles one day in 1960,
a white Rolls Royce cruised by me at about 95 miles an hour. It
was so damn quiet, it mesmerized me. A few weeks later, I saw a
Rock Hudson movie, and he was driving a Rolls in it. That did it.
I had to have one. But I didn't actually get around to ordering it
until several months later, in New York, when I was having a

glass of milk with a friend one morning, and he said, "What are we going to do today?" and I just sort of blurted out, "Let's do something different. Let's go downtown and buy me a Rolls Royce."

He was wearing some shorts and an old pair of sneakers and some old Army socks, and I had on a pair of raggedy dungarees and a T-shirt, but we figured, "What the hell, we're just going down to a car lot." We didn't realize they don't sell Rolls Royces in a "car lot," and when we got to the address on the East Side that we'd found in the phone book, it was a plush, second-floor office. We went up, and this secretary looks down her nose at us and says, "May I help you?"

"Yeah," I said, "I want to buy a Rolls Royce."

You could see right away she thought we were either drunk or pulling her leg. I mean, how many scruffily dressed, seven-foot black men come strolling in off the street in New York to buy Rolls Royces?

She disappeared for a minute, and came back with a very proper-looking British gentleman.

"Can I help you?" he asked me.

"Yeah. I want to buy a Rolls Royce. A convertible. I thought you might have one or two around that I could look at."

He said they didn't have any cars right there, and he invited me back into his office. Then he asked me my name.

"Chamberlain."

It didn't seem to ring any bells, but he left me for a few minutes, and he must have called someone who told him who I was; when he returned, he was ready to do business with me. He gave me a brochure and pointed to a picture and said, "Look at this car. It's a Bentley Continental Park-Ward 500 drop-head coupe."

"Wonderful," I said. "What the hell is that?"

He explained to me how a Rolls and a Bentley had the same engine, "but this particular Bentley has the most beautiful lines, and there are only three of them in the whole country."

I wasn't all that impressed with the picture frankly, but he said I should see it in person:

"We have a black Rolls convertible in our garage. Let's go take a look at it. Maybe there'll be a Continental there, too."

There was.

I carried a lot of cash around in those days, and I took one look at that Bentley, and reached in my pocket and pulled out $10,000, and said, "Don't go any further. That's what I want. Here's my deposit."

He told me the full price of the car, including shipping and tax and all, would be just under $30,000.

"That's OK," I said. "When can I get it?"

"About 16 months."

"I want it next week."

"I'm sorry, Mr. Chamberlain, but these cars are all custom made. If you're really in a hurry for it, I can special-order it. I might be able to get it in 13 months."

I didn't have much choice, and when the 13 months was up, my third year with the Warriors was just ending; I called the guy and told him I'd pick it up in London myself.

I often take friends to Europe with me, and that summer, I took a guy named Willie Gardner along. When we got to London, I saw my car sitting in the showroom window. It looked magnificent. I knew it had to be my car because the salesmen had said they made so few, and this one was just the model and heather color I'd ordered, so I walked in and said, "Give me that car right there."

One of the salesmen told me it was already sold.

"I know," I said. "I bought it."

That was eleven years ago. I still have that car. It's got about 185,000 miles on it now.

I had the Bentley shipped to Paris that summer, and me and Willie drove it all over Europe. It's a fantastic automobile, with unbelievable handling. I remember one time I was cruising at about 110 miles an hour on my way to the south of France, from Paris, about 4 o'clock in the morning, and me and Willie were talking, and all of a sudden I saw this sharp curve ahead of us. I knew I couldn't make the curve at that speed, and there are no gears in the car to brake it down that way, and I was sure we'd either spin out or go screeching off the road if I used the foot-brake. I figured it was all over for us.

They say your whole life is supposed to flash in front of you when you're about to die, but the only thing that flashed before me was the time I'd gotten caught in a wind-blown rainstorm started by a hurricane after my senior year in high school, and this big gust of wind spun my 1949 Olds around and slammed me into a telephone pole about two miles from Kutsher's and rolled me over and over and over. I thought sure I was going to die then, too, and I later heard there had been reports in Kansas that I actually *was* killed. But all that happened was my car got totaled —which was bad enough; I'd been saving my money to buy a new 1955 Olds to take to Kansas, and—with the '49 Olds to use as a trade-in—I had just enough to swing the deal. The junk-man gave me just $24 for my Olds, and I had to settle for a '51 Buick instead of the new Olds. Now, in France, it looked like I was going to wipe out my beautiful new Bentley the same way—and kill me and Willie in the process. Well, I hit the brakes and we went around that curve so smoothly I couldn't believe it—no screech, no spin-out, no wobble, no nothing. Fantastic!

The Bentley was something of a status symbol, too, of course, and me and Willie had fun taking turns playing "chauffeur" in Europe. We'd pull up to fancy nightclubs in Paris and Berlin, and watch the doormen come running over with dollar-signs in their eyes and treat us like royalty.

We were in Cannes, on the Riviera, when my wonderful summer began to fall apart. I got a call from Philadelphia saying that Eddie Gottlieb had sold the Warriors to a group of businessmen in San Francisco.

I immediately called Eddie and told him I hoped the sale hadn't been contingent on my playing in San Francisco because I wasn't going to.

"I think I'll just stay here in France; I really do," I told him. "I'm learning the language, and I love it here."

Naturally, I was the key to the deal—I was damn near the whole Philadelphia franchise—and Eddie talked his ass off, at trans-Atlantic telephone rates, trying to convince me to come back and play in San Francisco.

I wasn't upset about the deal because I had any great love for Philadelphia. How could anyone love Philadelphia? I've always had a great many close friends there, and I'll always be grateful for what I learned about basketball there as a child, but Philadelphia has most of the liabilities of both big city and small town, with very few of the advantages of either. I was already living in

New York part-time anyway, and early in the season, I'd told Eddie I'd like to be traded out of Philadelphia to some decent city. But when I had that great year and got along so well with Coach McGuire and we came so close to beating Boston, I'd changed my mind. I'd told Eddie after the season that I wanted to play in Philly one more year so we could win a championship for him and Coach McGuire. In fact, what bothered me the most about going to San Francisco was that I knew Coach McGuire wouldn't come with us, and I didn't want to have to play for another Neil Johnston. Coach McGuire had a son who was palsied, and the family wanted to stay on the East Coast, near all the doctors and other facilities they were taking his boy to.

Eddie finally talked me into coming back, though, and I got back to the States just in time for the annual Maurice Stokes benefit game at Kutsher's and the Rucker League games I always played in in New York with some of the other top college and pro stars and the best of the New York schoolyard players.

If I remember correctly, that's the first time I ever played against Connie Hawkins, who had just turned 20, and had been something of a legend in the schoolyards for several years already. Connie was 6 foot 8, and he had these incredibly long arms and huge hands, and he could do anything with a basketball except make it sing the national anthem. Connie had been expelled from Iowa in a betting scandal that he'd never had anything to do with, and both the NCAA and the NBA—which had banned him —were warning players not to play with him. I guess they figured we'd get contaminated or something. I played anyway, and I had my old friend Wally Choice on my team, along with Cal Ramsey, Russ Cunningham, and "Satch" Sanders. We beat Connie's team by 35 points or so in our first meeting, but the next time we played them, Connie was shooting and passing and blocking shots like crazy, and he hit a jump shot at the final buzzer to beat us by one point.

I'm a close friend of Connie's now—and one of his biggest fans. I think he may be the best one-on-one player in basketball history. But I wasn't the least bit surprised when he didn't eat the NBA alive, the way some people thought he would when they finally let him into the league. One-on-one isn't team basketball, and that's why so many of these schoolyard hotshots are either

145

disappointments in the NBA or don't make it at all. You pick up a lot of bad habits playing one-on-one in the schoolyards, and if you really pride yourself on that flashy kind of individual jukin' and jivin' with the ball, where you make more moves on one play than Bobby Fischer makes in one year, it can be awfully tough to adjust to the style of team play required to win games in the NBA. Connie doesn't play defense worth a shit, for example, and when his man burns him a couple of times—or when a tough, hard-nosed forward like Dave DeBusschere gives him a bad time at both ends of the court—he gets down on himself and loses the edge you have to have in this league. Earl Monroe is much the same way. Jerry West says he'd rather watch "Pearl" than any other player in the league; he says he'd pay $50 just to watch "Pearl" go one-on-one. I wouldn't pay 50 cents; I like basketball—team basketball—and that isn't it. But there are a quite a few flashy players like Connie and Earl in the league. Nate Archibald was probably one of the biggest names in the NBA last year—the first man ever to lead the league in scoring and assists in one season. And yet, I'm not awed by Nate either. Sure, he's good—damn good. But I remember the two years he played in Cincinnati with Norm Van Lier as the other guard, and everyone agreed that Norman was the better player. Now, Norman is playing for Dick Motta, a sound, defense-minded coach who believes in a balanced attack; Nate is playing for Bob Cousy, the old flash himself, and Cousy has built the entire offense around Nate at KC-Omaha. No wonder Nate's got all those great stats now. But did you notice that Nate's team finished last in their division last season, and Norman and the Bulls damn near knocked us out of the playoffs—with Norman doing most of the damage?

While I was playing with Connie and Guy Rodgers and Chink Scott and some of those other guys in the Rucker games that summer, my Bentley was being shipped over here from Europe so I could drive it to San Francisco. I really dig that car, but a lot of my black friends, particularly around Harlem, didn't think much of it then. They'd say things like, "Man, you can buy three or four Eldorados for what that cost you, Wilt." But I thought it was a class car, and I'd never been all that comfortable in my Eldorado. In places like Harlem, pimps drive the Eldorados, and I always had this uneasy feeling that anytime I saw a fine-looking chick and wanted to cop her, she'd figure I must be a pimp, too. I still have a Cadillac, but it's mostly for friends and houseguests to use. If I'm going some place where I don't want to drive my Bentley or my Maserati, I'll use the Dodge station wagon I got from *Sport* magazine last year as the most valuable player in the NBA playoffs; I won't use the Cadillac. Maybe I'm overreacting to the black-pimp-in-a-big-Cadillac stereotype, but that's the way I feel, and since I love driving—and spend so much time doing it—I figure I should drive what I feel most at home in.

I've done so much driving in this country in my Bentley now that there's hardly a city of any size that I can't find my way around in, without a map. I particularly like to drive cross-country—out there alone, racing the wind, with no one bothering me. I once drove the 1,620 miles from the Muehlebach Hotel in Kansas City to the freeway interchange in downtown Los Angeles in 18 hours and 12 minutes—an average of 90 mph. I've also driven from Harlem to Nob Hill in San Francisco (3,041 miles) in 42 hours flat, and from New York to Los Angeles (2,964 miles) in 36 hours and 10 minutes. I always thought those had to be some kind of records, but a friend of mine—Dan Gurney, the race-car driver—told me he once made the New York-to-Los Angeles trip in 35 hours and 53 minutes. Of course, Dan had another driver along with him, sharing the load. I always go alone.

I never stop for meals or sleep on my cross-country drives. I pack a hamper of gourmet sandwiches, and get a few gallons of orange juice and 7 Up, and I take off. I don't even get out of the car when I stop for gas; just "fill 'er up" and, whoosh! I'm gone. Although I don't take any passengers with me, I do take a bouquet of flowers along—just in case I happen to meet a pretty young lady along the way. I also take my telephone and a portable television set and a three-speed record-player along for company on those long, dreary miles through the flatlands of Kansas and Nebraska.

One of the few times I've ever driven coast to coast without trying to break any records was that summer of '62, coming from New York to San Francisco after the Warriors were sold. I stopped

147

in Chicago to see some people, and then I went by Lawrence to see Bob Billings and a few fraternity friends, and I just figured I'd drive until I got tired and then I'd stop for the night. But it started raining, and I didn't feel like getting out of the car in the rain, so I kept on driving and the next thing I knew, it was almost 2 o'clock in the morning and I was in Denver. I was going to stop overnight there till I remembered how all the trucks go over the Rocky Mountain passes during the day; I didn't want to get stuck behind them for half a day, so I decided I'd go ahead and slip over the pass and find a motel on the other side. I was really tired coming over the pass, and when it started to get light, these huge jackrabbits started lining up on the side of the road and jumping out in front of me and scaring the hell out of me. I got pissed at that, so I started driving on the shoulder, right near the damn things. Now *I* was scaring the hell out of *them;* you should've seen them run for the brush.

That little exercise seemed to refresh me, and I never did stop to rest. When I got just north of Sacramento, coming out of Reno, I saw this gray Thunderbird doing about 90, and I opened the Bentley up to about 135 and blew right by him. Then I saw a cop chasing us. I hopped off at the next exit and hid in a gas station. But the cop saw me get off, and he got off, too. As soon as I saw him whiz by me, I roared out from behind the gas station and back on to the freeway. I caught up to the Thunderbird a few miles later, and we jockeyed back and forth some, and when I finally looked over, I saw it was George Lee, a guy the Warriors had just gotten from Detroit. He was on his way to San Francisco, too. I honked and waved and, whoosh!, I was gone.

I got to San Francisco just in time for our first practice, and afterward, me and George and Wayne Hightower decided to go to North Beach for dinner and a show. It was raining like hell, and we were walking along Broadway, and this car full of girls comes by, and one of the girls throws open the back door and says, "Hey, Wilt, come on in."

Well, any time a good-looking girl invites me in out of the rain, I'm going to take her up on it—even if I do have to leave my buddies behind.

"Where you going?" I asked after I squeezed in between the five girls.

The driver, a dark, foreign-looking guy with a funny accent, said, "We're going to a party." The girls asked me if I'd like to come along. "Sure." When we got to the party, everyone was all excited about having me there—everyone except the foreign guy. He'd been the heavyweight boxing champion of Persia, and he'd been in the United States since 1952, but he didn't know Wilt Chamberlain from a sack of rocks. The guy's name was Jim Bryant, and he soon became one of the closest friends I've ever had. We've been to Europe together, and we've chased girls together, and we've stayed at each other's houses, and when he got married later and his wife had their second child, I had a great time visiting her in the maternity ward and freaking out the nurses by pretending to be her husband.

I think one reason Jim and I are so close is because he likes me for what I am, not who I am. He liked me before he knew I was rich and famous, and to this day, he doesn't treat me any differently. When you're in my position, that doesn't happen very often. Most people I meet either use me or fawn all over me, and I can't stand that. Jim doesn't even talk basketball much; he'd rather play dominoes—particularly if we're at his house and the loser has to wash the dishes.

Friends like Jim quickly helped me forget that I hadn't wanted to come to San Francisco at all, and like so many other people, I instantly fell in love with his city—with its European charm, with its California tradition, with the views of the Bay I had from the different places I lived in on Twin Peaks and Pacific Heights and Diamond Heights and right downtown. I could see the fog circling in around the Golden Gate Bridge, and for a while, I even rented a houseboat and lived on the water, just outside Sausalito. It was beautiful, absolutely gorgeous. San Francisco was a very romantic city, and I guess I was a very romantic young man then.

San Francisco was also a great restaurant town, and I'd always loved to eat, ever since I was a kid and my mother used to make her great home-made biscuits and country sausage and salt mackerel and chicken and dumplings and this special veal cutlet dish. She taught my six sisters to cook, too, and it was always a big production around the house when each of them got old enough to take over the cooking from the one before her. I

149

remember when Barbara cooked her first meal—hot dogs and baked beans; she put five cans of beans in this huge five-gallon kettle of water . . . what a gooey, runny disaster! But Barbara became a fine cook, in time. So did Delores. And Margaret. And Selina. In fact, on a scale of one to twenty, they'd all be at least fifteens, and Barbara and Delores would damn near be twenties. But it always took a while to break them in, and I remember telling myself I was sure as shit gonna be out of the house before Yvonne, my youngest sister, took over, and I'd have to go through that transition period all over again.

My mother taught me to cook, too, and I've become pretty good at it. I make a great potato salad, and I do OK with roast chicken and spaghetti and lemon meringue pie, too. That may not be the same as *chateau de boeuf Strasbourg en chemise* and *soufflé grand marnier,* but it's one way for a celebrity to avoid the hassle of going to a nice restaurant with friends and then being bugged throughout his meal by people who want him to shake hands and sign autographs.

In San Francisco, though, I was just starting to gain the sophistication and discrimination necessary to enjoy really fine food, and I liked going to some of the fancy continental places, restaurants like Ernie's and the Blue Fox and L'Étoile and La Bourgogne and, over in Sausalito, Ondine; I had a few personal favorites that weren't so well-known, too—places like Vanessi's on Broadway and the Barbary Coast and, for a good steak, Lew Lehr's.

San Francisco is a good drinking town, as well as a good eating town, and I started having a great time bar-hopping with some of my friends there, too. That's really when I pretty much stopped drinking hard alcohol. If you went to three or four spots in one night, and had a couple of drinks in each one, you could get drunk pretty often—and spend a helluva lot of money, as well. I just started drinking 7 Up and orange juice together or mixing lemonade and 7 Up and grape juice together, and drinking only wine and champagne on special occasions or for a formal dinner. I always got too much out of life to need the artificial high of booze anyway, but I still liked to prove I could hold my liquor every once in a while, and I had a couple of good challenges in San Francisco. Once I drank a whole quart of Old

Here I am at age 12, just before I grew my beard.

Photo by Stan Meltzer

One of the few pictures of me on a basketball court, *not* wearing
No. 13. I'm No. 5 here—in high school, back around 1954.

Uncle Willie on the Borscht Belt circuit, cracking up during a skit at Kutsher's Country Club in the Catskills in the early 1950s.

The best bellhop in the Catskills.

At Kutsher's in 1957 (left to right) Eddie Gottlieb, owner of the Philadelphia Warriors, the late Ike Richman, my friend and attorney, and Milt Kutsher.

With my good friend and teammate Bob Billings at Kansas in 1957. Bob was a straight-A student, but if I remember this moment correctly, I was helping him solve a complex calculus problem. Uh-huh.

The scourge of the airwaves on the "Flippin' with the Dipper" radio show, broadcast from K.U.

Clearing 6′ 6″ in the high jump. At Kansas, I lettered in track before I lettered in basketball.

Talking with another big man—novelist James Baldwin, in Harlem, in the early 1960s. (He's the one on the right.)

Courtesy Philadelphia Daily News

Photo by Dr. I. W. Schmidt, F.P.S.H.

Abe Saperstein, owner-coach of the Harlem Globetrotters, comes up short trying to measure me with a six-foot tape, in this publicity photo taken in 1958.

(ABOVE) Dunking during my rookie year (1959–60). Willie Naulls of the Knicks doesn't seem to be able to do much about it, does he?

A quick move toward the basket against the New York Knicks in my rookie year. That's my teammate Paul Arizin (11) looking on.

Poor Zelmo. Here I am, with San Francisco in 1964, dunking over Zelmo Beaty, then with the St. Louis Hawks. Some other pretty fair players here, too—Bob Pettit (9), Lennie Wilkens (14), and Cliff Hagan (16).

Beating Bill Russell to a rebound—can you believe that?—in 1969 game between the Celtics and the Lakers.

Photo by Jim Edwards

Happy Hairston (52) ducks behind my screen in 1972 game against Milwaukee. Greg Smith (4) gets hung out to dry.

Photo by Jim Edwards

Dunking against Houston's Elvin Hayes during 1972 game in Los Angeles.

Photo by Jim Edwards

Score one for me in the battle of the giants. I block Kareem Abdul-
Jabbar's shot in 1972 game against the Milwaukee Bucks. Others are
Gail Goodrich (25), Happy Hairston (52), Jim McMillian (5), Bob
Dandridge (10), and Jon McGlocklin (14).

I played the 1972 NBA championship game with a broken hand, but the Lakers still won—and I got a new Dodge as the most valuable player in the series. I was supposed to get a Challenger, but I asked for a station wagon instead, so I'd have a car for my dogs to ride in.

Kansas against UCLA, Lakers against Portland Trailblazers, me against Sidney Wicks, jumping center during 1972 game at the Forum.

Setting a screen for Jerry West against Chicago Bulls' Jerry Sloan during 1973 playoffs.

Photo by Mike Paladin

United Press International Photo

Referee Jack Madden and I have a friendly discussion about the weather and the high cost of beef. This particular beef cost me a technical foul in the third Knick-Laker playoff game, May 1973.

Knick Willis Reed demonstrates his affection for me during the 1973 playoffs. Willis picked up five personal fouls in trying to guard me in this game—but when the Knicks won the championship, he also picked up a new car as the most valuable player in the series.

On a Hollywood movie lot with Dick van Dyke and Elke Sommer in 1965.

One of my better investments—a harness horse I owned in 1967.

"OK, Richard, now why don't you . . ."

With David Eisenhower at the 1968 Republican convention in Miami.

Now, this is me playing the game I *really* like . . . volleyball.

Photo by Jim Edwards

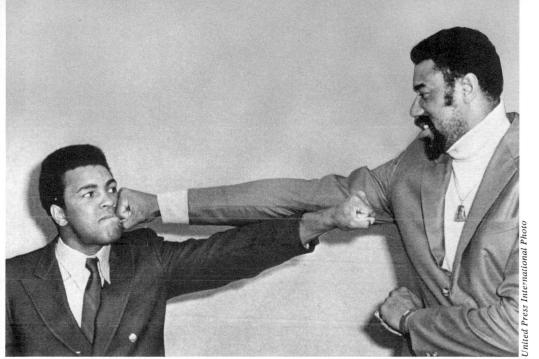

United Press International Photo

That's what I would like to have done if Muhammad Ali and I had been able to get together in the boxing ring.

Photo by Barry Bregman

Anyone want to race? This was taken at the Ontario Motor Speedway, but I've always thought I should try the European road race circuit.

Los Angeles Times *photo by Art Roge*

The early stages of construction on my house, in July 1971, when everyone said it couldn't be done.

Photo by Mike Paladin

Wine is the only alcoholic beverage I drink anymore, and this wine rack can hold 75 bottles.

Come up and see me some time. This spiral staircase took four months to complete, and is patterned after those circular boat stairways—only much bigger.

My Great Danes and I get ready for a swim. Their names are Thor, Odin, and Careem.

Finished, at last. My dream house—the possible dream.

Grand-Dad in about two hours, just to win a bet. Another time, I had a fantastic drinking bout with one of my teammates, Tom Meschery, in one of the hotel bars on Geary Street, during a team party celebrating our Western Division championship in 1964.

Tom was matching me drink for drink that day until the bartender said, "Hey, I got a good drink for you guys." He reached under the bar, and came up with some Ron Rico 151-proof rum. I downed a shot, and Tom got about halfway through his before his eyes started bulging out, and he set it down and gave up. Wayne Hightower had joined us by then, and when we left this place and went over to Pierce Street Annex, Tom told Wayne how I'd drunk him under the table. Wayne said he figured he could out-drink me, so I started all over with him. We drank hard for a couple of hours, and Wayne suddenly disappeared. Me and Tom went outside looking for him, and found him—all 6 foot 8, 240 pounds—draped around a street sign like a piece of spaghetti. He was really ripped. Tom wasn't doing so hot either. I just grinned, and drove them both home.

Tom and I and Al Attles and Guy Rodgers and Tom Gola were the only members of the Philadelphia Warriors who went with the team to San Francisco. Everyone else either quit or got traded or released outright, and after about 20 games, when Gola decided he didn't much like San Francisco, he was traded, too—at his own request—to New York. That made for a pretty unsettled team—nine new faces on a thirteen-man squad—and with Meschery out part of the season after breaking his wrist, we had a lousy year. We lost 49 of 80 games, and finished next-to-last in the Western Division.

I had another good year individually, but after the pleasures of the previous season, under Frank McGuire, it wasn't much fun playing for a loser for the first time in my career. I led the league in ten categories again, including scoring (44.8 points a game), rebounding (24.3 rebounds a game), field goal percentage (52.8 percent), and minutes played (3,808); I scored more than 50 points 34 times and over 60 nine times and over 70 three times. But it wasn't enough.

There were several reasons for our dismal performance—one of them being that San Francisco, for all its exquisite charm and fine food and cosmopolitan atmosphere, is an absolutely rotten basketball town. The people there tend not to be big sports fans—especially not big basketball fans. They seem to think they're too sophisticated for that, and they're too busy trying to be like New Yorkers, with their opera and ballet and theater and all. But—unlike New Yorkers—they don't seem to realize that you can like both sports and culture.

San Francisco had no great basketball tradition. The city's only real infatuation with the sport had come during the 1955–57 period when the University of San Francisco won 60 straight games and back-to-back NCAA championships, and—if anything—USF's record hurt us more than it helped us; Bill Russell and K. C. Jones, the stars of that USF team, were both playing with Boston, and anytime the Celtics came to San Francisco, the fans rooted for them, not us. But that's about the only time they rooted at all.

We got off to a bad start in San Francisco through no fault of our own—or of the city's. The San Francisco baseball Giants were in a torrid fight with the Dodgers that year for the National League championship, and the Giants came roaring from behind in the final days to tie for the pennant. Then they beat the Dodgers in a playoff. They lost the World Series to the Yankees, but there was so much rain, the Series was drawn out almost a week longer than usual. They were still playing baseball when we started our exhibition season, and the people in San Francisco who *were* rabid sports fans were far too preoccupied with the Giants to worry about us. They never did make the transition, and I remember —just before our league opener—we rode in a motorcade through town to City Hall, where we were supposed to be presented with the keys to the city. The City Council was planning something similar for the Giants, and the people on the streets got confused; I heard one guy looking at us ask his buddy, "Which one's Willie Mays?"

We averaged less than 4,000 fans a game our first season in San Francisco—and about a third of them were special $1 admissions. The Warriors never did draw well there; that's why they moved to Oakland. But the Warriors' owner, Franklin Mieuli, has to share the blame for the poor attendance. He knew as much about basketball as I do about phrenology. In our first season there, he never scheduled even one exhibition game for us in

152

San Francisco, and that was typical of the way he promoted and presented the Warriors. We played our games in a place called the Cow Palace, and that's just what it was. The damn roof leaked so badly that when it rained, I'd get a half-dozen drops of water in my eye every time I looked up for the center-jump. The San Francisco sporting press didn't dazzle anyone with its knowledge of basketball either. They were too busy trying to be cool and sophisticated. In our first game there, we beat Detroit, and I got 56 points, and the papers the next day said something like "he bears watching." I bore watching, all right; in the next four games, I scored 50, 46, 53, and 59.

Probably our biggest problem that first year in San Francisco was that our coach, Bob Feerick, didn't know much about coaching pro basketball. Bob was—and is—a great guy, and we're still good friends. He's general manager of the Warriors now, and I understand he's doing a damn good job. I also hear he was a good college coach at Santa Clara before he came to the Warriors. But he just wasn't much of a professional coach. Hell, he didn't even want the job. He only took it because they said they needed him. He must have told me at least a hundred times that he didn't want the job, and didn't think he was any good at it. He used to ask *me* to help him coach some times, and I just don't have the temperament to be a good NBA coach, so you can see we were in real trouble. In fact, Eddie Gottlieb—who came out to San Francisco with the team to serve as general manager for one year and help with the transition—felt so bad about our performance that he volunteered to stay on a second year. When the owner agreed—eagerly—Eddie replaced Bob Feerick with Alex Hannum.

Alex had wanted to coach us our first year in San Francisco, but when Frank McGuire decided not to come West with us, Eddie figured he should give the first shot to someone who was pretty well known in the San Francisco area. That someone was Bob Feerick.

Alex was a brilliant coach—second only to Frank McGuire among the eight coaches I've had in the NBA. He knew basketball, and he knew men. But I really wasn't all that excited about playing for Alex at first. When he'd coached at Syracuse, he was always baiting me and telling his players to push me around and yelling about me to the referees—saying I was walking with the ball and

153

violating the three-second rule and all. He also said he didn't think I should play almost 48 minutes every game and score so many points. But a funny thing happened when Alex took over the Warriors: He didn't say another word about the three-second rule or about my walking with the ball—and I led the league again in both scoring (36.9 points a game) and minutes played (an average of just over 46 minutes a game).

When Alex was first hired, people immediately tried to pit me and him against each other. He was my fourth coach in five years, and sportswriters started blaming me for the quick turnover. That was preposterous, of course, and Alex told me right away that he knew it. We became good friends, and remain good friends to this day.

Alex and I had a lot of good times together in San Francisco. He was a speedboat and water skiing freak, and he got a big charge out of scaring me to death the first time we went out in his boat. He went roaring over the water, twisting and turning and bouncing, and I was sure we were going to flip over and explode and drown. After that, I kept trying to get him to ride in my car with me, but he knew what I had in mind, so he had about 874 excuses and we never did it. We did water ski together a lot, though, and I think that helped build the strength in my legs, and enable me to continue playing 46 to 48 minutes a game, every game, at an age when most athletes are retired.

I think the best time I ever had with Alex was when we bet on the first fight between Sonny Liston and Cassius Clay (as he was known then), and I bet on Liston and lost, and had to take Alex and a friend out for a night on the town. We had a fine meal at Bimbo's 365 Club in San Francisco and saw a good show and closed up a few bars, and just had ourselves a helluva time.

But Alex and I did have our disagreements. Once he got so mad at me, he cleared the locker room and challenged me to a fight. Alex is about 6 foot 7, maybe 200 pounds, and with his shaved head and deep-set eyes, he can look pretty menacing. But I wasn't exactly quaking in my sneaks, and—fortunately for Alex—he's as smart as he is strong; we settled our difference with words, not fists. Sometimes I was right in our disagreements, sometimes he was. Since he was the coach, he usually got his way.

154

Like our first training camp together, in 1963, was in Hawaii, and he was giving each player $1.55 a day for cab fare. I told him, "I need $5. I'm Wilt Chamberlain, and people expect me to tip big." Alex just looked at me and said, "Fine. If you want to be Wilt Chamberlain, you can pay for being Wilt Chamberlain. You'll get $1.55, just like everyone else."

I had another one of my narrow escapes from death in Hawaii that year, too. Me and my roommate on the Warriors, Howard Montgomery, took these two girls to the beach for a nighttime picnic; I wasn't getting anywhere with my girl, but I could see he was about to get some action with his, so I asked my girl to go for a swim; I figured Howard could work better alone. The water was so nice and warm, I didn't pay too much attention to what I was doing and before I knew it, I was too far from shore, caught in a heavy undertow, and being pulled clear to Japan, for all I knew. I cut my leg on a coral reef, and kept going under, and I guess I thrashed around out there for 30 or 40 minutes before I finally made it to shore and collapsed on the sand. I'd damn near gotten myself killed trying to help a friend get a piece of ass—and he later told me he didn't even get it.

After Hawaii, the Warriors finished their training in Santa Cruz, a beautiful little community about 60 miles south of San Francisco. One day, after practice, Nate Thurmond and Wayne Hightower asked me if I'd like to go with them to the Newport Jazz Festival that night. Alex was working us hard—the hardest I'd ever seen—and after two practice sessions a day, I was too tired to go anywhere but bed. But Lamonte McLemore, who's now singing with the 5th Dimension, was working on a magazine story on the festival then, and he was going with Nate and Wayne. He kept telling me how many fine-looking girls would be there —including Kim Novak, who lived in Big Sur, about 50 miles south of where we were training. I'd always been a big fan of Kim's, so I agreed to go—and drive—on one condition:

"If me and Kim hit it off together, you guys are going to have to walk home."

Nate just laughed, and said, "If you get some action with Kim, we'll be glad to walk home."

Well, I met Kim at the festival, and we talked some, and when I saw Nate and Wayne in a night club later that night,

I caught their eyes and grinned and waved and said, "Have a nice walk."

Kim is a delightful woman, and the time I spent with her that summer is one reason I'll always remember my first training camp with Alex as a pleasant experience—despite the two-a-day practice sessions and the mini-Olympics he staged almost every day. He had us jumping and running and shooting, and competing against each other in every way possible. Even though I won most of the contests, Alex always kidded me afterwards that I complained so much about his conditioning program that I'd probably never go through training camp with him again. As it turned out, he was right. When he coached me later, in Philadelphia, I was so embroiled in contract talks that I didn't join the team until its final exhibition game of the preseason.

But Alex's training program had the Warriors ready for the season. We didn't have the world's greatest talent that year —"some of the slowest players and worst shooters in the NBA," one sportswriter said—but Alex took us from our 31-49 record and fourth place finish the previous year to a 48-32 record and the Western Division championship in 1964. I was still scoring a lot —I had over 50 ten times that season—but Alex had us moving more and looking for the open man, and he helped me in developing my passing ability, as well as my scoring ability. Because I'd always been so big and strong, coaches hadn't figured it was necessary for me to work on finesse and some of the subtle fundamentals necessary to be a good passer. I guess they thought scoring and rebounding was enough of a burden for me. Not Alex. He wanted me to do it all, and he was the first coach who really encouraged me to work on my passing in practice and use it during the game. I'd always been a fairly good passer, and my assists had been increasing steadily since my second year in the league—from 148 to 192 to 275; under Alex, with the opportunity to be a passer on a regular basis, I had 403 assists, tied for fourth best in the league with Jerry West. The only guys ahead of me were such all-time great assist men as Oscar Robertson, Guy Rodgers and K. C. Jones. No center had ever finished anywhere near that high in assists before, and with both Guy and me in the top five, you can see we were really playing good team ball.

The Warriors played about .500 ball for the first ten weeks of the season, while we were adjusting to Alex's style of play. Then, early in January, we went on a tear and won 16 of 21 games.

Just as we were getting that streak going, we broke for the annual NBA all-star game. The game was in Boston that year, and Walt Bellamy, the same guy who'd beaten me out for the all-NBA team in my third year—when I averaged 50 points a game—beat me out for the starting center position on the Western all-star team. I was way ahead of "Bells" in scoring and rebounds again, and my team was doing far better than his in the standings, but I guess this was another chance for some of the more jealous players in the league to stick it to me. There almost wasn't an all-star game that year, though. The players met beforehand to discuss some complaints they had about the NBA pension fund, and they agreed to strike and boycott the game if their demands weren't met. I thought they had some legitimate gripes, but I didn't think they were very well organized or presented, and I couldn't see how any purpose would be served by a last-minute strike that night. I finally got tired of listening to all their bullshit and said, "Well, I don't know about you guys, but I'm going out and play me some basketball." That seemed to end the strike. The other guys followed me out on the floor.

In the playoffs that year, the Warriors beat St. Louis in a tough seven-game series, then ran into Boston again. The Celtics were at the peak of their dynasty in 1964, on their way to their sixth straight world championship. Bob Cousy had retired after the previous season, and the rest of the guys were determined to prove they could win it again, without him. They had John Havlicek, Tom Heinsohn, and Tom Sanders playing about equal time at forward, the Jones boys at guard, and Russell at center. All those guys except K. C. averaged in double figures, and they still had guys like Frank Ramsey, Willie Naulls, Clyde Lovellette, Jim Loscutoff, and Larry Siegfried coming off the bench.

The Warriors were good, but not nearly that good. Guy Rodgers couldn't even score a basket in the first two games, and to make matters worse, we had severe injury problems going into the Boston series. Wayne Hightower and Tom Meschery were hurt, and all our guards were hurt—even reserves—and I had a goddam hole in my hand from falling on a loose screw sticking up out of our great Cow Palace floor. But Boston would've beaten

157

us if we'd all been healthy and playing the best ball we were capable of. They were just great.

As with both my previous playoffs against Boston, though, we had another near-riot. This one came in the second game, after Boston had dumped us, 108-96, in the first game. They were about 20 points ahead, and my old friend Clyde Lovellette was up to his usual tricks—yanking at my pants, elbowing me in the back, trying to trip me. I was pissed about the way things were going anyway, so when the officials finally called him for fouling me, and he came over to bitch at me and say I'd been the one who fouled him, I just let him have it—right on the chin. He crumpled to the ground like a rag-doll in a pool of blood, got to one knee like he was thinking of continuing the fight, took one look at me standing over him, and rolled over on his back, out cold. Both benches emptied, and the Boston cops had to come out on the floor to pull everyone apart. But several Celtics, including Russell, came over to me, and said they were glad I'd decked Clyde. They said he was a dirty player. Russell told me, "He's had it coming a long time, Wilt."

I made the free throw for Lovellette's foul, and wound up the game with 32 points, but Boston won, 120-101. We blitzed them, 115-91, two nights later in San Francisco, but that only delayed the inevitable. Despite a great game by Guy, the Celtics won the fourth game, 98-95. I got 27 points in that game and 30 in the next one—even though I gashed my hand badly on the rim—but Boston won, 105-99, to take the championship.

I went to Europe, as usual, after that season, and when I came back, I had a rather unusual surprise waiting for me—an offer to play professional soccer. Some guy met me at the airport, and said I'd been drafted by the new Atlanta team.

"I represent the New York team," he said. "We bought your contract, and we're prepared to offer you a six-figure contract to play goalie for us. You won't even have to quit basketball. Our season runs from late spring to early fall; it doesn't overlap with basketball at all."

The offer was very flattering. I was pleased that they thought enough of my general athletic ability to think I could play as a pro in a sport I'd never tried before. I also liked the idea that soccer was a big sport abroad. I really dug Europe, and I figured it wouldn't hurt me any to do something that would make me as well known there as I was here. But I also realized they were probably more interested in what my name could do for them than in what my feet could do for them. It wasn't my fear of this exploitation that finally led me to turn them down, though; it was my reluctance to sacrifice the freedom of my off-season time. Pro basketball is a very demanding, regimented way of life, and I'd come to cherish those few months, from May through August, when we weren't playing. I knew that if I agreed to play soccer, I'd be lucky if I had time to take a leisurely leak by myself the whole year.

As it turned out, it didn't make much difference whether I signed for that year or not. Things went so disastrously for me in 1964–65 that I might just as well have signed a contract to play the role of the bull in Madrid every Sunday afternoon during bullfight season.

We opened training camp and I took my routine physical examination in San Francisco, and was ready to fly to San Luis Obispo with the team for an exhibition game when I was paged at the airport. Some new doctor had given me my physical, and he'd seen something he didn't like, he said. He wanted me to come straight to the hospital.

When I got there, he told me my electrocardiogram showed I had a heart problem. I told him I'd been having stomach pains on and off all summer, and he said they might be connected. He had me check into the hospital. But I'd had sporadic stomach pains ever since high school, due primarily to an excess of calcium in my system. I'd even been ordered to stop drinking milk a few times to curb the condition. That didn't sound like a heart attack to me, and I sure as hell didn't feel like I'd had a heart attack.

Well, they kept me in that goddam hospital for almost a month, running one test after another. I had three regular doctors —Dr. Good News, Dr. Bad News and Dr. No News. Dr. Good News kept telling me I'd be out water skiing in a week. Dr. Bad News would tell me I might never play basketball again. Dr. No News just walked around the room shaking his head. Finally, the hospital called in one of California's top cardiologists. He said I shouldn't even think about basketball for a year. "Then," he said, "after all that rest, come see me, and we'll talk about it again."

159

But he made it pretty clear that he didn't think I'd ever play basketball again.

I was scared, I tell you. For a long time I couldn't even have visitors. Alex finally weasled his way in to see me, and he was really kind and considerate. I told him I'd be back. I just didn't buy that heart attack shit. I don't know who I was trying to convince—him or me—but after a while, I started believing what I said; I kind of adopted this "All Things Are Possible If You Only Believe" philosophy that some black minister had put on a record.

One day, I snuck out of my room and called my doctor in Philadelphia, Dr. Stanley Lorber. He's a gastroenterologist, and he said he didn't think I'd had a heart attack either, judging by everything I'd told him.

"You've always had an irregular EKG," he told me. "It's pretty common among young, black athletes, but it always panics white doctors who've never seen it before."

I went back to my room feeling a lot better, and as soon as I got a chance, I jumped out of bed and did 100 push-ups, just to be sure. Then I called Dr. Lorber again, and told him what I'd done.

"You better come back here, and let me take a look at you, Wilt," he said. "I don't think those guys out there know what the hell they're doing. I think you got stomach trouble, probably pancreatitis, not any damn heart attack. I just hope they aren't screwing you up with the wrong medications."

I told him I had been taking Demerol and nitroglycerin, "and me and this intern have been drinking some Crown Royal quite a bit. I've been kind of depressed, and he's been coming by with a bottle to cheer me up and keep me company. He says a little booze is good for a heart patient."

I think I could've heard Dr. Lorber scream then, even if I hadn't had a telephone connection to Philadelphia.

"He's right," he said when he calmed down, "but any booze at all is absolute murder for pancreatitis. You get your ass out of that hospital and back to Philadelphia in a hurry."

I did just that. But I had another pancreatitis attack on the plane, and when we stopped to make connections in Chicago, I got off the plane and called Dr. Lorber again.

160

"It really hurts," I told him. "I'm scared. What should I do?"

"Get back on the plane, and come to Philadelphia."

"But what if I die in the air?"

"Then I'll look pretty stupid."

When I got to Philadelphia, Dr. Lorber put me into his hospital. It didn't take him long to diagnose my problem as pancreatitis. That seemed more logical than cardiac trouble, so I accepted the diagnosis—and that's another reason why I don't drink hard liquor now; I'm under doctor's orders not to. But if I ever believed any of that bullshit the doctors try to promulgate about their own infallibility—and the exactitude of medical science—I sure haven't believed it since my experience in San Francisco. I even got Dr. Lorber to give me a few medical books, so I could read up on any other problems I'd had, and I got him to let me audit several classes at the Temple University Medical School, where he taught. I figured that if lots of doctors don't know their asses from their elbows, I better find out a little something about medicine myself.

About the time I rejoined the Warriors that season, around the first week in November, I got another shock. One of the things I'd always liked most about San Francisco was its liberalism and its cosmopolitan approach to racial questions. In Philadelphia, I'd always felt it bothered people when they saw me with a girl who wasn't black. In New York, I used to get pissed as hell when I'd see cab drivers refuse to pick up blacks. But except for one incident—when I tried to buy a house in Madera Heights, just north of San Francisco—I didn't see any of that attitude in the bay area. No one seemed to care if you were black or white or chartreuse with orange polka dots. Everyone seemed to be treated the same. Then, that November, some people put Proposition 14 on the ballot. Proposition 14 would have repealed the just-passed California fair-housing law, and, in effect, put racial discrimination into the state constitution.

I didn't know if the proposition would pass statewide, but—my own experience in Madera Heights notwithstanding—I was dead certain it would get clobbered in San Francisco. That shows you how stupid I was. Proposition 14 passed by a 2-1 margin statewide —and it even passed in San Francisco! The Supreme Court later ruled it unconstitutional, but that didn't assuage the tremendous

161

sense of disappointment and betrayal I felt on election night. I took the election personally—more personally than I had the incident in Madera Heights. It was as if the entire city of San Francisco, including my friends, had risen up as one, and said, "You're a nigger, Chamberlain. We don't want you in our neighborhood."

When I rejoined the Warriors that season, I'd missed all our exhibition games and our first five regular-season games, and the team was clearly in trouble. They'd had to change their whole style of play without me, and they'd lost four of those first five games, even though Nate Thurmond was already showing flashes of the brilliance that would soon make him one of the best centers in NBA history. In later years, when I had to play against Nate, I came to appreciate how tremendously talented he was. He's probably the toughest center of all for me to play against —tougher than either Kareem Abdul-Jabbar *or* Bill Russell. Kareem says the same thing—that Nate gives him his hardest games. But Nate wasn't mature enough yet to handle all the shifting around necessitated by my presence—and absence. In his rookie year, he was primarily a forward, playing about 25 minutes a game behind Wayne Hightower and Tom Meschery, and filling in at center only for the minute or two I missed. Then, when I got stuck in the hospital for so long in his second year, Alex had to shift Nate to center. When I returned to the lineup, it was back to forward for Nate. That's a tough way for anyone to break into the NBA.

I probably shouldn't have played right away when I got out of the hospital, but the owner of the Warriors—Franklin Mieuli— ordered Alex to "get Wilt back in the lineup right away." I'd lost 35 pounds and was pretty weak, and Alex argued that I should work my way back into shape first, for my benefit and for the good of the team, as well. I couldn't be expected to be very effective coming off a six-week hospital stay, with no exhibition games and hardly any training camp, but after my "heart attack" Mieuli had made up his mind he wanted to trade me; he was afraid I'd have another "attack" and lose all my market value before he could unload me, he told Alex, so he wanted me on the floor, scoring points, to show the teams he was negotiating with that I was healthy and not a bad risk for them. Alex said Mieuli told him to "play Chamberlain back into shape," regardless of how that might hurt me individually or the team as a unit.

So, under protest, Alex played me full-time right away. I played 33 minutes in my first game, and scored 16 points and pulled down 17 rebounds; four nights later, in my second game, I played the full 48 minutes—and scored 37 points. Less than two weeks later, I scored 62 points in our 122-106 victory over Cincinnati. Eleven days after that, I scored 63 points against Philadelphia. Then, on December 4, in a game against Boston, a 6 foot 10, 230-pound rookie named John Thompson accidentally elbowed me in the nose while we were battling for a rebound. Splat! He broke my nose. I missed two more games, and was so bored and frustrated during the week I was off, I decided to grow a goatee for the first time. When I returned to the lineup, on December 11, my nose was still so badly injured that I had to wear an ugly face-mask like the one I'd worn my rookie year. But I scored 40 points that first night back, and hit 58 four nights later.

In the first six weeks I played that season, I scored more than 50 points six times. Through the all-star break I averaged 38.9 points and 23.5 rebounds a game—*and played just a few seconds less than 46 minutes a game!* But the team was playing miserably. They couldn't make the adjustment from me to Nate back to me again, and with me not really in shape, we couldn't run as much as we had the previous year. Nor did we execute our pattern plays as well; I hadn't worked out with the guys since the previous season, and our timing was rusty. With Guy Rodgers, Al Attles, and Tom Meschery also having early-season injury problems, we lost our last 11 games in a row before the all-star game and went into the second half of the season in last place in the Western Division, with a 10 and 34 record.

That's when Mieuli traded me.

With Nate either stuck on the bench behind me or playing at the unnatural position of forward, trading me really wasn't such a bad idea for San Francisco. Nate was 23 then, five years younger than me, with his whole future ahead of him. If the Warriors could get some other good, young players for me, they figured they might have the nucleus of a helluva good team. But Mieuli was so anxious to dump me, he made a lousy deal. Everyone in the league knew he wanted to get rid of me, so no one had to make much of an offer. Mieuli wound up trading me to the Philadelphia 76ers for Lee Shaffer, Paul Neumann, and Connie Dierking. Hell, I'd scored more points and gotten more rebounds the previous year than all three of them combined; I'd had individual years when I scored and rebounded more than any of them would in their whole career. As Jim Murray wrote in the *Los Angeles Times* after the trade was announced:

> The San Francisco Warriors did everything but list him [me] in the Yellow Pages. It was a situation unique in sport. Man O' War was being dropped in a claimer. Jim Brown was going to be dealt off for a fifth-round draft choice. Babe Ruth was being put up for two relief pitchers and an old scorebook.

It was announced that Philadelphia gave Mieuli $300,000, plus Shaffer, Dierking, and Neumann, for me, but the figure was actually much lower—and most of it went to me, not Mieuli. He was behind in my salary, and I suspect that's another reason I was traded—I kept bugging him for my money.

What made the trade even more of a farce was that the key to the deal, from the Warrior's standpoint, was Lee Shaffer—and he never played a single game in San Francisco. Alex had coached Lee in Syracuse—before the Syracuse franchise moved to Philadelphia—and Lee had averaged about 18 points a game for him over two years. When Mieuli told Alex he was going to trade me, whether Alex liked it or not, he asked Alex what the team needed. Alex said we needed a good guard, and mentioned Shaffer, who wasn't even playing for Philadelphia that year. (I don't remember if he was hurt or holding out or just playing out his option.) Mieuli told Alex to talk to Lee and get his assurance that he'd come to San Francisco if the trade were made. Alex met with Lee and they agreed on contract terms, and Alex relayed the word to Mieuli that Lee said he'd be in San Francisco "the day after you make the deal."

Alex still wasn't very happy about it, but when we all went to St. Louis for the January 13 all-star game, Mieuli told him, "I'm not leaving St. Louis till I get rid of that son-of-a-bitch" —meaning me, of course.

164

Ironically, one of the teams Mieuli talked to the most about me was the Lakers. Bob Short was the owner of the Lakers then, and he told Mieuli he wanted to poll his players first to see what they thought about having me on the team. They voted 9-2 against it, and that was the end of that; I guess guys like Elgin Baylor and Jerry West were afraid I'd come to Los Angeles and take some of their glory away. In principle, though, I think Short had a good idea. I've never been one of those guys who thinks owners have no right to trade their players, but I do think a player —particularly someone who's given you many years of good service, like West and Baylor had done for Los Angeles—should be consulted on any major trades, whether the trades involve them personally or not.

Mieuli wound up running around from hotel room to hotel room in St. Louis, trying to swing a deal for me, and he finally made it—at 12:30 in the morning, during the post-all-star-game party, on the winding staircase of Stan Musial's restaurant. I understand it was one of the least confidential, most slapstick negotiations in NBA history. One referee, Joe Gushue, was going upstairs to go to the bathroom or something, and overheard the deal being made, and came down and told everyone at his table about it. But Mieuli not only hadn't told me he was trying to trade me beforehand, he didn't even have the class to tell me about the deal personally after it was made. Some sportswriter came running up to me with the story, asking for my reaction before I knew the deal had actually been made. In fact, the only reason I even knew there was a deal in the works at all was that Ike Richman, the co-owner of the 76ers, was a close personal friend, and he'd told me he was trying to get me to play for him.

As you might imagine, I wasn't all that enthusiastic about going back to Philadelphia after falling in love with San Francisco. Once again, I decided to quit. I had made some good investments in land and apartments and other ventures, and I figured I could make it financially without basketball. But, once again, Eddie Gottlieb—and Ike—talked me out of it.

When Eddie had sold the Warriors to Mieuli, in 1962, he was already negotiating to bring the Syracuse Nationals to Philadelphia. But that got stalled for a year, and by then, Eddie was in San Francisco, and Irving Kosloff and Ike had bought the

165

Syracuse team for Philadelphia. Even though Eddie was not part of the 76er ownership, he had returned to Philadelphia after his two years helping with the Warriors' transition in San Francisco, and he wanted to see me back in Philadelphia, too. So did Ike. He said the team—and the city—really needed me. The 76ers were playing only .500 ball, and they weren't drawing flies; the Eagles, as usual, were losing more games than they won; the Phillies had blown a 6½-game lead—and the National League pennant—in the last week of the baseball season. Ike said the Philly sports fans—never the world's most pleasant—were ready to hang every professional athlete in town.

Ike was more than a friend and attorney and prospective employer to me; he was like a second father. I agreed to come back to Philadelphia.

Before I left San Francisco, my friend Jim Bryant gave me the only surprise party I've ever had that really surprised me. He got one of the girls I was dating to take me to La Bourgogne for dinner, and he had it set up with the maitre d' there to keep him posted every 20 minutes or so on our progress; he even had the doorman phone him when we left. I took the girl back to my apartment, figuring to cop her one last time before I left for Philadelphia, and, instead, I found my apartment full of people. But it was great. What made it so amazing to me was that a friend from New York, Charlie Polk, had been staying with me for a few days, and he'd helped Jim coordinate the party, and I never did figure out what they were doing.

Most of the Warrior players and officials were at the party, and I think that was probably the last good time any of them had that whole season. Without me, the Warriors lost their first six games after the all-star break to run their losing streak to 17 straight—a record at that time. They wound up in last place in the Western Division, with a record of 17 wins and 63 losses —the worst record in the NBA in 11 years.

Lee Shaffer, curiously enough, never did report to San Francisco. Connie Dierking and Paul Neumann averaged about 19 points a game between them for the Warriors the rest of the 1964–65 season, and then Dierking got traded to Cincinnati. Two years later, the Warriors got rid of Neumann, too.

166

10

WHEN I JOINED THE 76ERS IN Philadelphia, after the NBA all-star game, Ike Richman didn't want to take a chance on my receiving anything less than a thunderous welcome in my hometown. He had people out giving away tickets on streetcorners and in schoolyards for our first game, and he organized groups of kids with banners and noise-makers, and when I was introduced before the game that night, the arena damn near fell apart from all the screaming and stomping and whistling. I like to think at least some of that emotion was genuine, but I didn't know anything about what Ike had done then, and I was really moved.

Ike had good cause to do everything he could to make me feel welcome. He knew I was apprehensive—if not downright hostile—about having to play that season for the 76ers coach, Dolph Schayes. Schayes was one of the reasons I was so reluctant to come back to Philadelphia in the first place.

Back in 1960, when I wrote that story for *Look* about all the roughhouse treatment I'd had in my rookie year, Dolph wrote a story for another magazine, calling me an "immature . . . stubborn . . . crybaby" who was "pampered" by the officials. Then, the next season, when I started having trouble with my free throws, Dolph had gone around telling everyone, "It's ridiculous; any high school kid could do better. . . . He's just too lazy to practice. That's all it takes—practice."

Dolph had been a fantastic foul shot himself all through his 16-year NBA career with Syracuse and Philadelphia, and he'd led the league in free throw percentage four times. His career record was about 85 percent, and even though his field goal percentage was way down around 38 percent, he had been an all-time all-pro—just a few hundred points behind Bob Pettit then as the second-highest scorer in NBA history. But Dolph was much like my first pro coach, Neil Johnston—a great player who became a lousy coach (though I have to admit that Dolph was generally more decent and fair-minded than Neil. That, in fact, was part of Dolph's problem; he was just too nice a guy to be a good coach.)

The first thing Dolph did when I joined the 76ers was have me practice free throws. I must have shot 400 a day. And I usually made about 80 percent of them. Then, during the games, I reverted to my old habits and hit about 50 percent, and Dolph finally realized that my problem wasn't laziness.

The 76ers played well when I first joined them. We won nine of our first eleven games after the all-star break—including a 104-100 victory in Boston that broke the Celtics' 16-game win streak, one game shy of what was then the NBA record. Bill Russell took 15 shots against me that night without scoring. A week later, we played Boston again—in Philadelphia, before a record crowd—and we beat them again, 118-105.

I was averaging 30 points a game, and Hal Greer was averaging 20, and the team was starting to jell, despite Schayes' manifest ineptitude. Then Hal and our other starting guard, Larry Costello, both got hurt, and I had another acute attack of pancreatitis. We slumped back to the .500 level, and finished third in the Eastern Division, 22 games behind Boston.

Fortunately, our first opponent in the playoffs was Cincinnati, and their star—Oscar Robertson—was also injured. We smashed them three out of four games, and now—for the fourth time in my six-year NBA career—it was time to play Boston.

168

In the first game, in Boston, the Celtics' full-court press—and their rabid fans—completely demoralized our guards; we threw the ball away a dozen times in the first half alone. Boston won, 108-98. Two nights later, I outscored Russell, 30-12, and out-rebounded him, 39-16, and we won, 109-103.

The Celtics' press and my own poor play beat us in the third game. I went 24 minutes without a basket and committed several turnovers, and we got blown out, 112-94. But we evened the series at 2-2 the next night with a 134-131 overtime victory.

Before the fifth game, *Sports Illustrated* published the first article in a two-part series I'd done for them several weeks earlier with Bob Ottum, one of their staff writers. Bob had promised me that the series wouldn't be published until July—well after the NBA season was over. When it came out in the middle of the playoffs, I was really pissed; as we'd expected, the stories created quite a furor, and I'm not sure the 76ers ever got back in stride during the playoffs.

Bob called me to apologize for the timing—and for the title his editors put on the series, "My Life in a Bush League." I hadn't approved the title, and I didn't like it. Neither did my teammates or my coach or most of the other players in the league—or the NBA office itself. I got fined for what they published. What got me so mad about that was that I'd always assiduously avoided criticizing other players and coaches in the NBA, even when guys like Bob Cousy and Neil Johnston and Dolph Schayes were putting the rap on me, and sportswriters were practically begging me to answer back. Those guys didn't have any legitimate gripes against me. They were just jealous because I was breaking their records and getting all the attention and making more money than they were. But none of them got fined. Then, when I said some things about the league that needed to be said, I got fined. If you compared the NBA in 1965 with the NFL and the two baseball leagues, you'd see that the *Sports Illustrated* title probably wasn't so far off, after all. It's only in the last three or four years that conditions in the NBA have approached those in professional baseball and football.

But there are some things you're just not supposed to say. I mean, when have you heard a Jerry West or a John Havlicek or an Elgin Baylor or a Walt Frazier be really critical of anything?

They'd rather play it safe—and be hypocrites. I've heard all those guys say things in private they wouldn't say in public. But I just can't be that way. I've always prided myself on having the courage to be honest and say what I think—even eight or ten years ago, when it was far more risky for an athlete to be outspoken than it is today. That's one reason I've been so unpopular —the villain of the NBA, the superstar you love to hate.

In that *Sports Illustrated* story, I said I was tired of being treated as a villain, tired of having my every move criticized, tired of being pushed and shoved by other centers who were protected by the officials, tired of men like Dolph Schayes and—most of all—tired of the regimentation and sub-par playing conditions and constant public attention of NBA life.

"Defeat and victory all smell exactly the same in a pro basketball dressing room after a while," I said. "You get so you don't feel any elation. You just feel beat. . . . Basketball burns you out."

For a sports superstar who was supposed to be bubbling over with gratitude for every second he got to play, those were pretty harsh words. I could understand why some people (including Dolph Schayes) got upset.

The day after the magazine came out, the 76ers looked ragged against Boston. We got beat, 114-108. But we won the sixth game, 112-106, even though I played almost the whole last quarter with five fouls.

Then came the seventh game.

Boston led, 110-103, with less than two minutes to go. Then I hit a tip-in, two free throws and a dunk. It was 110-109. But there were only six seconds left, and it was Boston's ball out of bounds. Incredibly, Bill Russell—supposedly the greatest clutch player of them all—threw the ball into a guy-wire attached to the basket, and the ball caromed out-of-bounds. It was our ball— with five seconds left to get a basket and win the championship. We called time out. Schayes gave us the play: Greer, our best outside shot—with 28 points already that night—would pass the ball in to Chet Walker, then duck behind a Johnny Kerr screen, take the return pass and fire away from 15 feet. But Hal never got the shot off. His in-bounds pass had too much arc, and John Havlicek reached over and slapped the ball to Sam Jones, and we lost the game—and the championship.

I'd outscored Russell, 30-15, and outrebounded him, 32-29, and he'd come within an eyelash of being the goat of the game. But, once again, he was the winner, and I was the loser; the Celtics went on to whip the injury-riddled Lakers four times in five games to win the NBA title.

The off-season wasn't much better for me that year than the playoffs had been.

I had been living in New York during the season and in San Francisco during the off-season, and a flash fire destroyed my San Francisco apartment one day while I was in New York for a benefit game; when I got back to San Francisco, all that was left was one small metal box full of girls' phone numbers. (Thank God, some of them were winners!)

About the same time, I got stopped by a cop in New York, and he damn near shot me. I'd bought a nightclub in Harlem several years earlier—Big Wilt's Small Paradise—and after I'd worked 18 hours a day one off-season, learning the business, I'd brought in a friend to manage the place for me. I always try to stop by when I'm in New York, and I was on my way back from there to my apartment, on Central Park West, when this cop started following me. He pulled me over, and said, "Let me see your license, boy." I gave him the license, and asked him what the problem was.

"Be with you in a minute, boy," he said.

He kept calling me "boy," and I didn't like it much. I told him my name was on my driver's license, "and I'd suggest you use it."

This was just a few nights after the Watts riot, and cops everywhere were even more uptight than usual around blacks. He pulled his gun out of his holster, stuck it in the window about six inches from my head and cocked it. I said, "OK, mother-fucker, you cocked that thing, you might as well pull the trigger."

Then I started to get out of the car.

Fortunately for me, the cop backed off. He pulled his gun away and apologized, and I snatched my license back and roared off, with him still standing there, holding his gun.

It wasn't until I got home and got into bed that I realized how

171

close I'd come to getting my head blown off. I didn't sleep too well that night, and the next morning, I reported the officer to his precinct captain.

A few days later, I was telling Hank Stram, the coach of the Kansas City Chiefs, about the incident. We were at Kutsher's, in the Catskills, where Hank and I both had summer camps for kids, and he just laughed and said, "You ought to get into a safer line of work, Wilt."

"Like what?"

"Like pro football."

Now it was my turn to laugh. But Hank was serious. He said he'd always been an admirer of mine, and he thought I had the size and speed and agility to make a great flanker. I thought about it—for ten seconds—and said, "Thanks, but no thanks. It's a little late for me to start all over in another sport."

That same week, I signed a new three-year contract with the 76ers.

Although I'd been making more than $100,000 for several years by then, this was the first time any clubowner publicly admitted he was paying me that much. Bill Russell responded by demanding that Boston pay him $1 more—$100,001—and the papers made a big deal out of Bill's one-upmanship. I was rather amused by it all, since I was making considerably more than $100,001. I was glad to let Bill have the publicity; I wanted the money.

From the time I first came into the league, other players had resented my salary. When the $100,000 figure was announced, some of them really got mad. They acted as if I were taking money out of their pockets. Just the opposite was true. I drove salaries up for everyone. That's why the men who owned the clubs I played for were so reluctant to admit just how much they were paying me. They knew that other players would begin pointing to my salary, and demand more money for themselves. That's exactly what happened, of course, the owners' subterfuge notwithstanding. When I came into the league, no one was making more than $25,000. Now the *average* is $60,000—and even rookies sign contracts for four and five times that much. Bob Pettit is one player who recognized my role in that change. He said I was responsible for the same kind of breakthrough in basketball salaries that Babe

172

Ruth had been responsible for in baseball salaries. In fact, early in my career—when I signed my first $100,000 contract—Pettit got wind of it, and walked into the Hawks' front office, and asked Ben Kerner, the Hawks' owner, "Don't you think I'm worth half as much as Chamberlain after playing in the league as long as I have?"

Kerner tore up Pettit's $26,000 contract on the spot, and gave him a new one—for $50,000.

Armed with *my* lucrative new contract—and the conviction that the 76ers were going to have a great year—I went into the 1965–66 NBA season in a buoyant mood. For the first time in my career, I actually felt our personnel was as good as Boston's—finally!

At guard, we had Hal Greer, one of the all-time top scorers *and* assist men; Larry Costello, another good assist man, and Wali Jones, a flashy little playmaker who got a little too flashy at times, but was a good man for our particular team. We were also three-deep at forward, with Chet Walker, a strong 6 foot 7, 220-pound, three-year veteran who was getting better every year; rookie Billy Cunningham, who soon became the best forward in the NBA in my book, and Luke Jackson, a big, brawny second-year man who helped me out tremendously on the boards. For back-up, we had guys like Gerry Ward, Dave Gambee, and Al Bianchi coming in off the bench. All we needed was a decent coach—and we were so strong, not even Dolph could hurt us much during the regular season.

I averaged 33.5 points and 24.6 rebounds a game, and led the league in both categories that year. I also finished seventh in assists. Hal finished sixth in scoring and tenth in assists. Chet and Billy both averaged in double figures. The 76ers won 55 of 80 games—including six of ten over Boston—and finished first in the Eastern Division, ahead of Boston for the first time.

The only thing that marred the season to that point was the death of Ike Richman. Ike rooted for the 76ers as loudly and frentically as any fan, and on December 3—in Boston—he suffered a heart attack and died during a game. We won the game for Ike—119-103—but Philadelphia was never the same for me again; I had lost one of the dearest friends any man could have.

In the playoffs against Boston that year, we were flat. I don't

173

know why, but we were. In the first two games, Hal scored only 21 points total—less than half his season average—and Boston won both games easily, 125-96 and 114-93, with hot outside shooting and a devastating fast break. Red Auerbach outcoached Dolph something terrible in those games and in the rest of the series—making smarter substitutions, mapping better strategy, using his time-outs more shrewdly, knowing just how to motivate his players. We managed to win the third game, 111-105, and almost tied the series in the fourth game when I blocked a Russell layup in the final seconds of regulation play to send the game into overtime. If we could've won that one, we might have won the series. But we couldn't—and we didn't. The Celtics won, 114-108, and came back two nights later to eliminate us, 120-112—even though I had again outscored Russell by a 2-1 margin, and outrebounded him as well, throughout the series.

In the locker room after that fifth game, a Philadelphia sportswriter named Joe McGinniss told me I'd missed 17 of 25 free throws in the game, and asked me if I thought I was responsible for the loss. I'd just scored 46 points—exactly the same number as our other four starters combined!—so I thought the question was a little out of line; I didn't even bother to answer him. He asked me the same question again, only this time he added, "Don't you think you might have hit a few more of those free throws if you hadn't missed practice this week?"

I had missed one practice that week—just one—because I had the flu, and the press had played it up big. They had always resented my living in New York, first with the Warriors and now with the 76ers; they thought it was an insult to Philadelphia (which, I guess, it was—a richly deserved insult), and when the sportswriters had asked Dolph where I was that day I was sick, he had mishandled the situation, as usual. I had called and told him I was sick, but he just shrugged at the reporters, and said, "Who knows?" The press had a field day with that—another example of the double standard I'd always been subjected to. Bill Russell missed more practices than I ever dreamed of missing, but no one ever criticized him for it; Tom Gola had lived in New York before I even joined the Warriors, but no one ever accused him of insulting Philadelphia.

That's why, when McGinniss asked me about missing practice

in the dressing room after the fifth game with Boston, I just glared at him and didn't answer. When he asked the question for the third time, I exploded. McGinniss became famous three years later when he wrote *The Selling of the President*, but if Chet and Billy hadn't restrained me that night, he wouldn't even have lived to write the story of that game. I really wanted to kill him—and I damn near did; Chet and Billy had to use all their strength to hold me back.

That summer, just about six months after Ike Richman had died, another older man who'd been a good friend and advisor died—Abe Saperstein of the Globetrotters. I was in Europe at the time, and—through some intermediaries—I was offered an opportunity to buy a piece of the Globies and become president of the company. I considered it—and might even have taken it—but the 76ers had fired Dolph Schayes and hired Alex Hannum, and now I knew we were going to beat Boston for the championship in 1967, and I didn't want to miss that for anything.

Alex's decision to come to Philadelphia was gratifying to me on several counts. The most obvious, of course, was that I liked him as a man and respected him as a coach, and knew he'd take us to the championship. But the press was saying I'd been responsible for the 76ers' firing Dolph. They forgot that Dolph had been fighting with the other players on the 76ers before I even joined the team. They also forgot what we all knew—that Dolph Schayes was a piss-poor coach. On his next coaching job, in Buffalo, he had a 22 and 60 record his first year, and set a world record his second year—he was fired after one game! But it made better copy to say "Chamberlain Fires Schayes" than "Schayes Stinks," so that's what the papers said; they said I'd had five coaches in seven years and was "devouring them like aspirin tablets." So why did Alex come to Philadelphia if I was so tough on coaches? He'd coached me for two years in San Francisco; he knew what to expect. Surely, he wouldn't step into an impossible situation, just looking for trouble. It was a ridiculous charge against me, and Alex—as he had in San Francisco—told me so.

Alex had also coached several of the other 76er players a few years earlier, when both he and the franchise were in Syracuse, and he quickly reestablished rapport with them, and reinstilled in the rest of us the almost small-town closeness and friendship the team had had in Syracuse.

175

We became the closest team I've ever played on—much closer off the court, for example, than the Laker teams I've been with since then. In fact, I'm still a lot closer to two of the guys I played with on the 76ers—Chet Walker and Billy Cunningham—than I am to any of the Lakers.

On the floor and in the locker room, the 76ers and Lakers were both very close teams—cohesive units concerned about each other as individuals, given to constant banter and repartee. But I hardly ever see any of the Lakers socially between seasons, and I don't really see that much of them between games either. When I was with the 76ers, we usually went over to Pagano's Italian restaurant on Chester Street after most of our games to have dinner together, or at least visit among ourselves for a few minutes. We also had parties at each other's homes almost every month or so. At one party, around Halloween, I came dressed as a Persian, with a turban and all, and Alex came as a Japanese karate expert, and we ribbed the hell out of each other—as we usually did.

Another time, on a road trip, Alex and I raced from the San Francisco Airport to our hotel downtown. I was ahead of him when I spotted a cop up ahead. I zipped off the freeway before Alex knew what was happening—and the cop stopped him and gave him a ticket. I circled back to another on-ramp, got back on the freeway and, whoosh!, I zoomed by Alex and the cop at about 100 miles an hour, waving and honking. Alex later told me the damn cop was so mad, he almost threw his flashlight at my car as I went by.

I've always enjoyed being a prankster, and the relaxed, easygoing mood we were all in that season led me to exercise those inclinations almost daily—and not just on my coach and teammates.

I had two big Great Danes then—Thor and Odin—and I used to like walking them through Central Park late at night, after midnight, when I had trouble sleeping. You can imagine the startled looks I got from late-night lovers and other strollers when they saw this huge black man and his monstrous dogs come marching by.

I lived in a high-class, 12th-floor apartment on Central Park West then, and when Thor and Odin were young and small, the landlady there kept telling me how "cute" they were. But they grew quickly—and so did her apprehension. Finally, I started playing tricks on my neighbors with the dogs. I'd pick a time like 5 or 6 o'clock in the evening, when I knew the lobby would be crowded, and I'd put them in one 12th-floor elevator, and I'd get in the other. When I got down to the lobby, I'd jump out and hide around the corner to see what happened when the door to the other elevator opened. Thor and Odin would come bounding out like giant wolves, hot after dead game; you never saw so many grown people running and screaming in your life.

I was evicted from the building, but my stunts with the dogs were typical of the kinds of pranks I and the other 76ers played on each other—and unsuspecting bystanders—all the time. With all the short trips we took in those days—to places like Boston and Baltimore and New York—we often went by bus or train or a chartered DC-3, rather than by commercial jet, and that kept us together, isolated from other passengers, much of the time. We got to know and like each other so well, we felt comfortable needling each other and playing outrageous practical jokes on each other. If a guy tried to catch up on his sleep in an airport, waiting for a late flight, we'd steal his shoes. Once, I remember, Billy Cunningham fell asleep in the car while we were parked somewhere, and everyone else piled out and threw cherry bombs into the car. Billy said it was the best goddam alarm clock he'd ever had.

Al Domenico, our trainer, was often the ringleader in the pranks. He liked to fill his bag with heavy equipment that he didn't really need, then make some rookie carry it all over the country for him on road trips. He also liked to give guys the wrong room keys when we checked into a new hotel—and deliberately wake them up two hours early for a morning departure, then watch them stalk angrily around the hotel lobby, wondering why everyone else was "late."

Al gave me a large, very realistic rubber rat one time, and I used to scare the shit out of some of the guys with it. I used it on Matt Guokas once, during his rookie year, and he had nightmares about it for a week.

Probably Al's best stunt that year came when we were down in some small Southern town for an exhibition game, and he put the bus driver up to warning us to stay in our hotel rooms and just order room service " 'cause this is one bad KKK town." After we

177

checked in, Al and Billy and Chet Walker got all dressed up in sheets, and went from room to room, scaring the shit out of all of us. Hal Greer got so scared, we almost couldn't get him to leave his room for the game that night.

One day, we all decided to give Al a taste of his own medicine. We wrapped him up between two mattresses, taped the whole thing together with tape from his trainer's kit and dumped him out in a parking lot in some abandoned shopping center on a Sunday afternoon.

One of the things that enabled us to do things like this to each other was that there were no cliques on the 76ers. When I'd first joined the team, in January 1965, there had been two distinct cliques—blacks like Hal Greer, Chet Walker, and Luke Jackson in one, whites like Al Bianchi, Larry Costello, Dave Gambee, and Johnny Kerr (all from the old Syracuse franchise) in the other. By the 1966–67 season, Kerr and Bianchi were gone and Costello was injured; me and Wali Jones had started loosening up the other blacks on the team, and Billy Cunningham had loosened up the other whites. We became one happy family—me and Wali going to the movies together, Billy and Hal playing golf together, Dave and Luke drinking beer together. Hell, to show you how close we were, Billy and Chet were just about the closest friends on the team, even though Chet is a black man and Billy is a white man from North Carolina—and even though a lot of people thought Billy should have been starting at forward, ahead of Chet, instead of coming off the bench as our sixth man. But there wasn't an ounce of jealousy or resentment between them. (If there had been, I would've known; they were my two best friends on the team.)

All of us had our individual quirks and shortcomings, of course, but instead of exploiting them to hurt each other—and the team—we tried to help each other. Like, I've always enjoyed copping girls in situations where I have to make my move quickly or be unusually imaginative or meet some other challenge. Instead of resenting my success with the ladies, the other 76ers encouraged me and even helped me out. I remember one time, we had an exhibition game in Albuquerque, and I met this sensational girl, and it didn't look like I'd have time to cop her before our plane left. Wali Jones volunteered to rent a car and drive us to the airport, and she and I made love in the back seat on the way there. We weren't quite through when we got to the airport, so Wali just parked the car within walking distance—but not peeping distance—from the terminal and left us alone. The car was a compact—a Ford Falcon—and it took some real ingenuity on my part to make things work. But it wasn't nearly as difficult as the time Chet helped me with a girl on a flight from Chicago to Los Angeles later that season. She was a stewardess—absolutely gorgeous—and we got to rapping, and she let me know she'd like to make it with me right then—38,000 feet in the air. I took her back into the rest room, and we did it, half standing and half leaning, in what must have been a double world fuck record—the smallest space and the highest altitude . . . with Chet standing guard outside the door, whistling loudly to cover any sounds of pleasure that might filter back to the other passengers.

Chet and Billy and Luke and Hal and all the rest of the guys got along so well together that year I'm not sure I can remember a single incident where there was any real friction in the whole season. In fact, me and Alex had the only big beef that I can think of now. Alex always came into the dressing room to tell us how great we were after each victory, and he always shook damn near every player's hand, even if some of us hadn't had particularly good games. But when we lost, he didn't shake anyone's hand—not even the guys who played well. I've never believed completely in the "It's-not-who-wins-but-how-you-played-the-game" school of thought, but I do think there's at least an element of truth in it, and after one of our rare losses—when I'd played extremely well—Alex didn't say a word to me. I got pissed. The next night we won, and he was back shaking hands. I refused to shake with him. "If you can't shake my hand, win or lose, I don't want any part of your handshakes," I told him.

I was serious about what I said, and I think we both remembered it for a long time. But it didn't create any lasting rift between us; Alex and I and everyone else were too happy with the way we were playing to let something like that happen.

We were a loose and happy and cooperative team that season because we were a winning team. But you never know which comes first; did we win because we were close, or were we close because we were winning? I suspect it's a little of both. I also think I learned some valuable lessons that year that contributed to both the victories and the closeness.

Under Alex, in San Francisco, I had begun to do other things besides score, and my scoring average had been coming down steadily since my third year—from 50.4 points a game to 44.8 to 36.9 to 34.7 to 33.5. But I still considered myself a scorer, first and foremost, and I still led the league in scoring every year—and in money and publicity, as well. Some of the other players couldn't help resenting that, and while I kept telling myself they were pros and should act accordingly, some of them weren't too happy about playing with me.

I was 30 years old when the 1966–67 season began, and I was maturing as a man, and learning that it was essential to keep my teammates happy if I wanted my team to win. I not only began passing off more and scoring less, I also made a point of singling my teammates out for praise—privately and publicly. I'd always done that some—back in my rookie year, I remember one game where I got 55 points and 29 rebounds, and kept telling the sportswriters that Andy Johnson, not me, was the hero of the game—but I had never made a deliberate, all-out effort at it before the 1966–67 season.

I realize now that this is the kind of thing that helped make O. J. Simpson's teams at USC and Bill Walton's teams at UCLA so successful. The same is true of Joe Namath and the Jets. O. J. and Bill and Joe always praise their teammates. They remember the name of every guy who throws a key block or makes a good assist or a good defensive play, and they tell the player—and the press—all about it. That can't help but make the player try even harder next time, instead of maybe letting down, subconsciously, because he's tired of being ignored and hearing how great you are all the time.

I was just learning this lesson in 1966, and it was reflected in my statistics. I took only 1,150 shots that season—less than half what I'd been averaging since I came into the league, and only about one-third as many as I took the year I averaged 50 points a game. Not only was I shooting less, but I was shooting more selectively; I hit 68.3 percent of my shots that year—better than anyone had ever done before. I wound up averaging 24.1 points a game—15 points under my career average to that point;

for the first time in my eight-year NBA career, I didn't lead the league in scoring. I finished third. More important, instead of me averaging 40 points a game, and only one other guy on my team averaging much over 20 or so, we had a great scoring balance. Hal Greer averaged 22.1, Chet averaged 19.3, and Billy averaged 18.5. Luke Jackson and Wali Jones also averaged in double figures. That's the kind of balance Boston always had, and I had told myself before the season began that if I averaged 24 or 25 points a game, that's the kind of balanced scoring we'd get. We had the players and we had the coach, and I knew there was no reason we shouldn't go all the way if I was willing to sacrifice my image as a prolific scorer—which wasn't actually much of a sacrifice anyway. I'd already proved I could outscore everyone. That was no longer much of a challenge. Being a passer and a feeder was.

I finished third in the league in assists that year with 630, behind Guy Rodgers and Oscar Robertson—and ahead of such great playmakers as Jerry West, Lennie Wilkins, K. C. Jones and Richie Guerin. No big man had ever finished that high or had that many assists before in the history of the NBA. I also led the league in rebounding—for the sixth time in eight years. That meant that of the four most important categories—scoring, rebounding, assists, and field goal percentage—I finished first in two and third in the other two. That was something else no other player—big or small —had ever done before. But, like I said, ours was a team performance that year, not a one-man show. Hal, Chet, Billy, and I *all* finished among the top 15 scorers; Chet finished sixth in field goal percentage; Wali Jones finished seventh in free throw percentage; Chet, Billy, and Luke had more rebounds than any other three-forward combination in the league.

The 76ers really were an awesome team that year. We won our first seven games, lost one, won eight straight, lost one, won 11 straight, lost one, won another 11 straight, lost one, then won nine more before Larry Costello got hurt. That meant our record in our first 50 games was 46 and 4—still the best in history. We were about ten games ahead of Boston in the Eastern Division by then, and—with Larry out for more than 30 games—we sort of eased up some. But we were so strong that year, we even won easily when we didn't play our best.

181

I can remember one game we won against the Lakers when I didn't play the whole second half. It was in Los Angeles, in March, and I had two technical fouls called on me late in the second quarter and I was ejected—by referee Norm Drucker, the same official who'd thrown me out of a game in Los Angeles during my rookie year. When I walked outside into the Sports Arena parking lot this time, they were starting to unload the animals for the circus that was opening there the next day. I went over to get some sympathy from the elephants when, all of a sudden, this lion gets out of his cage and comes charging at me. That scared the elephants almost as much as it scared me, and when they started snorting and pawing and milling around, I didn't know whether to be more afraid of them or the lion. The trainer finally got the lion back into his cage, after getting cut up pretty badly, and then the elephants quieted down. I later heard that that same lion had attacked the trainer a couple of nights earlier, and it had taken 150 stitches to close his wounds. If I ever needed proof of my old coach's warning about the dangers of losing my temper and getting thrown out of a game, that was it; I never argued that much over an official's call on me again. That was the third—and last!—time I've ever been ejected from an NBA game.

Philadelphia wound up the 1966–67 season with 68 wins and 13 losses—the best in NBA history until my Laker team won 69 and lost 13 in 1971–72. The 76ers finished eight games ahead of Boston in the Eastern Division that year, and after all those years of waiting for a championship, our victory over them in the play-offs was almost anticlimatic. We were so clearly better than the Celtics that year, that we knew we would win—and win easily.

We were probably a little overconfident—and looking ahead to Boston—when we opened the playoffs against Cincinnati; the Royals beat us, 120-116. We stormed back to win the next game, 123-102. We won the third one easily, too, and I tied Bob Cousy's all-time playoff record with 19 assists. After we beat Cincinnati again in the fourth game, it was time for Boston.

We crushed the Celtics four out of five games—by an average of almost 15 points a game—and our scoring was as balanced as it had been all season. In the first game, Hal scored 39, and Wali and I had 24 apiece. In the second game, Chet had 23, Wali had 22, Hal had 17, Luke and I had 15 apiece, and Billy had 13. In

182

the third game, Hal had 30, Wali had 21, I had 20, and Chet had 18. That gave us a 3-0 lead. Boston nipped us in the fourth game, 121-117, but we came back to slaughter them, 140-116, in the fifth game, with Hal getting 32, me 29, Chet 26, Wali 23, and Billy 21. In the dressing room after the game, all the players were screaming and whistling and pouring champagne over each other; it was an incredibly wild celebration. But I didn't take part in it. Beating Boston just assured us of the Eastern Division title, not the world title. We still had to beat San Francisco to win that, and I wasn't about to get cocky now and blow it. I told the guys to cool it for a while.

As it turned out, San Francisco was slightly tougher for us than Boston—but only slightly. In the first game against them, I had 16 points, 33 rebounds, 10 assists, and nine blocked shots, and all five of our starters scored in double figures. That pretty much set the pattern for the series. We had five men in double figures in every game—and six men in double figures twice—and we beat the Warriors, four games to two. At long last, we were the NBA champions.

I felt great. During the regular season, I'd answered all those critics who always said I couldn't do anything but score and that I was a disruptive influence on my team. Now, in the playoffs, I'd answered the critics who said I was a loser who'd never win a championship. But there were three delicious bits of irony surrounding the championship and its immediate aftermath, and I'll probably remember them as long as I'll remember the championship itself.

Irony No. 1:

The press, quite accurately, called the championship a team victory. They said we had beaten Boston because we were a better team than the Celtics—"not necessarily because Chamberlain was better than Russell." Of course, they'd never taken that approach all those years Boston beat my teams. They'd never said Boston won because they were a better team—"not necessarily because Russell was better than Chamberlain." When Boston was winning, it was always Russell who was responsible, Russell who made the Celtics a great team, Russell who beat me. But they wouldn't give me the same credit for our victory.

183

Irony No. 2:

Rick Barry had kind of replaced me as the superscorer in the NBA that season. While I was busy passing off and rebounding and setting screens for my teammates, Rick was burning up the league. He averaged 35.6 points a game—best in the league—and he scored more than 50 points in six different games. In the book he wrote a few years later, though, Rick had a few unkind words to say about me. "Wilt is a loser," he wrote. "He is terrible in big games." So how had Rick Barry performed in the "big games" against us in those 1967 playoffs? Well, in the last game, when the Warriors were only down by a point, with four seconds to go, Rick went up for an easy jump shot at the right of the key; if he had made it, the series would have been tied at three games apiece. But he choked, lost his balance, and threw up a shot that missed by about 28 miles—and we were the champions.

Irony No. 3:

After we won the title, I was presented with the prestigious John Wanamaker award in Philadelphia. Having waited so long for my first championship, I had a lot of things I wanted to say in my acceptance speech. But I got laryngitis, and couldn't say a word —one of the few times in my life I can ever remember being speechless.

After all the championship celebrations in Philadelphia, I took off for my annual summer tour of Europe. I was just starting to gamble for big stakes then, and when I met Jim Brown in London, he and I and another friend went over to a casino to try our hands at the crap tables. We played about like the 76ers had played during the season. In 35 minutes, we were $225,000 ahead. We lost some of it back, but I still won about $65,000 myself, and Jim and the other guy did pretty well, too. We actually broke the bank. They had to close the casino, and pay us off the next day— 50 cents on the dollar.

When I got to Italy a week or so later, I used some of my crap table winnings to buy myself a present—a $26,000 Maserati Ghibli. I had the car flown back to the United States in time for me to drive it to the Maurice Stokes benefit game at Kutsher's, but I almost didn't make the game. A small-town cop stopped me for speeding and took me to the local magistrate—a nearsighted, wizened old man who asked *me* how much I thought my fine should be. I'd been going about 125 miles an hour, so I had no idea what he had in mind. I suggested $20, figuring he might be thinking of at least $100. But he said, "How about $10?"

"Great."

Then the cop stepped up and said "Magistrate, this is Mr. Chamberlain."

The magistrate brightened immediately. "Oh, Mr. Chamberlain. My wife and I are big fans of yours."

I was in a hurry to get to the game, but I couldn't risk getting the guy mad at me and maybe throwing me in jail for reckless driving, so I decided to humor him. I thanked him and told him how much I'd always liked his little town.

He nodded. "Yes, my wife and I watch you on television every week. We love you."

Every week? We played on TV some, but it wasn't even every month, no less every week. I couldn't figure out what he was talking about.

Then the cop spoke up again. "Magistrate, why don't you come outside, and take a look at Mr. Chamberlain's beautiful car."

We all walked outside—with the cop guiding the magistrate by the arm—and the magistrate walks right up to the car and starts squinting and patting it. "My, this sure is a nice car," he says. "I didn't know you doctor fellows made so much money."

Doctor fellows? Suddenly, it dawned on me. The half-blind old coot thought I was *Richard* Chamberlain, the guy who played Dr. Kildare on television. I'd heard the saying "Justice is blind" before, but I never knew that's what it meant.

I decided to split—before the guy asked me to take out his appendix or something.

That was the last amusing moment I had during the summer of '67. I was soon embroiled in the longest, nastiest contract holdout of my career.

When I had agreed to return to Philadelphia in 1965, one of the reasons I had done so was that Ike Richman had promised me a piece of the team. He and Irv Kosloff each owned half the team, and Ike promised me half of his half—25 percent. He couldn't put it in writing then, he said, because NBA rules prohibited a player from owning part of any team. But Ike and I had never had to put anything in writing anyway; we were friends, and we trusted each other implicitly. Then, when Ike died, Kosloff said he had no knowledge of our agreement—and he had no intention of giving me 25 percent of the team, then or ever. Kosloff also said that several harness horses Ike and I had bought together had been bought by Ike as part-owner of the 76ers, not Ike as a private individual. A 50 percent interest in the horses also belonged to the team now, he said.

I'd first gotten into the horse business early in my career, when I bought a nag named Spooky Cadet for $3,500. He won only one race in the two years I owned him, and when I sold him, I got only $2,000 back. But the rest of the horses I bought—under Ike's guidance—were money-makers. On one—Rivaltime—I tripled my money. Another one, Richman Hanover (named for Ike), cost me $100,000—one of the highest prices ever paid for a pacer in Pennsylvania. Naturally, I wasn't very happy about having to give up half our horse investment to the Philadelphia 76ers. And I was livid with rage over Kosloff's refusal to honor my deal with Ike.

Kosloff and I argued about that through the whole summer after we won the championship, and I finally decided I couldn't play for the man any more if that's the way he was going to treat me. But I had one year to go on my three-year contract. In mid-October, the day before the 76ers' final exhibition game—and less than a week before the 1967–68 league opener—Kosloff and I reached an uneasy truce: I would get a cash settlement in consideration of my deal with Ike; my old three-year contract would be torn up, and I would sign a new one-year contract at an announced salary of $250,000. The cash settlement was sizable, but it was nowhere near the $2 million to $3 million my 25 percent of the franchise would have been worth then, so I wasn't exactly thrilled with the settlement. But I agreed to it for one reason—Ike had been so good to me and had done so many things for me, I didn't want to tarnish his memory with bitterness.

I told Kosloff I'd sign the one-year contract with one condition—that I be free after that year to retire or buy my own team or go back to the Globies or do anything else I wanted to do (except, of course, sign with another NBA team). My official contract, filed with the NBA office, had the required reserve clause in it, binding me to the 76ers for at least one year beyond that, but I trusted Irv's word that he would ignore that, and let me go my own way when the season was over. It was an unprecedented concession for an owner to make to a player, and I was feeling pretty good about it when we finally signed the contract.

Still, I didn't go into the 1967–68 season with any great enthusiasm. I've always been the kind of person who needs specific, concrete goals and challenges; with them, I'm the most competitive guy in the world; without them, I tend to be lackadaisical. I'm just not naturally competitive and aggressive. I don't have a killer instinct. In the past, I'd always been able to set challenging goals for myself—whether it was selling $200 worth of junk in one day as a kid or leading the league in scoring as an NBA rookie. But by my ninth year in the NBA, there really weren't many goals I hadn't already reached. I'd led the league in damn near everything more times than I could count. I'd broken my own records year after year. I'd even been on a championship team. What else could I do? With my attitude toward Philadelphia and Kosloff, I just wasn't in the mood to work hard at dreaming up some new goal. I couldn't just go through the motions, though; I had too much pride in myself—and too much affection and respect for my teammates—to do that. So I decided I'd lead the NBA in assists. That was the only category, except free throws, that I'd never led the league in, and it was the one category that no other center had ever led in either. For basketball's greatest scorer to lead the league in assists would really be something, I thought. It would be like Babe Ruth leading the game in sacrifice bunts or Jim Brown leading the league in blocking.

The 76ers began the 1967–68 season well again, winning their first five games easily, with me passing off, and Hal and Billy and Chet doing most of the scoring. Then, in our eighth game— against San Francisco—I passed off so much, I didn't take one shot the whole game. We won the game, but the way the press wrote it up, you would have thought I'd just been found guilty of raping my sister or something. When we lost five of nine games at the end of November, the howl in the Philadelphia papers became unbelievable. It was all my fault, they said. I had to score more if the 76ers were going to repeat as world champions. So, the next day, I went out and scored 52 points and got 37 rebounds.

I was really mad that night; I hit 22 of 29 from the floor, including my last 15 shots in a row—even though half the Seattle team was hanging on my back.

We won that game, and when I reverted to my playmaking role, we continued to win. We won 15 out of 16. But the fans were accustomed to seeing me score, and so they grumbled about my averaging "only" 20 points a game or so. In mid-December, one of the Philadelphia sportswriters got to talking to Alex, and they decided I wasn't scoring because I *couldn't* score any more. I was too old, they said; I'd lost a half-step, and couldn't beat my man anymore. That's just the kind of challenge I like. The day that story ran, we were in Chicago, and a friend back in Philly called me and read it to me. I got 68 points that night. The next night, we played in Seattle. I scored 47. Three days later, we played Seattle again. I scored 53. I figured I'd proved my point, and I went back to being a passer.

Actually, I was more valuable to the team as a passer than a scorer. We had plenty of guys who could score. Some of them had to score to be happy. I didn't. The more shots I took, the fewer shots they could take. Someone did a study of the relationship between my shooting and Hal's that year. In the games where I took less than 12 shots, Hal averaged 27 points a game. When I took 12 to 15 shots, he averaged only 18. When I took 16 to 20 shots, his average dropped to 13.5. When I took more than 20 shots, he averaged only 10.

After that three-game splurge in mid-December, I only had one other game all season where I scored more than 40 points. That game was against Los Angeles in the last week of the regular season. I got 53 points—and I wanted every one of them; I'd pretty much decided I'd like to play for the Lakers the next season, if possible, and I wanted to show them I could still score—just in case they had any doubts.

I averaged 24.3 points a game that year, almost exactly what I'd averaged the previous year, and the 76ers had only one more "bad" spell the rest of the season—losing five of ten games in the first three weeks of January. We won 25 of our last 30 games, most of them by such big margins that I could pretty much do what I wanted out there without hurting the team. If I wanted to score—like I did in that game against the Lakers—I could do it. If I wanted to pile up assists, I could do that, too. I was battling Lennie Wilkens of the Hawks for the league lead in assists through most of the season, and I remember a few games when I'd tell whoever was hot on my team, "Look, I'm just going to pass the ball to you for a while. I keep setting these other guys up, and they keep blowing easy shots. How am I going to beat Wilkins that way?" I wound up beating Wilkens by a good margin—702 to 679—and I probably got more satisfaction out of winning that title than almost any other. It was my way of answering those people who said I was a selfish gunner and a freak who couldn't do anything but dunk.

The 76ers had only two unsettling moments during the last month or so of the season—one minor, one major. The minor one came Feb. 17 in San Diego. San Diego was the worst team in the league that year, and they'd lost 17 straight when we came to town. That tied the league record San Francisco had set in 1965—when Alex was coaching the Warriors. If we could beat San Diego, which seemed a cinch, Alex would "lose" that record—happily!

We had had a tough game in Los Angeles the night before—winning 135-134 in double overtime—and a lot of the guys had partied all night afterwards. Hal got stinking drunk, and Billy and a couple of the other guys had too much beer, too. My folks lived in Los Angeles then, in a 40-unit apartment building I'd built, and I spent the night with them. When I got to San Diego the next day, a couple of the 76ers looked like they were still hung over. But they weren't resting, trying to shake it off. They were out playing golf—something you should never do on the day of a game, drunk *or* sober. I got real pissed at them, but they didn't take me too seriously.

"It's the Wilt Chamberlain Memorial Golf Tournament," Billy told me.

Well, we got our asses kicked in San Diego that night. Late in the third quarter, we were behind 86-68—the best team in basketball was behind the worst team in basketball by 18 points! The guys started to feel ashamed then, and tried to pull themselves together. We put on a helluva rally. But the booze and partying and golf were too much. We lost 111-106.

We only lost three more games the rest of the year; San Diego lost their next 15 in a row. If we'd beaten them that night, they would've lost 33 straight!

Our other unsettling moment that season was far more serious.

On March 27, we played New York in the third game of the Eastern Division semifinal playoffs. The game went into overtime. On the first overtime play, I tapped the ball to Billy. He drove toward the basket, ran into one of the Knicks and fell down. He broke his right wrist in three places, and was out for the rest of the playoffs. We won that game, in double overtime, and we beat New York, four games to two, but now we were in trouble against Boston.

We had won 62 and lost 20 that year, and finished eight games ahead of Boston again. If it hadn't been for the NBA's screwy playoff system, we would've already been the champs—without playing New York *or* Boston. I never could understand that playoff system. You play 82 games, then you start all over. It's not like baseball, where the teams that meet in the World Series don't play each other all year. In the NBA, you play every other team six or eight or ten times, and—six months later—you still have to prove you're the best.

Going into the Boston series, Billy wasn't the only 76er who was injured. Luke Jackson had pulled a hamstring in his left leg. So had Matty Guokas, our No. 3 guard. I hurt my knee in the playoffs, too. But we still should've beaten them. We were a much better team. Alex didn't have us playing our best ball, though; he was thinking about Oakland, not Boston. Alex was a California boy, and that's where he wanted to live and work. He'd only come to Philadelphia because he couldn't stand Franklin Mieuli in San Francisco, and there were no other coaching jobs available on the West Coast. He had an agreement with Irv Kosloff that he could leave if one opened up. Alex said Kosloff had also promised him he could have final approval over the 76ers' general manager. But Kosloff named Jack Ramsey the general manager, over Alex's strong objections, and Alex had little respect for Ramsey. During the final weeks of the season, Alex was spending as much time looking for another coaching job as he was working with the 76ers. By playoff time, he had all but agreed to take the head coaching job with Oakland of the ABA. You could see he was distracted, not concentrating—and he later admitted as much to me.

The day before our first playoff game with Boston, Martin Luther King was assassinated. Red Auerbach called the Boston players together, and they talked about whether or not they should play the game or ask for a postponement. They agreed to play. The day of the game, they came to Philadelphia together, united in their grief—and in their determination. But Alex didn't think to call a player meeting. Most of us didn't see each other until we got to the locker room that night. Then we started wondering if we should play or not. Like Boston, we were grief-stricken. But we were confused, bewildered, uncertain. It showed that night. The balance we had relied on all season evaporated. Me, Hal, and Chet scored 91 of our 118 points, and Boston beat us.

Because of Dr. King's funeral, we had five days off before the next game. That gave us time to regroup. We beat Boston in that game, and we beat them in the next two as well. We were ahead, three games to one, and we only needed to win one of the last three games to take our second straight Eastern Division championship.

We never got it.

With Luke and Billy both hurt, we just couldn't get enough scoring out of our forwards to beat Boston. In the seventh game, they beat us, 100-96, and—again—everyone said it was my fault. In earlier losses to Boston—in other years—I was blamed for shooting too much and not playing team ball. This time, they said I didn't shoot enough, particularly in the second half, when I didn't take one shot from the field. But I was playing the way we'd played —and won—all year. I was passing and rebounding, and I out-rebounded Russell, 34 to 26. Boston had half their team guarding me. Russell was behind me, and K. C. Jones and Sam Jones would collapse back on me. That left my teammates open for easy eight-to-ten-foot jump shots. I kept passing the ball to them, but they kept missing. Hal hit only eight of 25 shots. Wali hit eight of 22. Matty hit two of ten. Chet hit eight of 22. Those four guys took most of our shots, and hit less than a third of them. But I got the blame. A couple of years later, when Chet and I went to Europe together, he got all choked up one day in Stockholm, and told

191

me he'd always felt guilty about that. He'd missed four or five lay-ups in that game, and the other guys had blown cinch shots, too, but none of them had come forward to accept the blame for the loss; they'd all let me be the whipping-boy.

"We were wrong," Chet said. "We took the easy way out. We always did that with you around. You overshadowed the good things we did, and you obscured the bad things we did. I guess we figured that was a fair trade."

ALMOST AS SOON AS THE 1968 playoffs were over, Alex announced that he was leaving the 76ers to go coach Oakland in the ABA. Kosloff knew I wanted to leave, too, but he figured he might be able to keep me by offering me the head coaching job. When I turned it down, he asked me whom I thought he should hire.

"Frank McGuire or Bill Sharman," I told him.

Sharman had taken over the Warriors after Alex left, and he'd turned them around right away. Even though we'd beaten them in the 1967 playoffs, I thought he'd done a good job, and I'd heard good things about him. But Bill had already agreed to become the coach of the Los Angeles Stars in the ABA, and he didn't want to come to Philadelphia. Coach McGuire had returned to college by then, and had a long-term contract with South Carolina; he was reluctant to leave that security. When Kosloff didn't make him much of an offer, Coach McGuire also said no.

It was pretty clear to me that Jack Ramsey, the guy Kosloff had hired as general manager, wanted to be head coach *and* general manager. It was also pretty clear that one of the first things

Ramsey wanted to do was get rid of me. I don't think it was necessarily anything personal, but Ramsey had been a successful college coach, and he was convinced he could win in the NBA the same way—with small, quick, fast-breaking teams. He didn't think he needed a big man, and he didn't particularly want one. Then, when he started to get an inkling of just how much money the 76ers were paying me, I really became expendable. He figured he could buy a wagonful of his kind of ballplayers if the team didn't have to carry my salary.

Ramsey didn't try very hard that summer to sign me for the next season. Neither did Kosloff. Kosloff was a quiet, taciturn man, and he and I never did get along well. He was one of those owners who likes to use his star players as social ornaments—inviting us to parties and dinners where he could tell everyone we were friends and bask in our limelight. I've always detested that parasitic attitude, so I invariably turned him down. That didn't make things any warmer between us.

We negotiated salary half-heartedly through the spring and early summer, but since I didn't want to go back to Philadelphia, and neither Kosloff nor Ramsey wanted me back that badly, neither of us was willing to compromise much. I decided it was time for me to take affirmative action, and I began looking for an opening. Surprisingly, it came in Los Angeles, about a month or so after our season ended—and it touched off about two months of incredible intrigue.

When I'd first lived in Los Angeles—briefly—in 1959, I hadn't liked the city at all. I had the same complaints about its sprawl and lack of identity that most Easterners have. But I'd lived in the suburban flatlands then, and on my many subsequent visits to Los Angeles, I spent more time in the hills and on the beach, and I grew to love the beauty and informality of Southern California. Everyone there seemed to be "doing his own thing" long before that phrase became fashionable. Girls were prettier and less inhibited and more independent, and even the guys seemed more free and open and honest. I think my budding love affair with Los Angeles probably paralleled my own personal growth process. The first city I'd fallen in love with had been New York—big, vibrant, exciting, full of just the sort of action a gawky rookie ballplayer in his early twenties would find irresistible. Then, after I'd been to

194

Europe several times and began to appreciate fine food and cosmopolitan charm, I'd been swept off my feet by San Francisco. But by the spring of 1968, I was a mature, 31-year-old man, more interested in being myself and meeting other people than in playing any pseudosophisticate's role. I liked the fact that people in Los Angeles didn't feel compelled to wear coats and ties everywhere, and that they didn't judge people by their cars and clothes and breeding like people in New York and San Francisco tended to do.

I also had a couple of other reasons for wanting to play in Los Angeles. One was movies—I've always been a big movie fan, and I thought I might like to get into that business after I retired from basketball. Playing next-door to Hollywood certainly wouldn't hurt that ambition any. Even more important, my mother and father and several of my sisters and brothers had lived from time to time in my apartment complex in Los Angeles, and now my father was there, dying of cancer. He and I had always been close, and I wanted very much to be near him in his last days.

I'd made my first, abortive attempt to interest the Lakers in me in March, 1967, when I'd invited a Los Angeles basketball writer named Merv Harris up to my hotel room in Pittsburgh when the 76ers and Lakers were there for a game. I knew Merv was on pretty good terms with Jack Kent Cooke, the Laker owner, and I asked him—in strictest confidence—to let Cooke know I might be interested in leaving Philly and coming West. Merv passed the word to Cooke, but Jack is a man who believes in propriety and protocol; he called Kosloff first to ask his permission to talk to me. Kosloff refused, and that ended it—until May, 1968.

I was in Los Angeles then, talking to Alfred Bloomingdale, the president of Diner's Club, about a franchise deal for me and Diner's-Fugazy travel bureaus. One thing led to another, and I kidded him about how much easier our business dealings would be if I played in Los Angeles. He laughed and said Jack Kent Cooke was "a good personal friend."

"I'll see what I can do," he said, still laughing.

"Please do," I told him. And I *wasn't* laughing.

Bloomingdale talked to Cooke, and Cooke again called Kosloff. This time, Kosloff gave him permission to talk to me, and Jack invited me to his house. But he had several advisors there with him—his attorney and his accountant and, I think, the Laker general manager, Fred Schaus—and I told him I really didn't think he needed all that help to talk to me.

A day or two later, Jack called me back, and said he'd like to have me over for dinner again—"alone."

We ate and talked well into the night that time, discussing our Bentleys, our European travels, our feelings about women and food and politics and people in general. We even found time to discuss basketball a little. I decided I liked Jack, and when I left, he suggested we keep in touch—and that I use a code name ("Mr. Norman," my middle name) any time I called his office. He was afraid some other clubowners would hear about our negotiations, and join the bidding themselves.

After a few more private meetings between Jack and me, we decided it was time to bring the advisors back in and get down to details. I asked my accountant, Alan Levitt, to fly in from Philadelphia, and he and I and my Los Angeles attorney, Sy Goldberg, went to Jack's house for a meeting.

When we started talking salary that night, we got into some pretty big numbers. What made them even bigger was Alan's assurance that we could develop good tax-shelter investments to ease the burden of my 70 percent tax bracket.

But I was also in contact with another NBA team—the Seattle SuperSonics. I had met Sam Schulman, the Sonics' owner, in a Beverly Hills discotheque called the Factory one night before my first contact with Jack, and Sam and I had joked around about my playing for Seattle. When I'd told him I was serious, he had backed off some. I guess he was afraid he'd be accused of tampering with me while I was still under contract to Philadelphia. But once I'd started negotiating with Jack, I'd passed the word to Sam that he didn't have to worry about that any more; I was definitely leaving Philadelphia, and it was just a question of where I'd play and how much I'd get paid. Sam said he wanted to talk to me.

The night after Alan and Sy and I met with Jack and his attorney, we had dinner with Sam. In the beginning, I'd liked Sam better than Jack. Jack had seemed a little too straitlaced and too demanding and dominant for me; Sam was a swinger, an easy rider. As I got to know Jack better, I came to like him

196

more, but at that point, I thought Sam would be easier to play for. When he topped Jack's offer to me by about 35 percent, I *knew* he'd be easier to play for! The next morning, Sam came to our hotel suite, and gave Alan a letter of intent, spelling out the details of his offer.

Now I had a real problem: Did I accept Jack's offer of Los Angeles or Sam's offer of more money? For a variety of reasons, I wanted to play in Los Angeles. I also knew that even if I chose Seattle, Schulman might not be able to offer the 76ers enough good players to close the deal, and all our negotiations and agreements wouldn't be worth a damn. The Lakers were an established, first-class team, with several good players available to trade for me; Seattle was a one-year-old expansion team that had just finished next-to-last and had a lot of guys with names like Al Tucker, Tom Kron, Henry Akin, and Plummer Lott.

But I was attracted by the seeming hopelessness of the Seattle situation. I liked the city, and I liked the idea of trying to play a central role in turning an expansion loser into a big winner. I finally decided Sam's offer was just too good to turn down. I telephoned Jack, and told him I wouldn't be joining the Lakers.

"I won't tell you where I'm going or how much they're paying me," I told him. "I don't want to play you off against the other guy. That's not the way I do things."

But Jack found out who had made the offer, and what it was, and he called Sy, and they talked all day on the telephone. When they were through, Jack had matched Sam's offer. Sy called and told me.

"Shit," I said. "Now what do I do? I'm doing my best not to start a bidding war, and these guys are determined to have one anyway." I thought a few minutes. "OK, call Jack back, and tell him I'll accept his offer. Then call Sam, and tell him I'm not coming to Seattle. Make it firm. Tell them both this is final."

This was late on a Saturday afternoon, and that night, Jack had to go to a wedding—his attorney's daughter was getting married. He told Sy he'd have his attorney call Sy right after the wedding. That, as I soon learned, was the way Jack worked. Weekends, holidays, special occasions, and illness meant nothing to him. Business not only came before pleasure; business excluded

197

pleasure—because, for Jack, business *is* pleasure, his whole life. But Sy told him he'd refuse to accept the call from Jack's attorney, Clyde Tritt, that night.

"You may not mind interrupting Clyde with business on one of the most important nights of his life," Sy said, "but I sure as hell do. Tell him to call me tomorrow morning—after 11."

Jack resisted 20 minutes before giving in.

When Sy and Clyde spoke the next morning, they confirmed the details of the contract that Jack and Sy and Alan and I had previously agreed on. Clyde said he'd have the contract drawn up.

Then, two days later, I got a call from Bill Sharman. He had taken the coaching job with the Stars, and he wanted me to meet with him and Jim Kirst (their owner) and Jim Hardy (their general manager).

More to accommodate Bill than anything else, I agreed to the meeting. I wanted to play in the ABA about like I wanted to become a monk, but the ABA had just lured Rick Barry from San Francisco to Oakland, and they were feeling pretty cocky —until I told them I wanted $1 million to make the jump. I didn't really want to leave the NBA, so I figured I'd ask for some ridiculous amount, and that would be that. Besides, the figure wasn't really all that outlandish. The guys who ran the ABA were all loaded, and their teams were all doing miserably. When they told me they thought I could probably make the league a success, singlehandedly, I told them there was no reason the Stars should carry the burden for the whole league. I suggested they have every team kick into a pool to pay me.

While they were polling the league on that, Cooke was pressing me to sign with him. I wanted to, but with $1 million hanging fire, Sy and I decided we should stall. Then the ABA called back again. They wanted another meeting. We met in the Biltmore Hotel on July 3 with Hardy, Kirst, ABA Commissioner George Mikan, and the leader of the ABA owners, William Ringsby of Denver. They all checked into the hotel under assumed names, so no one would know they were in town—or why. I'd gone through some similar cloak-and-dagger stuff a few years earlier, when the ABA was just being formed, and the founders were trying to sign me up, and I hadn't been at all impressed then with the way they handled themselves—or the way they had tried

198

to exploit my name. I wasn't much more impressed this time either, and as we haggled back and forth, I decided I really didn't want any part of the ABA.

"Screw the ABA," I told Sy. "Let's sign with Jack."

But the ABA wanted time to draw up a formal offer, and poll the other league-owners again, so I didn't give them a definite "no" that night. The next day, one of the owners who didn't want to contribute to a common pool for me leaked a story to the papers in Miami that I was negotiating with the ABA. That got the other ABA owners upset. It also damn near screwed up my arrangement with the Lakers. When Cooke and Kosloff had agreed to the trade, subject to Cooke and me working out contract terms, the deal was that the Lakers would give Philadelphia Archie Clark, Jerry Chambers, and Darrall Imhoff, plus cash, for me. But between my prolonged negotiations with Jack and the leak of the ABA story, Archie figured out what was going on. He hadn't signed his 1968–69 Laker contract yet, and he told Jack he wouldn't sign unless he got a big raise. Archie had averaged almost 20 points a game for the Lakers the previous season, and he looked like a potential superstar. But he had only been in the league two years, and his demands were way out of line. He had Jack over a barrel, though, and he knew it. Without him, the 76ers wouldn't make the deal. Finally, Jack gave in.

When Jack officially announced that I was coming to the Lakers, he grinned at the press, and said, "Mr. Chamberlain has been kind enough to renew my contract as president of California Sports, Inc."

The 76er officials were in equally good spirits when they announced the deal in Philadelphia. Ramsey figured Imhoff would be the kind of center he wanted. Chambers would be a quick, aggressive forward, and Clark would be their top scorer and next superstar. They were giving up one starter, and getting three in return.

But, as Irv Kosloff has since admitted, my departure was the beginning of the end for the 76er franchise—and it was mostly Jack Ramsey's doing. The year after I left, Ramsey traded Chet Walker to Chicago. Two years later, he traded Archie Clark to Baltimore and Wali Jones to Milwaukee. He also bungled contract negotiations with Billy Cunningham and let Billy jump to Carolina of the ABA. By the end of the 1972–73 season, the 76ers were the worst team in the history of the NBA. They had an all-time record 20-game losing streak, and—ironically—at one point in that streak, their overall mark was four wins and 46 losses . . . exactly the opposite of the 46-win, four-loss mark the 76ers had had with me in 1967, the year we won the world championship.

But I had more important things than the 76ers—or the Lakers—to think about that summer of 1968.

For the first time in my life, I got involved in politics—real politics—at the highest level. I endorsed and campaigned for Richard Nixon, and worked hard to get him nominated for President at the Republican convention in Miami.

I had first met Richard a few years earlier, on a plane ride from New York to Los Angeles. He wasn't the President then, of course, and we were on a first-name basis almost immediately. To this day, I think of him as "Richard," not "the President" or "Mr. Nixon," although I'm sure I'd address him properly, as "Mr. President," in a public situation. On that flight to Los Angeles, we sat next to each other the whole way, and I remember being tremendously impressed by his intellect and his grasp of world problems and his willingness to see things in global, rather than just national, terms. That, I thought, had been President Johnson's trouble. He had been an expert in domestic issues, but he didn't understand what went on abroad and how everything tied together. Although I'd never gotten into politics much before, I'd always felt that we couldn't solve our problems unless we realized the same problems existed all over the world. Whatever happens here affects what happens in France and Italy and Russia and Africa, I thought, and Richard seemed to feel the same way.

Looking back on it, I suspect I was also subconsciously influenced to back Richard by several things he and I had in common. Throughout his political career, he'd been called a "loser"—the guy who could never win the big one. Me too. He had been shafted by the press quite a bit. Me too. He had a penchant for beating the other guy at the other guy's game —whether it was politics or poker or burning the biggest out-house in California atop the annual Whittier College bonfire. I'd never burned any outhouses, but I, too, liked to beat the other man at his game—whether it was drinking more vodka than

200

the Russians or making more assists than Oscar Robertson and Jerry West.

Richard and I had something else in common. The prevailing public opinion was that Richard wasn't very smart. Why? Because he wasn't very loquacious; he didn't speak smoothly and eloquently. That's why he lost to John Kennedy in 1960. Kennedy was a better speaker in the television debates, and the voters decided he must be smarter, too. You run across the same thing in sports. People say Muhammad Ali is smart, for example, because he's such a good talker. Well, Muhammad's a good friend of mine, but if you get him off two subjects—religion and boxing—he doesn't know enough to string three intelligent sentences together. But Muhammad doesn't let his ignorance get in the way of his loquaciousness, and the general public tends to equate loquaciousness with intelligence.

The public also tends to think most athletes are stupid. I first started running into that in the classroom, in college, when teachers would automatically give me a poorer grade than the other students in the class just because I was an athlete. It wasn't that they didn't like athletes in general—or me in particular. They just assumed that anyone who participated in sports must not be very smart, and they graded athletes accordingly.

People think that because we use our bodies to make a living, we must have empty heads. They don't realize how much you have to use your mind to be really successful, year after year, in professional sports, and sportswriters and sports announcers —who should be enlightening the public—only help perpetuate the image of the athlete-as-mindless-animal. When they interview you before or after a game, they rarely ask the kind of intelligent, incisive questions that might elicit intelligent, incisive answers. Instead, they come into the dressing room after a guy like John Havlicek has scored 40 points against you, and they ask such brilliant questions as, "Do you think Havlicek hurt you tonight?" Or they come in before a sixth playoff game, when you're ahead three games to two, and they ask you, "Would you guys like to wrap it up tonight?" No, of course not; we'd much rather blow the sixth game and have to play them again—and maybe lose everything!

After you've been asked questions like that thousands and

thousands of times, it's no wonder your only response is a monosyllabic mumble. And that, unfortunately, is all the public has to judge your intelligence by. It's no wonder, I guess, that when a fan sees you in an airport or a restaurant somewhere, all he can do is ask you the same stupid sports question he's heard everyone else ask you over the years. OK, I understand that they don't very often get a chance to talk to Wilt Chamberlain, and they're a lot more interested in what I think of Kareem Abdul-Jabbar and Bill Russell than what I think of Richard Nixon and Ronald Reagan. But inherent in that attitude is the implication that I don't have anything worthwhile to say on anything but basketball. I see that attitude time and again when I or my teammates do post-game interviews or television commercials. It's particularly true of black athletes; all we have to do is make it through without stuttering or saying "ain't," and people start praising us as if we'd just written and delivered the Gettysburg Address.

Like so many other athletes—and like Richard Milhous Nixon—I've always resented that supercilious putdown of my intelligence. But when I announced my support of Richard, almost all my black friends were surprised—and angry.

"How could you back a Republican?" they asked me.

Well, I've never paid much attention to labels and stereotypes. In sports, I root for individual players, not teams; in politics, I vote for the man, not the party. Still, that didn't satisfy my friends. They could understand my supporting some Republicans, they said, "but not Nixon. He's never done a thing for the black man."

But I'd marched alongside Richard at Martin Luther King's funeral, and I'd been impressed with the way he'd handled himself then—the dignity he had, and the way he didn't try to exploit his presence politically, like so many other politicians had done. I also had the idea that most presidential nominees of major parties in America really aren't all that different from each other. The extremists on both ends are weeded out in the primaries and at the conventions, and by the time a guy gets the nomination of the Democrats or the Republicans, he's no wild-eyed radical or reactionary.

Besides, any President is so ham-strung by constitutional limitations and congressional opposition and carryover commitments from previous administrations that he really can't do things a whole lot differently than the guy he's running against.

I know there are exceptions, but they're rare. Harry Truman was probably one. He integrated the troops and pushed the first tough civil rights bill through Congress and proposed the first Medicare legislation. But I really don't think John Kennedy did things much differently than Richard would have done them if he'd been elected in 1960—and I don't think Richard has done things much differently than Hubert Humphrey would have done them if he'd been elected in 1968.

Some blacks thought I backed Richard because I was getting paid for it; some thought it was because I "had it made," and didn't care much about other, poorer blacks. Neither was true. I didn't get a penny for helping Richard, and I hoped to use my contact with him to help other blacks. What my endorsement of Richard really boiled down to was that I respected his intelligence and his foreign policy experience and—most important of all—I knew him personally. If I was going to get involved in a political campaign, I wanted to be on the inside, where I could see just what was going on and how major policy and personnel decisions were made; if Richard won, of course, I figured I'd have some input at the White House, a chance to talk to the top man about some social and political issues I felt very strongly about.

I was especially hoping I could convince Richard to take the lead in trying to solve the overpopulation problem—probably the biggest problem in the world today, the way I see it. I figured that if he would throw the prestige of his office and the power of this country behind some sweeping birth-control programs in the more backward countries, we might make some real progress in that area.

I also wanted to talk to Richard and some of his major advisors about other international problems—and about doing more to provide equal opportunity for the black man in America. I even had some ideas on a few other domestic issues. Euthanasia is one. I think it's cruel to keep some baby alive when it's born with so many mental and physical abnormalities that it can't possibly enjoy life. I feel the same way about prolonging life for some sick old person who's in constant pain—the way they did with President Truman last year. Some people say it's humane to preserve life, but under some circumstances, I think the only humane thing to do is end life. We need laws to make that possible.

We also need new laws on the "victimless crimes" that don't really hurt anyone—gambling, prostitution, marijuana, and pornography. I think all of these must be controlled, but not outlawed altogether. Gambling and pornography should be kept away from children, for example, and prostitutes should be required to have frequent medical examinations, and marijuana should be subject to the same restrictions as alcohol. But to make all these illegal —forbidden—only increases their attraction, particularly to the young. Since human nature will always provide a market for these things anyway, making them illegal just opens the door for organized crime and other undesirable elements to control them —thereby robbing the government, and the people, of vast sums of money that could otherwise be collected in tax revenue, to be spent on important social programs. Even worse, when you let criminals control pornography, prostitution, gambling, and marijuana, you invite them to commit other, far worse crimes to perpetuate their control—crimes like smuggling, robbery, burglary, white slavery, loan-sharking, . . . and murder.

As it turned out, I was deceiving myself about having much input in the White House after Richard was elected. This was my first look at high-level politics, and I was pretty naive; I didn't realize how insulated the President of the United States is after he's elected. Richard sends me a card or letter every now and then, congratulating me on a championship or a great game, but I've had about as much opportunity to influence him as I have had to influence the Pope.

Does that mean he exploited me? Sure. All endorsements and testimonials are exploitation, though. When I do a commercial for Volkswagen, they're exploiting me to sell their cars, and I'm exploiting them to make money for myself. It's the same way in politics. Richard and the Republicans exploited me to get black votes, and I exploited them to provide black input—and to learn something about the political process. And I learned quite a bit indeed; I had a rare opportunity to see a presidential campaign from the inside. I had a hospitality suite at the Hilton during the convention, and I met and talked to almost every important

204

person in the Republican Party. Of all the thousands of people there, I was one of only about a half-dozen or so who was given a special lapel button that permitted me to go directly to Richard's room and see him and his top advisors whenever I wanted to. In fact, some of the old pols in the party got a little jealous of my close relationship with Richard, and when he was scheduled to fly into Miami for the convention, they had a meeting behind my back to decide who would meet Richard at the airport. Naturally, they left me off the greeting committee. When I heard about it and confronted them, they hemmed and hawed and said they'd reserved a "special" place for me at the front door of the hotel, after everyone got back from the airport.

I had enough to keep me busy in Miami, though, and I didn't worry much about the games everyone was playing. One night, I even took the big Ohio delegation out for a talk and a cruise on Biscayne Bay at a time when they were still thinking about casting their ballots for Nelson Rockefeller.

I worked on delegates from several other states, too—both black delegates and white delegates—but my primary responsibility was to convince the 78 black delegates and alternates to vote for Richard. My most difficult—and most important—job in that regard came after Richard picked Spiro Agnew to be his vice president. I was for Rockefeller or Mark Hatfield or John Volpe or Jim Rhodes—almost anyone except Agnew. Most blacks at the convention felt the same way, and several of them threatened to walk out if Agnew were nominated. The black delegates from Maryland—Agnew's home state—had their walk-out planned, and it was up to me to persuade them to stay, so Richard—and the Republican Party—wouldn't be embarrassed on TV.

I did my job, but I wasn't too happy about it. After the convention, I went to see Richard.

"How can I sell Spiro to black people?" I asked him.

"Don't judge Spiro until you've talked with him," Richard told me. "He's done some good things for blacks. I'll set up a meeting for you in San Diego in a couple of days."

Well, I met with Spiro. I told him he should say "black," not "Negro," and say it like he means it and isn't afraid of it. I also told him he should say "law and order and justice," not just "law and order"—and mean it. We talked for quite a while, and he kept telling me how liberal he was and how much he'd done for blacks in Maryland and how much he agreed with everything I was saying.

The next day, Spiro had a meeting with a group that had a lot of blacks in it. Do you know that dumb fuck must have said "Negro" and "law and order" 10,000 times? I'm sitting right there, looking at him, and sliding further down in my chair every minute. I finally walked out.

The next day, I told Richard, "You gonna have some problems with Mr. Spiro."

I taped a few interviews with Richard after that, and they used them in black areas, but I didn't do too much campaigning after the convention. I was disillusioned by Agnew.

I've been pleased with many of the things Richard has done since he took office—ending the war in Vietnam and going to Russia and China in particular. But I haven't thought much of his Supreme Court appointments or his choice of John Mitchell as Attorney General. After he was elected, Richard started surrounding himself with guys like Mitchell and H. R. Haldeman and John Ehrlichman, and—as the Watergate scandal subsequently showed—that was a horrible mistake. I was also pissed off when Richard had our astronauts put an American flag on the moon. Outer space is supposed to be for all mankind, not just Americans. I was disappointed in Richard then.

I guess that my ambivalence over his performance was one reason I didn't campaign for him again in 1972. Besides, he didn't need me then. All the blacks who had been bad-mouthing me for endorsing him in 1968 realized he'd be an easy winner this time, and they all jumped aboard the bandwagon.

I learned a few lessons the hard way in my brief fling at politics, but it was a valuable experience. I think the biggest lesson I learned was that politics isn't much different from anything else human beings do. It's no mystic, saintly art; it's just life. All the bickering and infighting and maneuvering for access to the candidate wasn't much different than the way people act around athletes and movie stars and other celebrities. When I saw Ph.D.'s and other people of that caliber volunteering to wash dishes and run errands, just so they could say they were close to Richard and his top advisors, it reminded me a lot of the starry-eyed groupies and go-fers who hang around sports arenas. In fact, while I was wooing delegates in Miami and trying to keep Nixon delegates away from Rockefeller and Reagan campaign workers, I was repeatedly struck by another similarity between sports and politics; what I was doing seemed just like what the professional football scouts had done with top college prospects just before the NFL-AFL merger. Brad Pye, a black sportswriter and sportscaster from Los Angeles, worked with me on the campaign, and he said the same thing. He'd been one of those pro football "babysitters" who was supposed to keep good prospects hidden from the rival league, and he said he felt like he was doing the same job all over again in Miami. When you get right down to it, what we did wasn't all that different from what college recruiters had done to get me 13 years earlier. You smile a lot and you promise a lot, and you say and do whatever is necessary to convince the delegate (or athlete) that your candidate (or college) is the closest thing to God (or Heaven) on earth.

12

ON OCTOBER 31, 1968, TWO weeks after I began my first season with the Lakers, my father died. It's difficult to explain just how deeply a man is affected by his father's death. Even if you're a wealthy, successful, independent man in your 30s, as I was then, it's a shattering psychological blow. Your father is your best friend, your teacher, your advisor in everything from affairs of the heart to affairs of the pocketbook. He's the one man who's always been there, for as long as you can remember, and—suddenly—you'll never see him again, never be able to ask his advice again, never be able to make up for all those times you forgot to say "thank you" and "I love you." For the first time in your life, you're truly alone —and you feel a little apprehensive, abandoned, deserted.

Unfortunately, my frame of mind going into the season was pretty shitty, even before my father died. Everyone, it seemed, was speculating that the Lakers would be a dissension-ridden team because of me. The team had two other superstars—Jerry West and Elgin Baylor—and the "experts" were all saying that we couldn't possibly play together harmoniously. We'd need three basketballs in the game to keep us all happy, they said; we'd be so busy trying to outscore and upstage each other that we wouldn't have time for cohesive team basketball.

That kind of speculation tends to be self-fulfilling, particularly when you're dealing with athletes or other performers who have big egos and thin skins. The Laker players were probably more susceptible to that pressure than most because they'd come so close to winning for so long. In the seven years before I joined them, they'd won the Western Division championship five times and lost to Boston in the finals every time—twice in the seventh game; guys like Elgin and Jerry were anxious to find any scapegoat they could for their failures, and—having been through much the same experience myself in Philadelphia and San Francisco—I was also more willing than I should have been to look for someone else to blame at the first sign of trouble.

Surprisingly, Jerry and I actually got along pretty well—and still do—both on and off the court. I think some people may have assumed we would be at odds because our backgrounds and life-styles are so different. Jerry's a small-town white boy from West Virginia; I'm a big-city black from Pennsylvania. Jerry's a husband and father; I'm a swinging bachelor. Jerry's a modest, fairly quiet, self-effacing sort of guy who never has a harsh word for anyone else—at least not in public; I'm a loud extrovert who's not afraid to say something good about myself—or something bad about someone else—when the occasion warrants it. Because of these differences—and others—Jerry and I could never become bosom buddies. But we didn't become mortal enemies either. He did his thing, and I did mine, and we've always been on good terms with each other.

On the court, our styles are as radically different as they are off the court. That tends to help the team, though, not hurt it, because our skills complement each other. Jerry is primarily an outside shooter; I work primarily under the boards. Jerry likes to gamble on defense; I like to play back, under the basket, where I can bail my teammates out if they gamble and their men get by them. Contrary to what the "experts" predicted, I didn't cut down any on Jerry's scoring—or Elgin's either, for that matter. They both averaged almost exactly the same my first year with the Lakers as they had the year before I joined them. In fact, if you

209

check the statistics, you'll also find that, with me playing that first year, Jerry's assists went up about 15 percent and his minutes played went up about 25 percent and his defense got better, too. Jerry doesn't have to score to be effective, and he knows that. If I lightened his scoring burden some, he was grateful, not resentful; that just meant he could concentrate more on play-making and defense and leadership—and be even more valuable to the team.

I don't mean to imply that Jerry and I always got along famously. We didn't. It was only natural that two veterans, both proven superstars, would come into conflict occasionally. We each had our own habits and preferences and our own way of doing things, and there were times when we clashed. I think Jerry probably envied all the records I'd set and all the money I made, and he was probably a bit sensitive about my "invasion" of his turf; Los Angeles was "his" town, and here I was, coming in to challenge him. He'd always been the highest-paid, most popular Laker; I took one of those titles away from him before I played my first game. Would I take the other one away, too? I'm sure he worried some about that.

But I was also envious of Jerry. Throughout my career, I'd been cast as a villain. I was booed in almost every arena my teams visited. Not Jerry. He did just as much to defeat the other teams as I did, but where I got jeers, he got cheers. He was everyone's favorite, and I know I resented that. It also bothered me—and came to bother me much more in subsequent years—that Jerry was never willing to be as outspoken in public as he was in private. But we didn't let those things affect us too much that first year, and I like to think Jerry and I are friends today, despite our differences.

Unfortunately, I can't say the same thing for the Lakers' other superstar, Elgin Baylor.

On the surface, you would think Elg and I would have been more likely to become friends than Jerry and I. We were both black, both raised in big cities in the East, and we'd played together occasionally and talked to each other on the phone quite a bit when we were in college. But Elg and I, unlike Jerry and I, had too much in common.

Elg is an extrovert—a garrulous, fast-talking guy who loves to be the center of attention. Until I came to the Lakers, he was just that. He was the team captain, the team wit, the expert card-player. He had nicknames for everyone, and everyone loved him; he was the one man around whom the entire team revolved. Then I stepped into the picture. Like Elg, I was accustomed to being the center of attention wherever I was. Like Elg, I was garrulous, a jokester, a good card-player. My sheer size and bulk commanded attention and respect from others. My loud, deep voice did, too. So did my record in basketball—and my eagerness to talk (or argue) about any subject under the sun.

In college, I'd gotten far more publicity than Elgin. In the NBA, the same thing happened. I outrebounded him every year, and outscored him every year but one, and I even had more assists than he did. I'd also been on one championship team, and he hadn't been on any, and I think he was really tired of playing second-fiddle to me. He sure didn't want to have to play second-fiddle to me on the Lakers, too, so tension between us was inevitable. It came in a hundred little ways—needling each other in card games, trying to top each other with pranks and wisecracks, jockeying with each other for the limelight, both on and off the court. It was a continuing game of one-upmanship. I even remember one instance where we had a hassle over soft drinks. The Lakers had always kept small cups of Gatorade and Coca Cola in the locker room for the players to drink. I wanted 7 Up, my favorite soft drink. I got it. A few days later, Elgin walked into the dressing room and said, "I want grape soda or I'm not going to play." It could've been a funny line. But it wasn't. It just fanned the fires of bitterness between us. The other players tended to side with Elgin at first, and that hurt me more than they realized; I guess I've always had a persecution complex anyway—because of all the abuse I've taken over my size, my candor, my free-throwing, and the "Wilt's-a-loser" bullshit—and I probably exaggerated the other players' reactions to my struggles with Elgin. But as the season wore on, the players and the press began to gravitate more toward me; then it was Elgin's turn to get uptight.

Unfortunately, our on-the-court styles only exacerbated the tension between us. Elgin was almost exclusively an offensive player. Defense was something Elg did only to help pass the time between shots—like Ted Williams thinking about his next time

211

at bat when he was supposed to be playing the outfield. Elgin was not a great outside shot, but he had incredible moves and body control, and he loved to drive toward the basket, go up into the air, stay there until everyone else came down, then do a corkscrew and a double pirouette and drop the ball in the basket. He was fantastic at that, the best I ever saw. There was only one problem; I, too, was most effective under the basket on offense, so I could rebound and dunk and get tap-ins. That meant Elg's maneuvering room there was severely constricted. Instead of driving in there with just one man to beat, he had to worry about my man switching off, too—and about me and both defenders getting in his way.

A smart basketball coach—a man like Frank McGuire or Alex Hannum or Bill Sharman—would have devised some offensive tactics to capitalize on both our assets and defuse a potentially explosive situation. But we didn't have a smart basketball coach that first year. We had Butch van Breda Kolff, the worst coach I've ever had.

Van Breda Kolff may have known a little more about coaching basketball, from a technical standpoint, than either Dolph Schayes or Neil Johnston did, but he was so ignorant of basic human relations that he was an utterly hopeless coach.

I suppose I should have known what was coming when my trade to the Lakers was first announced, and someone asked van Breda Kolff if he thought he'd have any trouble with me. His answer was something like, "I can handle him." Well, I've always thought you "handled" horses; you work with human beings. But "handle" is exactly the way van Breda Kolff looked at it. He was an ex-Marine, and he had this compulsion to prove he was the boss. The first thing he did with me was tell me to play the high post on offense—out around the free-throw line, instead of under the basket. He said that would enable Elgin to drive. I was a higher scorer and better rebounder than Elgin, though; I didn't see why I should sacrifice my position for him. Even though I'd already abandoned my role as a big scorer, I was still averaging more than 20 points a game, and my rebounding was critical to any team I played for. How could I rebound if I was playing at the free-throw line? Besides, I'd already changed my entire style of play just two years earlier—going from scorer to feeder in Philadelphia—and I didn't like the idea of van Breda Kolff arbitrarily deciding I'd have to change again, and leave the position I'd played for my entire college and NBA career.

I tried to talk to van Breda Kolff about the situation—to reason with him and discuss some possible compromises and alternatives. It was only his second year in the NBA, and it was my tenth year. I thought I might have a few ideas worth listening to. But he wasn't interested in listening or discussing. He was the coach, and he figured it was his job to coach and our job to play —not to ask questions or make suggestions.

He was stubborn, and then I got stubborn, and—on February 3, in Seattle—the whole thing blew up in our faces. Van Breda Kolff was walking down the corridor toward our locker room, bitching out loud that I wasn't hustling. I was bitching out loud that he didn't know shit about making substitutions. He whirled on me, and told me to shut my mouth. I told him that no one talked to me that way. The next thing I knew, we were at each other's throats. It took Elgin and damn near half the team to pull us apart.

The newspapers heard about the confrontation, and it was all over the sports pages. Word came down from the Lakers' front office that we weren't to talk to the press about the situation anymore. Anyone who violated the gag rule would be fined $1,000.

Things quieted down for a bit after that, but the tension was eating away at the team. Everyone was looking over his shoulder at everyone else. Finally, I suggested we have a team meeting and air our grievances—without van Breda Kolff there. It was pretty clear by then that he wouldn't be back the next year, and I saw no reason for us to build up lasting animosities that even a new coach might have trouble breaking down.

At the meeting, I said that one of my complaints was that some of the guys—particularly Elgin and Jerry—often seemed more interested in scoring points than winning games. Some of the other guys on the team said their biggest gripe against me was that I frowned and glared at them when they made mistakes; my expressions were so obvious to the fans, they said, that it embarrassed them. We all chipped in with a few more complaints, and everyone promised to pull together and play more like a team.

We did seem to play better after that, but van Breda Kolff

kept sniping away at me. He even benched me a few times. He was so determined to break me that he ignored the rest of the team. Then, when he saw he couldn't break me, he got so frustrated, he started screaming and nagging at everyone. But he was just a rotten coach. He didn't know how to substitute effectively. He didn't know how to motivate and coordinate his players. Worst of all, he wasn't the kind of man you could respect off the court.

Among other things, van Breda Kolff drank pretty heavily— at home and on the road. I can remember times when the players literally had to pick him up off the floor, from between two bar stools, and carry him off to bed.

I think the one thing he did that was most indicative of his personality was the way he conducted his pregame "strategy" sessions. Instead of coming into the locker room 30 or 40 minutes before game time, like most NBA coaches do, he wouldn't show up until just a couple of minutes before we were supposed to go out on the floor to warm up. Then, instead of discussing any special tactics or matchups he had in mind for our opponent that night, he'd just laugh and joke and stage a farting contest. That's right, a farting contest! We had one player who had a stomach problem that made him fart a lot, involuntarily, and van Breda Kolff often used that to make fun of him and get the contests started. I'm no prude, but I found that such a gross, tasteless thing to do that I lost all respect for the man. So did everyone else on the team. Only, as usual, when the sportswriters came around to ask questions about team morale, no one but me had enough balls to say what he really thought. Elgin and Jerry and everyone else on the team had lost respect for van Breda Kolff, too, but none of them would admit it publicly. Jerry and Elgin were afraid of involvement in controversy. They thought it would besmirch their public images as decent, traditional, clean-cut young sportsmen. Besides, I was the villain—the athlete who was "difficult to handle" —and since the public sided with van Breda Kolff, they didn't want to be caught on the wrong side. They did go to the sportswriters secretly, though, and tell them about things like me and van Breda Kolff going at each other in Seattle. Then, when the sportswriters asked what was going on, I was the only one who would speak for the record. So all the newspaper stories talked about the feud

214

between me and van Breda Kolff, and made it look like I was responsible for the dissension. It was my first year in Los Angeles, and I got blamed for breaking up the "happy Laker family." What happy Laker family? The Lakers, like any other professional sports team—or any other group of men who are thrust together almost constantly for eight solid months—had their own tensions and jealousies and animosities long before I came to Los Angeles.

I didn't bust up any love affair between Jerry and Elgin, for example. They were never all that close, despite what the press tried to imply later. There was a natural rivalry between them for the role of the team's most important player, and that kind of rivalry rarely produces warm friendships—particularly when both players are as intensely competitive as Jerry and Elgin. I don't imagine their relationship was helped any by Elgin's realization that, for all his records and his popularity with the fans, he wasn't making nearly as much money as Jerry. Nor was Elgin likely to be thrilled by the kid-gloves treatment Jerry always got —and still gets—whenever he's injured. Jerry usually misses a lot of games—about 20 that year, 30 the year before, 15 the year before that. I don't think he's ever played in every game in any one season. Most of his injuries were serious, but even with minor injuries or nagging colds, he'd miss a game or two now and then. Elgin was expected to play every game unless he was virtually crippled, and that bothered him. Like the difference in their salaries, he attributed it to race—and he was right. In sports, blacks are looked on as superhuman (or subhuman?) athletes (animals?) who should always be able to play. Little things like pulled muscles and flu attacks aren't supposed to affect them as much as they do the more tender (and valuable?) white athletes.

Because Elgin's knees were so bad near the end of his career, his presence in the line-up placed an added burden on Jerry—particularly on defense, where Elgin had never been all that good anyway. I don't think Jerry was very happy about that, especially since Elgin was still more or less acknowledged as the team leader. Each of them had led the team in scoring five times going into my first season with the Lakers, and they practically finished in a dead heat that year. Jerry averaged 25.8 points a game, and Elgin averaged 24.8 points a game.

215

With me adding another 20.5 points—and 21.1 rebounds—a game, the Lakers managed to overcome all the friction and dissension and petty bickering among ourselves—and with van Breda Kolff—to win ten of our last thirteen games and take the Western Division championship by seven games over San Francisco. We won 55 games and lost 27 that year, the best record the Lakers had ever had—just as my first year with the Warriors and my first year with the 76ers had produced the best years those teams ever had.

Jerry and Elgin both finished in the top ten in scoring, and Jerry also finished in the top ten in assists and free throws. I led the league in rebounding and field goal percentage—and the Lakers had the best attendance in their history.

In the playoffs, we were sluggish and lost the first two games to San Francisco, then blew them off the court four straight times, including a 118-78 rout in the last game. We destroyed Atlanta in four out of five to win the Western Division finals, and came home to play Boston for the championship.

By all rights, Boston shouldn't even have been in the finals that year. They'd finished *fourth* in the Eastern Division—behind Baltimore, Philadelphia, and New York—and we'd slaughtered them in one late-season, nationally televised game, 108-73. Cousy and Sharman were gone by then, K. C. Jones was gone, Tommy Heinsohn was gone, Bill Russell and Sam Jones were in their last year. The dynasty was crumbling, but the bizarre NBA system enabled the Celtics to make the playoffs.

Baltimore was the power in the East that year. They had the best record in basketball and one of the best young players in the NBA in rookie Wes Unseld of Louisville. I beat Unseld in every department that year—scoring, rebounding, shooting percentage, assists, and minutes played—but everyone was so impressed with his taking Baltimore from last place to first place that he was chosen the most valuable player in the league. Then, in the first round of the playoffs, Baltimore choked; the Knicks bombed them four straight. Boston, meanwhile, ripped Philadelphia, four games to one. In the Eastern Division finals, Boston beat New York, four games to two—winning twice by just one point—to earn the right to play us.

Our first game against Boston was one of the most exciting

and artistic in NBA history. Jerry said afterwards that he thought it was so good, he wished he could have been just a fan in the stands for that one. I felt the same way, but I was glad Jerry was a player, not a fan; he scored 53 points, and we won, 120-118. We won the second game, too, 118-112, with Jerry hitting 41 and Elgin 32. Boston won the third game, 111-105, when Elgin hit only four of 18 from the field, and he and Jerry combined hit only one for 14 in the fourth quarter.

The fourth game was as sloppy as the first game had been artistic, but we led, 88-87, with 15 seconds to go when Elgin threw the ball away. Sam Jones missed a jumper, and I slapped the rebound to Elgin. He stepped out of bounds with the ball, and now Boston had one more chance, with seven seconds left.

They in-bounded the ball, and we played tight defense. Sam Jones got the ball. He slipped, and made a desperate lunge, just to get the ball into the air. It hit the front rim, bounced around and fell in. Even Sam admitted it was an incredibly lucky shot. He said he didn't think the ball had a chance to reach the basket, but he thought Russell might be able to tap it in. He didn't realize until the buzzer sounded and he walked to the bench that Russell hadn't even been in the game then! Bill, the player-coach, had benched himself during the final seconds so there would be five good free-throwers in the Boston line-up, just in case we fouled anyone.

We returned to Los Angeles tied at two games each, and the Lakers immediately jumped ahead, three games to two, with a 117-104 victory in the fifth game. I outscored Russell, 13-7, and outrebounded him, 31-13, but it was a Pyrrhic victory. With less than three minutes to play, Boston's Em Bryant knocked Jerry off stride, and Jerry pulled a hamstring muscle in his left leg. With him hurting, we lost the sixth game, 99-90.

Going into the seventh game, we were worried. Jerry was the key to our offense, and he wasn't fully recovered. But Jack Kent Cooke was confident we would win. He had the USC band there, in the corridor, ready to march on to the floor and lead a victory celebration, and he had thousands of multicolored ballons hanging from the ceiling in huge nets, ready to be cut loose the instant we won.

The band never played, and the balloons never fell.

217

Jerry scored 42 points, and I hit seven of eight from the floor, but everyone else was ice cold. Elgin hit only eight of 22, Keith Erickson hit only two of 11, Johnny Egan hit only three of ten, Mel Counts hit only four of 13. Except for Jerry and me, the team shot a miserable 20 percent. In the third quarter alone, the Lakers missed 15 straight shots, and the Celtics jumped into a 17-point lead. Then we started to rally. With five minutes left in the game, we cut their lead to nine points. I had 18 points and 27 rebounds, but when I came down with number 27, I banged my knee into something hard. It hurt bad, like when you bang your crazy-bone against a wall as hard as you can. I had to be helped from the floor.

Frank O'Neill, the Laker trainer, sprayed some local anesthetic on it—we call the stuff "don't-hurt-no-more"—and after just about a minute, the pain went away. I signaled van Breda Kolff that I was okay and wanted to go back in. But the team had played well with Mel Counts filling in for me, and we'd cut Boston's lead to three points. Van Breda Kolff figured he could win without me—and win his petty personal battle with me in the process. Twice more, I signaled I was ready. Finally, he just said, "We don't need you."

He was determined to prove he was the boss, even if it cost the Lakers the world championship. And that's exactly what it cost. When the final buzzer sounded, Boston had won again, 108-106—the seventh time the Celtics had beaten me for a championship, and the sixth time they'd beaten Jerry, Elgin, and the Lakers for a championship.

I'm not sure I was ever as angry at one man as I was at Butch van Breda Kolff that night. By refusing to put me back in the game, he had not only humiliated me, he had deprived me and my teammates and the Laker fans of an NBA championship. With me in there for the last four minutes, I think we could have won. But van Breda Kolff wouldn't give me—and us—that chance.

I have to admit that I got a vengeful, almost sadistic sort of pleasure this last season when van Breda Kolff did something very similar for Phoenix and got fired. Like my other lousy coaches —Neil Johnston and Dolph Schayes—van Breda Kolff didn't exactly work his way into the Basketball Hall of Fame after we

218

parted company. He went from the Lakers to the Detroit Pistons, a team with such good players as Dave Bing, Jimmy Walker, Walt Bellamy, and Terry Dischinger, and he promptly coached them into the Eastern Division cellar in his first two years there. In his third year, he just up and quit after about two weeks. Then, last season, he was hired to coach Phoenix—a potential super team, with players like Connie Hawkins, Charlie Scott, and Dick Van Arsdale. The Suns split their first six games under van Breda Kolff, then played the Lakers in Los Angeles. We got a big lead—as big as 19 points—and van Breda Kolff got mad and decided his stars weren't playing the way he wanted them to play. So he benched them—and Phoenix rallied. With a little better than two minutes left in the game, they cut our lead to seven points. But instead of putting his starters back in to try for a victory, he did exactly the same thing he'd done with me four seasons earlier; he kept his reserves on the floor and his starters on the bench, just to prove he was the boss. Phoenix lost the game (just as the Lakers had lost that seventh game in the 1969 playoffs), and that was the last game van Breda Kolff ever coached for Phoenix (just as that playoff game was the last game he ever coached for Los Angeles). The Phoenix management fired him the very next day—after only seven games on the job—with the understatement of the year:

"It was obvious there was no communication between the players and the coach."

Van Breda Kolff wasn't the only man who left me with a bitter aftertaste from that 1968–69 playoff loss to Boston, though.

Not long after the season ended, Bill Russell announced his retirement and went on a speaking tour. In Wisconsin, before an audience of college students, he started talking about race relations, and suddenly switched subjects.

"Wilt copped out in the last game," he said. "Any injury short of a broken leg or a broken back isn't good enough. When he took himself out of that game, when he hurt his knee, well, I wouldn't have put him back in the game either."

When friends told me what Bill had said, I was shocked—and hurt. Other people had been saying the same thing, but I hadn't let them bother me. They were just ignorant fans who either had a hard-on for me or were disappointed because the Lakers had lost another championship. Bill was different. Or, at least, I thought he was. He was a friend. He knew me, and he knew the game. Hell, he'd had the same thing happen to him in the 1958 playoffs. He'd hurt his ankle, and had to come out of the game, and St. Louis beat Boston for the championship. I sure as shit wouldn't say he copped out then, and he shouldn't have said I copped out in 1969.

Because Bill and I were such fierce rivals for so many years, a lot of people assumed we were always enemies. But that wasn't so. In fact, we were such good friends that when I played in Philadelphia and the Celtics came to town for the playoffs, I'd often pick Bill up at the airport. When my teams went to Boston, he'd pick me up. We had dinner together quite often, too, and we'd even go over to his house before playoff games, and play with this huge complex of electric trains he had.

I think the only time we had anything remotely approaching a personality clash before 1969 was in my rookie year, when someone asked Bill if he thought I was fast enough to play in the NBA, and he said he'd heard I was pretty slow. When I read that, I challenged him to a foot-race, with the loser to donate $5,000 to the winner's favorite charity. Bill didn't accept my challenge, and—until 1969—that was the last time he ever came close to criticizing me. In fact, we used to kid each other a lot about the feuds the press tried to start between us.

In retrospect, I think the Celtics' domination of my teams in all those playoffs—and all the things everyone used to write about "Russell the winner versus Wilt the loser"—probably created a subconscious tinderbox of resentment in me. Although Bill and I remained good friends, it took just one big spark—like his statements about me copping out in the 1969 playoffs—to ignite the fire and kill our friendship.

The astonishing thing, I think, is not that our friendship died after that, but that it had lasted as long as it did, under the intense pressure of ten years of championship competition and daily newspaper accounts of our battles.

Even after Bill made his comments about me in 1969, I wanted to shrug it off and remain friends. After all those years, I didn't want us to finally fall into the trap of becoming the enemies the sportswriters had tried to make us ever since I came into the league. When the newspapers started calling me for my reaction to Bill's comments, I swallowed my pride and my resentment, and refused to strike back at him. I suppose I should have called Bill immediately myself and asked him for an explanation, and tried to smooth things out. It was ridiculous for us to become enemies now that he was retired, after we'd been friends all the time we played against each other. But I didn't call him. I got stubborn, and decided he should call me. He owed me an explanation and an apology, and I wasn't going to go begging for it. Bill soon made it clear that he had no intention of explaining or apologizing for anything, though. For awhile, it seemed like everytime he opened his mouth, it was to rap Wilt Chamberlain. He even wrote a piece for *TV Guide* saying I wasn't a challenge for him at all after my rookie year because he'd proven he was better than I was.

Russell didn't let up either. He's still knocking me, particularly on television, when he helped cover the NBA "Game of the Week" the last two years. Bill's an extremely bright guy, so his digs aren't always obvious. He knows that sophisticated, fair-minded fans would resent that; so he's sly. Sometimes, he just denigrates my play by implication and innuendo—or downright omission. Like, throughout the Lakers' 33-game win streak two seasons ago, he never had me on TV as his pregame or halftime guest, even though everyone said I was the key to our success. He didn't even interview me when ABC telecast the game in which I broke his career rebound record. Same thing this last season. We had one televised game in Milwaukee where I made Kareem Abdul-Jabbar miss 14 of his first 19 shots, and—in the first quarter alone—blocked shots by three other Bucks. Russell didn't say a word. Then, the first time Kareem blocked a Laker shot, Russell started raving, "Now *that's* playing defense."

Russell had his own radio sports talk show in Los Angeles until he went to Seattle, and friends told me he was also slipping in a rap-Wilt line there, too, whenever he could.

I've tried to analyze his behavior, but I haven't gotten very far. At first, I thought he might have made his 1969 comments on the spur of the moment, then felt guilty about it afterward. That would explain why he didn't want to confront me in an interview situation. But it wouldn't explain why he kept rapping me four years later—unless he decided that as long as he'd gotten himself stuck in that situation, he might as well exploit it, and give people something to talk about. That just didn't sound like the Bill Russell I'd known so well for so long, though, and I finally decided he had just been spoiled by all those NBA championships; he actually seemed to think the Celtics' playoff wins over my teams made him a better man than me—a better human being—and that gave him the right to sit in judgment on me, like some omniscient God.

To Bill, winning at basketball was everything. He said so himself during one of his potshots at me. "What it's all about is winning and losing," he said, "and he [meaning me] has done a lot of losing." Bill had never been a loser. His high school teams won 49 of 52 games. His college teams won 57 of 58—and two NCAA championships. His Boston teams won 11 NBA championships in 13 years. To Bill, every game—particularly every championship game—was a challenge, a test of his manhood. He took the game so seriously that he threw up in the locker room before almost every game. But I tend to look on basketball as a game, not a life-and-death struggle. I don't need scoring titles or NBA championships to prove that I'm a man. There are too many other beautiful things in life—food, cars, girls, friends, the beach, freedom—to get that emotionally wrapped up in basketball. I think Bill knew I felt that way, and I think he both envied and resented my attitude. On the one hand, I think he wished he could learn to take things easier, too; on the other hand, I think he may have felt that with my natural ability and my willingness to work hard, my teams could have won an NBA championship every year if I was as totally committed to victory as he was.

He may have been right. But I don't think so. I think his teams usually beat my teams for the simple reason that he usually had better teammates and/or better coaches then I did. No less an authority than John Wooden, the great UCLA coach, said the same thing earlier this year in his own book. Coach Wooden wrote:

> Had Wilt been surrounded by the playing cast that Russell was with the Boston Celtics, and had he had a Red Auerbach as coach, his team might have won all those championships.

222

I wish I had won all those championships, of course, but I really think I grew more as a man in defeat than Russell did in victory. Sure, I realize that may sound like rationalizing, and—to a certain extent—it probably is. But the people who've been close to Richard Nixon in recent years have noticed that his defeats in 1960 and 1962 had precisely that kind of effect on him. When you lose, you're forced to confront yourself as you really are, way down deep inside. You gain insights and a perspective on yourself and others—and life in general—that a guy who always wins just never gets. It may sound like sour grapes, but I really think Bill is a shallower man for all his basketball triumphs, and rather than my being angry or envious over his victories and his gloating and his raps at me, I feel sorry for him.

Much as I would like to have won a few more of those playoff games against Boston, I wouldn't trade my self-awareness and peace of mind for all his world championship rings and playoff checks combined.

13

ONE DAY SHORTLY BEFORE I began the 1969–70 season—my second with the Lakers—I was talking to Kareem Abdul-Jabbar about what he could expect as a rookie in the NBA. He'd just led UCLA to three straight NCAA championships, and everyone was predicting he might lead Milwaukee to *ten* straight NBA championships.

"Don't look too far ahead and count too much on the future," I told him. "This is a funny game. Anything can happen. Injuries can stop you at any time. It can all end like the snapping of a twig."

Little did I realize that I was talking about Wilt Chamberlain, not Kareem Abdul-Jabbar.

Going into that season, I had missed only 12 games in ten years, and I'd led the league in minutes played nine of the ten years. I'd always prided myself on giving my employers—and the fans—their money's worth, and those records made me just as happy as my scoring and rebounding and assist records. But all that came to an end in the ninth game of the season—like the snapping of a twig.

224

It was the third quarter of a game at the Forum in Los Angeles, and we were comfortably ahead of Phoenix. Jerry passed me the ball on a fast break, and I drove toward the basket. All of a sudden, my right leg caved in. I crumpled to the floor in pain. Oh, God, my knee hurt. I had torn my tibial tubercle—a tendon in the knee—and the pain was excruciating. It took five guys to help me hobble off the floor, into the Laker locker room. The team doctor, Dr. Bob Kerlan, took one look at my knee, and ordered an ambulance to rush me to the hospital. He and Dr. Frank Jobe operated on me the next day.

I was 33 then—getting old for most athletes—and the doctors weren't sure I'd ever be able to play again.

The body doesn't heal quickly—or fully—as you grow older, they said, and even if I did recover physically, the psychological scars of so traumatic an injury might never heal. I might always subconsciously favor my right leg; that would cost me my speed and my mobility. The best I could possibly hope for, the doctors told me, was an arduous, year-long rehabilitation program that might enable me to test my knee at the beginning of the next season. It was absolutely certain, they said, that I wouldn't play again in the 1969–70 season.

That, of course, is just the kind of challenge I love—being told that it's impossible for me to do something. But this was a more difficult—and different—challenge than any I'd ever taken on before. Even though I'd always prided myself on having a good, quick mind, my body was the one thing I'd always been able to count on to do what had to be done. I was fast and strong and durable, and there was very little I wanted to do that I couldn't do—whether it was run or put the shot or play basketball or high jump or lift weights or bowl or. . . . Now my body had failed me, and it was up to my mind to make my body respond. I had to will myself to get well—all the way well—and I was determined to do it that very season, in less than five months.

The Lakers, I knew, had a good enough team to make the playoffs without me. The Western Division wouldn't be too tough that year; all the power was in the East. If I could be ready by the end of March, I could join the team in time for the playoffs—and maybe even help us win the championship. With Bill Russell retired, Boston didn't figure to go anywhere, and I didn't think

225

Milwaukee—with Kareem in his rookie year—was strong enough yet to go all the way. I figured we'd probably have to play New York or Baltimore in the finals, and I thought we could beat either of them. I went to work on my rehabilitation program.

The hardest part of the program was the beginning—the week I spent in the hospital, lying flat on my back. I'd always been an active guy, and that inactivity was murder. I couldn't move much, I couldn't go anywhere, I couldn't do anything.

Once I got out of the hospital, though, I didn't have too much trouble with the cast—at least not after they put a second one on. The first cast was too tight, and I woke up in the middle of the night one time with the thing a deep shade of sticky red; it had squeezed the blood out of my leg.

Once we got that squared away, I learned to adjust and compensate for the extra weight and bulk of the cast, and I was driving and hopping around in no time.

The only real problem I had with the cast was in making love. Maneuvering my size body with a normal size girl can be difficult enough sometimes—particularly in tight quarters—but trying to drag that cast around without breaking the girl's leg (or decapitating her) was a real effort. After I worked out a pretty good technique, I found that some girls actually liked me better in a cast. I guess they thought it made for an exotic erotic experience.

The doctors kept my cast on for almost eight weeks, and I can still remember what happened the day they took it off. With the cast on, I'd gotten into the habit of jumping backwards into bed and flopping that heavy old right leg down in front of me. Well, the first time I tried that without the cast on, I thought I was going to die. The cast had held the knee rigid; without it, the leg hit the bed and bounced up and bent halfway back at the knee. I was sure I'd torn the tendon again. The pain was unbearable. I decided right then that I'd never play basketball again, I'd never walk again, I might never even get up out of that bed again.

The doctors assured me I hadn't done any damage, though, and they gave me a rigorous running and weight lifting program. But their program was designed to get me ready for the next season; I wanted to get ready for the playoffs *this* season. Whatever they told me to do, I doubled it. If they said I should run five miles,

I ran ten; if they said I should lift ten pounds with my leg, I lifted twenty.

Before long, I had an established pattern. Every day, I'd drive to Dr. Kerlan's office about midmorning for whirlpool treatments to restore the movement and flexibility in my leg. Then I'd go home and lift weights with my leg for an hour. It was what they call "resistance" weight lifting—sitting on the edge of a table and lifting a heavy boot again and again and again. I started with about 12 pounds, and built up to about 150. After weight lifting, I'd rest a few minutes, then drive to the beach, and walk eight or ten miles through the sand. I'd walk pretty fast, without stopping, and it usually took about three or four hours to finish. That helped me to get back my wind and stamina, and it also strengthened the leg and knee. Like the weights, the sand offered "resistance."

When I got home from the beach each afternoon, I'd do another hour of weight lifting. Before bed, I'd lift for another hour.

I spent about ten hours a day, seven days a week, trying to rebuild the leg, and sometimes it was as discouraging as it was painful. In the beginning, every time I bent the knee, it felt like someone was running a hot ice pick through the joint. It was just brutal. But when I began to see some progress—when the pain lessened a little, and I was able to increase the weight—I knew I was going to make it. I started to get excited by even the slightest sign of improvement. Like, it was a 17-minute drive from my house to the doctor's office. At first, that was too far for me to go without stopping; I couldn't keep my leg bent for that long without a lot of pain. But after awhile, I could make the drive easily.

I think the thing that really saved me was the beach. After I ran on the sand for several weeks, I met some people and became friendly with them. They were all volleyball players—damn good ones—and they kept trying to talk me into playing with them. When I asked the doctors about it, they said it might be good therapy—both physically and emotionally. It was more than good therapy; it was a godsend.

Most people seem to think the only thing I got from volleyball was the idea of wearing my gold headband in basketball. I did get that idea from volleyball—old rags and T-shirts wrapped around my forehead seemed a great way to keep the sweat from

227

pouring down my face on the beach. Now headbands are quite the rage among school kids who play basketball in Southern California. But the idea for the headband is far from the most important thing I took from volleyball to basketball. Playing volleyball in the sand not only helped me rebuild my right knee and leg muscles, it made *both* my legs stronger than ever. Legs are almost always the first part of the body that go bad in a professional athlete as he grows older, and I'm convinced that my volleyball —even more than my water skiing—is what has enabled me to continue playing 46 to 48 minutes of NBA basketball every game for the last three years, at an age when most athletes are either retired or just spot players.

But volleyball gave me far more than two strong legs, as important as that is. I grew to love volleyball. It's now my favorite sport. I play it all day, almost every day, during the off-season, and I like it better than basketball. I'm sure that's at least partially because volleyball is still comparatively new to me; it's still a challenge. There are a lot of guys who are better at it than I am, and I have to work hard and learn a lot to hold my own in top-caliber competition. Basketball, after 20 years, is no longer that challenging. There's very little I haven't done—and done often—in basketball.

I also made a whole new group of good friends playing volleyball—friends like Gene Selznick—and I've always felt that good friends are the most valuable commodity on earth. With them, you can be happy, even if you're poor and sick. Without them, you can't be happy, even if you have perfect health and all the money in the world.

But the most important thing I gained from my long period of rehabilitation and my first volleyball experience was a sense of security and inner peace and self-satisfaction that I'd never known before. Away from basketball for the first time since junior high school, I was forced to do some serious thinking about myself and my life—to take stock of Wilt Chamberlain, the man.

In many ways, I'm a different man today than I was before my injury. I'm more mellow, I guess. I decided then that I'd done my best in basketball—setting record after record and leading team after team to their best seasons ever—and that would have to be good enough. I was through getting upset with all my critics

228

all the time; I was through having to prove myself, again and again and again. Over the previous three or four seasons, when I'd been more passer than scorer, I'd let it bother me whenever someone said I wasn't scoring more because I *couldn't* score; I'd made a habit of going out and scoring 50 or 60 points two or three times every season, just to show them I could still do it if I wanted to. But I haven't done that anymore since 1969. I'm the greatest scorer in basketball history; why should I have to prove anything to anyone? As long as I know I can still do it, what do I care what anyone else thinks? As for my teams not having won more championships, well, I'm satisfied that playing against better teams with better coaches and better luck had something to do with that. If that doesn't satisfy the fans and sportswriters, and they want to blame me, there isn't anything I can do about it, so why let it bother me? No one as sensitive as I am can become impervious to criticism, of course, and I still gripe some when I think I've been subjected to a bad rap. Since my injury, however, my reaction to unfair criticism has come more as a matter of principle—to set the record straight—than as an emotional counter-attack. Now, once I've said my piece, I forget it, rather than agonize over it.

But the changes in my emotional makeup went beyond basketball.

For one thing, I became less materialistic. Ever since I'd started making good money and getting exposed to *la dolce vita,* I had eaten in the best restaurants, and worn the best clothes, and carried a wad of big bills around with me. I've never believed in credit cards or checking accounts—to this day, I don't have any of either—and I used to go out at night with $5,000 or $10,000 or more stuffed in my pants pockets.

Friends were constantly warning me that someone might try to hit me over the head and rob me. I had a smart-ass answer to that, of course:

"Anyone who wants to hit me over the head would need a step-ladder," I told them. "If I see some guy walking toward me on a dark street with a step-ladder, I'll know just what he wants."

But once I started playing volleyball regularly, I stopped carrying large sums of money on me. I might go out at night now and not have $20 in my pockets. I still enjoy an occasional foray into *haute cuisine,* and I have a couple of antelope suits that cost me $3,000 each, but I don't go in that much for expensive food and clothes any more either. The reason, I think, is that when I was playing volleyball, I found myself standing on the beach in bare feet and a $2.98 pair of shorts, day after day, having the time of my life, with a bunch of people who probably wouldn't earn as much money in their whole lifetime as I earned in six months. I'd play all day, and maybe spend 50 cents on some lemonade. I couldn't play basketball yet, so I had an awful lot of time to myself to think about things then, and I came to realize just how little I actually needed, in the way of material comforts, to be happy. I might have come to that realization without volleyball, but volleyball provided the vehicle or the impetus or whatever you want to call it. I found out that after 20 years of being the center of attention in high school and college and the pros, I really didn't need basketball *or* attention *or* money to be happy. Suddenly, winning NBA championships and beating Bill Russell and flashing $100 bills around didn't mean that much to me anymore. Don't get me wrong; I'm not saying I took a vow of poverty. I still get great pleasure out of negotiating big-money contracts, and I still insist on being paid what I'm worth, and I still appreciate many of the things that only money can buy—a fine car and a beautiful home and a chance to travel; I want to have enough money to be able to enjoy those things. But I learned that summer what I should have known all along—that they're luxuries, not necessities; that, if I have to, I can live quite happily without them.

With that attitude, I suppose it would have been natural for me to use my knee injury as a justification for retiring from pro basketball right then. But I wasn't ready to retire. I still liked basketball, and I'd been going to almost every Laker game during my rehabilitation period, trying to stay close to the guys on the team and letting them know how much progress I was making toward complete recovery. Besides, I had given myself a challenge—returning to the lineup before the season was over—and I wasn't about to quit without having met that challenge.

All the armchair experts had their own theories about my return, of course. Some of them said I was jealous that the Lakers were playing so well without me. Others said Elgin Baylor had returned to form in my absence, and that I didn't like the idea of him getting all that attention. Some people even said I couldn't wait to get back on the floor so I could show everyone I was still better than Kareem, despite the great rookie year he was having. I suppose there might be a little truth in all those theories—but not much. The Lakers weren't playing all that well without me; they were in second place in a weak division, with a 44-35 record, as compared with a first-place finish and a 55-27 record the previous year. Elgin may have been playing better without me in the lineup, but you sure couldn't prove it from looking at the statistics; both his scoring and his rebounding averages were *down* slightly from the previous year. As for Kareem, well, I'd spent ten years having everyone pit me against Bill Russell all the time; I wasn't about to start all over with Kareem. I figured I'd do my thing, and he could do his thing, and I wasn't going to worry about who everyone said was better or more valuable.

The doctors checked my knee periodically throughout my rehabilitation period, and they were astonished by how quickly I recovered. They attributed my progress to my good overall physical condition and my dedication and hard work, and even though they would have preferred that I wait until the next season to play basketball again—"just to be on the safe side"—they gave me permission to rejoin the Lakers for workouts on March 10. A week later—with three games left in the regular season—I was ready to play for the first time in more than four months.

I had gotten an unbelievable amount of really warm fan mail in the hospital and at the Laker office, but even that didn't prepare me for the tremendous ovation the fans gave me when I was introduced in the lineup for the first time. Although I didn't realize it then, that seemed to mark a watershed in my relationship with the fans. My injury and my comeback had turned me from villain to hero. I still get booed in places like Boston—where they'll never forgive me for challenging Russell—but I started getting cheers almost everywhere else; I sometimes even get more cheers than Jerry West now when the lineups are introduced in Los Angeles. It's almost as if my injury freed me of that Superman image, and proved I was mortal after all; people could suddenly identify with me. I think my comeback also helped. It showed I was willing to work hard and endure pain and sacrifice, and that destroyed the false image I'd always had of being a big guy who was lucky to have everything fall into his lap just because he was seven feet tall.

As time went on, the fans responded even more favorably toward me. With Lew Alcindor becoming Kareem Abdul-Jabbar, the fans had a new villain to jeer; his political and religious views and his seeming disdain for the press and the public made my earlier "sins" seem trivial by comparison. Kareem filled what one Boston sportswriter called "an important void in a sports fan's life" in a column he wrote about me.

"The continuing passion play that is pro basketball demands there be a Mr. Evil," he said—and now Kareem is it. Having been through the same thing myself for so long, I feel sorry for him. As I grew older and more sophisticated, I came to realize—and I'm sure Kareem realizes—the fans really aren't booing you because you beat their teams; they're booing your lifestyle, not your basketball. They're jealous of all your success and money and prestige; they resent your fancy house and expensive sports car and all those good-looking girls they just know you're screwing, and since they can't steal your girls or wreck your car or burn down your house, they boo you and knock you. It's cathartic for them, I guess—particularly if they're frustrated in their own lives. If a guy has a shrew and a house full of squalling brats at home— and a dreary, monotonous 9-to-5 job—it's easy for him to be bitter about your success . . . and to console himself and cop out for his own inadequacies by telling himself that the only reason you're so successful is that you're a seven-foot freak.

I occasionally get this kind of flak from the fans, even now, but, for the most part, they seem to be on my side—at last. The irony of the situation, of course, is that this respect and affection from the fans didn't come to me until I had decided I could live without it. During all those years when I was being jeered as a loser and a selfish gunner, I could have used that kind of encouragement and support. Now, when I had finally come to peace with myself, and decided I wasn't going to worry about it any more, it was there—in abundance.

I did—and still do—appreciate the way the fans began treating me at the end of that season, and I have to admit I was flattered by the concern many of them displayed over whether I should actually return to the lineup for the playoffs. They were worried that I might reinjure myself, and they wanted me to wait until the next season. Of course, there were other fans who thought the Lakers were playing effective basketball without me; they were worried that my return might so disrupt the team's rhythm and change their style that they wouldn't be able to adjust in time to win. But Jack Kent Cooke wanted me back right away, and most people seemed to agree with what Jerry West said:

"We get outrebounded every night, but we wouldn't with Wilt. With a guy like that, if you're going bad defensively or offensively, he can pick you up by himself."

I played the last three regular-season games with the Lakers, and we won two of them. Then came the first round of the play-offs—against Phoenix, the same team I'd been injured against way back in November. We won the first game, 128-112, and things seemed to be going smoothly. But we hadn't fully adjusted to having me back at center, in place of Mel Counts or Rick Roberson, a rookie, and our timing and coordination were both off badly. Phoenix whipped us in the next three games—by an average of 12 points a game—and suddenly, we were just one defeat away from elimination.

It was time to go to work.

In the fifth game, Jerry and I scored 36 points each, and we won, 138-121. In the sixth game, Jerry had 35 points and 12 steals, and I had 26 rebounds and 12 blocked shots. We won again, 104-93. That evened the series at three games each. In the seventh game, Jerry and Elgin and I all played like everyone had hoped we would when I first joined the Lakers. Jerry scored 19 points and had 15 assists. Elgin had 25 points and 14 rebounds. I had 30 points, 27 rebounds, 11 blocked shots, and six assists. We destroyed Phoenix, 129-94.

Atlanta was next, and Atlanta had always been a bruising, physical team. This year was no exception. They pushed and shoved and elbowed us all over the floor, and then complained when the officials called a lot of fouls on them. Richie Guerin, the Atlanta coach, even started threatening Jerry and Elgin. After the first game, he said there would be "a lot of blood spilled on the floor" in the next game if the officials kept calling so many fouls on the Hawks. "Baylor and West won't be around to shoot 18 or

233

20 fouls," he said. But Richie didn't threaten me. He knew better than that. And I told him that if his guys started knocking Jerry or Elgin around, I'd take care of their whole damn team.

We won the series easily, in four straight games, and the only game that was even close was the third one. We won that, 115-114, in overtime—after I hit two free throws (that's right, two *free throws*!) to tie the game with 13 seconds remaining in regulation play.

So now it was the Lakers against New York for the world championship. We thought we had the better team—I still feel that way—but New York seemed fated to win that year. They were Destiny's Children—a Cinderella team with fanatic fans, a longtime last-place team that suddenly made good—just like the New York Mets had done in baseball a few months earlier.

We split the first two games with the Knicks, then lost the third game, in overtime, despite Jerry's 61-foot shot to tie the game, just as the buzzer sounded at the end of regulation play. People in Los Angeles still talk about that fantastic shot. But they seem to forget that Jerry couldn't buy a basket in overtime. He missed five straight, and we lost, 111-108. The fourth game also went into overtime, and we won, 121-115, to tie the series at two games each. Then came the pivotal fifth game. We led by 13 points at the half, and the Knicks' center, Willis Reed—in pain and ineffective—had left the game in the second quarter, and was on the bench with a hip injury. All we had to do was hold any part of that lead, and we'd go back to Los Angeles with a 3-2 lead and a chance to win the championship before our home fans. We got a little too confident too soon. We let down a little and started to play conservatively and it killed us. New York got psyched up, and went crazy. Jerry, who'd averaged 34.5 points for the first four games, took only two shots—and missed both of them—in the second half. As a team, we took only 26 shots in the second half. New York had a smaller, scrambling, gambling team in there, and the more they harassed us, the worse we played. We had 30 turnovers!

Our coach's strategy didn't do much for us in that second half either. Joe Mullaney was our coach that year, succeeding van Breda Kolff, and he was a good coach and a good man. I liked him and respected him. Unlike van Breda Kolff, he was more

234

interested in winning games than proving he was boss. But Joe helped us blow that game. In the first half, I'd hit seven of nine field goals and had 18 points and 12 rebounds. With Reed out in the second half, the logical thing to do was get the ball in to me. The Knicks had a couple of forwards, 6 foot 6 Dave DeBusschere and 6 foot 7 Dave Stallworth, alternating on me, and neither one of them could possibly contain me. DeBusschere is a great forward, but I've got seven inches and 50 pounds on him; there's no way he's going to stop me—unless my teammates don't get the ball to me in a good position to shoot. That's exactly what happened. They either held on to the ball or shot it themselves or let the Knicks pick off their bad passes. When they did get the ball to me, I was in bad position—which was my fault as well as theirs. I hit on two of the three shots I took in the second half, but I only got seven more rebounds, and I let DeBusschere get good position on me too many times. We all played like zombies, and we got beat, 107-100.

In the sixth game, I decided I'd had enough of being a passer and feeder. If we were going to win, I had to score. I hit 20 of 27 from the floor, scored 45 points and pulled down 27 rebounds. We won, 135-113.

Then came the seventh game in Madison Square Garden. Reed wasn't supposed to play, and when he came limping out on the court and started warming up with the Knicks, just before the opening tipoff, the fans went berserk. When he hit the first two baskets of the game, I thought they were going to tear the building down, right then and there. That gave New York an incredible emotional lift. But neither that nor Reed himself is what beat us. Willis didn't score again the rest of the game, and he got only three rebounds; I had 21 points and 24 rebounds. But I missed 10 of 11 free throws, and the other Lakers only got the ball in to me often enough for me to take 16 shots (and make 10) from the floor. What beat us that night was a combination of several things —not the least of which was the subconscious, unspoken, but nonetheless inescapable feeling everyone on both teams had that no matter what the Lakers did, individually and collectively, the Knicks would find a way to win, and we would find a way to lose; we all just seemed to feel that New York was destined to win. Maybe I was imagining things. Maybe I was the only one who felt that way. Maybe it just seemed like destiny was with the Knicks because I'd become more philosophical and had changed so much, emotionally and mentally, in the course of that year, and winning a championship no longer seemed all-important to me. But I really did get the impression that all the other Lakers—and all the Knicks —felt the same way about the seventh game, particularly after the way we'd blown that fifth game. I have to give credit to the Knicks, though. They didn't just stand around waiting for destiny to hand them the championship. They hustled all the way, and they played brilliant defense, and they used their great poise and balance and precision passing to find the open man every time on offense. Their coach, Red Holzman, is the best in basketball, and their leader, Walt Frazier, is a superb clutch player. He whipped Jerry's ass that night—as he often does. Walt got 36 points and 19 assists (an all-time playoff record!), and he must have stolen the ball right out of Jerry's hands five or six times in the first half alone. But the papers somehow forgot to mention who won that particular duel; all they talked about was how poor, crippled Willis Reed "beat" Wilt Chamberlain.

The game wasn't even close. The Knicks led, 69-42, at the half, and they won going away, 113-99.

For the fifth time in my career—and the third year in a row —I'd lost an NBA championship or a chance at a championship in the seventh game; for the third time in *their* careers, Jerry and Elgin (and the Lakers) had lost an NBA championship in the seventh game.

But even that was better than we were able to do the next season. Hell, we not only lost again in 1971, we didn't make the final round of the playoffs at all.

Part of the problem, early in the season, was team morale. Our coach, Joe Mullaney, had a sound knowledge of basketball, but his gentle, easygoing ways—and a few odd personality quirks —made some of the players think he was just a nice, absent-minded old bumbler. Like, he couldn't remember his own players' names sometimes. He'd call Jim McMillian "Elg," and call Elg "Mac." When we kidded him about it, he'd say, "All you black guys look alike." With Joe, that wasn't a racial slur, as it would have been with some men. He wasn't prejudiced at all; he was just

236

kidding. Hell, he even got the white guys mixed up. He'd call Gail Goodrich "Jerry," and call Jerry "Gail."

Some of the Lakers who had been the most resentful of Butch van Breda Kolff's harsh, tyrannical tactics were so glad to have a mild-mannered gentleman like Joe around that they overreacted to the change and took advantage of him. Discipline, at times, went to hell. And, as usual, Wilt Chamberlain got the blame.

I missed one practice around Christmas time that season because I had trouble making airplane connections from Philadelphia, where I'd gone to visit my mother. Unfortunately, Joe considered it a particularly important practice. We'd lost four of our last six games, and he wanted to work hard on a few things and put in four or five new plays. I got back to Los Angeles in time for our next game—on Christmas night, against Boston—and Joe came over to me in the dressing room and said he wasn't going to start me.

He said he wasn't mad at me, but he felt he had to bench me for two reasons—(1) I didn't know the new plays he'd put in at practice, and (2) the other guys might think he was giving me special treatment if he didn't discipline me for missing an important practice. I understood his position, but it was the first time in my career that anything except an injury had kept me out of the starting lineup, and I was furious. I went looking for Fred Schaus, the Laker general manager. When I told Fred what had happened, he promised to talk to Joe and straighten things out. But I missed the first ten minutes of the game—and that was all it took for the rumor-mongers to start howling about a feud between Joe and me. If Joe had handled the situation better—starting me, then taking me out after a few minutes—he would have achieved his objective without that happening; the players would have realized he was disciplining me, without it being so obvious to the fans.

But the damage was done, and now the team was embroiled in a public brouhaha that hurt our play. We lost our last game in December and our first three games in January—the third one to Cincinnati, one of the worst teams in the league. We played that game in Omaha, on national television, and we got slaughtered, 146-112. That kind of thing will happen occasionally in the NBA, even to the best of teams, and for the rest of the season, we

237

jokingly referred to the game as "the Omaha disaster." Fred Schaus had watched the game on TV back in Los Angeles, though, and he didn't think it was so funny. When we got to Cleveland for our next game, he was there waiting for us.

In the dressing room before the Cleveland game, I asked the ballboy to go get me a hot dog. It's something I often do if I don't have time to eat in the afternoon, and it's a habit that's given rise to some wildly exaggerated stories about my devouring a dozen hot dogs and two whole chickens just minutes before a game. On this particular night, two or three other guys on the team also ordered hot dogs. But when Schaus got into the dressing room, the ballboy had just set the box of food down by me. Fred took one look at me calmly munching a hot dog—with several other hot dogs by my side—and he exploded. That, he said, was why we were losing: We were too complacent, too busy feeding our faces and thinking about other things and not concentrating on basketball. Our loss in Omaha was a disgrace, he said. Well, it just so happens that I'd played my best game of the year in Omaha. I'd had my season high—41 points—and I'd gotten 23 rebounds, so I didn't really think he was talking to me. But everyone else on the team looked scared to death. Throughout his tirade, no one moved or spoke; the hot dogs stayed in the box next to me, getting cold. When I gestured to a couple of the other guys, Jim McMillian and Rick Roberson, to take theirs, they made faces like "Me? A hot dog? I wouldn't order anything like that." Finally, I picked up the box and extended it toward Fred and said, "Hey, Fred, want a hot dog?"

That pretty much ended his locker room lecture.

We did start to play better basketball after that meeting, though. We won the game in Cleveland, and we won our next game, and from mid-January through early February, we won 11 out of 13.

Then, on March 2, Buffalo's Bob Kauffman—a hard-nosed, 6 foot 8, 245-pound forward—crashed into Jerry while Jerry was lunging for a bad pass. The minute Jerry hit the floor, we knew he was hurt bad. He'd torn the ligaments in his right knee, and immediate surgery was ordered. Bad knees had already sidelined Elgin for the year, and with Jerry gone now, too, we just didn't have enough firepower left to beat the best teams in the playoffs.

238

I had fully recovered from my knee injury, and I averaged 20 points a game that season, and led the league in rebounding again with 18 a game. But I couldn't do it all by myself. We lost eight of our last 11 games in the regular season, then—somehow—pulled ourselves together to beat Chicago, four games to three, in the first round of the playoffs. I've never seen guys play harder than my teammates did in that series. We were outmanned and outgunned, and we won anyway. In the seventh game, I had 25 points and 19 rebounds and seven blocked shots, and everyone in our starting lineup scored in double figures.

As it turned out, that was our last hurrah.

Our next opponent was Milwaukee, the team with the greatest record in basketball that year—66 wins and 16 losses, then the second-best mark in NBA history. The Bucks clobbered us in the first two games, 106-85 and 91-73, and before the third game, Keith Erickson—the man who was filling in for Jerry—had to be rushed to the hospital for an emergency appendectomy. Now we had three starters out of the lineup. Incredibly, we managed to win the third game, 118-107. But Milwaukee blitzed us in the next two games, 117-94 and 116-98, to advance to the final round, where they beat Baltimore four straight for the world championship.

I think I probably played some of the best basketball of my career in that five-game Milwaukee series. The Milwaukee fans thought so, too. I'm not sure I've ever been cheered as much on an opposing court as I was in Milwaukee the three times we played there. When I left the last game, they gave me a standing ovation. I'd outplayed Kareem in almost every game, and instead of resenting me, they were applauding me. Two years earlier, that wouldn't have happened; this was just another indication of how my knee injury and my comeback had "humanized" me for the fans, and made them into my friends instead of my enemies. I was beginning to get some inkling of how good and warm Jerry must have felt all those years, being everyone's favorite and getting the fans' cheers wherever he played. I would love to have talked to Jerry about that then, but I couldn't. He wasn't with the team for the Milwaukee series. While we were busting our asses, against insuperable odds, Jerry was on the East Coast, serving as the television color man for the Eastern Division playoffs between

239

New York and Baltimore. I know he couldn't play for us, but I thought he could at least have sat on the bench to give us moral support. I could just imagine what people would have said if I'd done what Jerry did. They would have resurrected all those old stories about what a selfish son-of-a-bitch I was, and how I didn't get along with my teammates and didn't give a damn how the team did, as long as I got my scoring records. But Jerry was an "untouchable." He had the image of being a selfless team player, and when you live in the public eye, once you get an image—good or bad, deserved or not—it's usually yours for life. Jerry's image was good, and no one said a word about his not having been with the Lakers for the playoffs.

Fortunately, with my new attitude, I was more bemused than angry about this; I looked on it more as an irony than an injustice. In fact, I suspect that this is one time in my career I might not have spent too much time worrying about Jerry *or* the loss to Milwaukee, even without that change in my outlook. I had another little project I had been thinking about, on and off, for several years, and shortly after the playoffs, it looked like it might finally come to fruition. The project was a fight with Muhammad Ali.

I had first been approached about becoming a boxer back in 1959, when a Seattle fight promoter named Jack Hurley said he thought he could get me a heavyweight championship fight with Floyd Patterson. Hurley had done just that with an amateur nobody named Pete Rademacher in 1957—gotten him a world championship bout with Patterson in Rademacher's *first* professional fight. Hurley said he knew Floyd's handlers would go for a Patterson-Chamberlain fight, and he was sure I'd have a chance to win.

"I've watched you play basketball," he said. "You're quick and strong and you move well. We can teach you the rest. It'll be a sensational attraction. Everyone will want to see the fight. We'll all get rich."

I was just finishing my first year with the Globies then, and I wasn't interested in becoming a fighter. If I hadn't been able to get mad enough to hit back at the opposing centers who had pushed me around in college, I didn't see how I could possibly get mad enough to deliberately beat someone up in a boxing ring. Besides, I was looking forward to joining the NBA; I wanted to play pro basketball, not fight. Hurley kept in contact, though, and—from time to time—he tried to talk me into becoming a fighter.

Then, in 1967, when Muhammad Ali was the heavyweight champion, several people came to me with a proposal:

Cus D'Amato, Floyd Patterson's former manager, would train me in secret for six months. I'd have no warmup fights, no exhibitions, just one big bout—Wilt Chamberlain vs. Muhammad Ali for the heavyweight championship of the world. I had a lot of respect for Cus as a boxing man, and I really liked him as a person, but I told him I was afraid to fight a professional fighter like Muhammad.

"That's good," he said. "If you weren't smart enough to be afraid, I wouldn't have anything to do with this; he'd kill you. But with your attitude, I think you can beat him."

"But I'm no fighter," I told him.

"That's OK, too. We're not going to train you to be a fighter. We're going to train you to fight one man. We won't talk about anything or work on anything except what you'll need to beat Ali. You'll have three things going for you—size, strength, and surprise. We'll look at all the films of Ali's old fights, and break them down, minute-by-minute and punch-by-punch. By the time you step into the ring with him, you'll know exactly what to expect from him. But he won't have the vaguest idea what to expect from you. He's never fought anyone as tall as you before. He won't know how to handle you. With your height and your reach, you should be able to keep him away pretty easy. With your strength, all you'll have to do is bide your time and land one good punch. It'll be lights out. You'll be the champ. Then you can retire and count your money."

It was an intriguing scenario. I said I'd think about it.

One of the first things I did was contact George Gainford, Sugar Ray Robinson's old trainer. I had always been a fan of Sugar's, and I thought Gainford was probably one of the most knowledgeable boxing men around. I laid the story on him. He said, "Wilt, it just might work. If you work your ass off, you just might beat him."

It sure was tempting. Fighting Muhammad would combine the two kinds of challenges I'd always responded to—doing something

241

everyone said couldn't be done, and beating another man at his game.

I told Cus and the others I was ready to sign.

We contacted Bob Arum (Ali's attorney) and Mike Malitz of Main Bout Inc., the company in charge of the closed-circuit TV rights for all Muhammad's fights. They were all in favor of the fight. Jim Brown was a 10 percent stockholder in Main Bout Inc., and he was so excited by the idea, he said he'd quit them and be my manager. We even had a tentative date and site for the fight —June 29, 1968, in the Houston Astrodome.

I was just starting my last season with the Philadelphia 76ers then—it was November, 1967—and Ali's people wanted to get the final details of the fight worked out. We had a meeting in Loew's Midtown Hotel with Muhammad and his trainer, Bundini Brown, and a couple of his advisors. The 76ers' trainer, Al Domenico, was there, too, kind of as my "second."

Bundini, it turned out, was dead set against the fight. He kept jumping up on a chair to show Muhammad how hard it would be for him to fight someone as tall as me. Nothing got settled that day, but I later heard that Bundini's apprehensions had been relayed to Herbert Muhammad—Ali's manager and the son of Muslim leader Elijah Muhammad. Herbert vetoed the fight.

Ali and I bumped into each other from time to time after that, and we always kidded about fighting. He and I—and Joe Namath —are easily the most controversial and charismatic athletes in the world, and since Joe wasn't about to fight either of us—or our sisters, for that matter—a fight between Muhammad and me seemed the best way to produce the biggest box office event of all time.

Then, on November 26, 1970, I got a telegram from Chris Dundee, whose brother Angelo had been with Ali for most of his career.

The telegram was sent from Miami, and it said:

"Would like for you to box Muhammad Ali during Super Bowl Week here. Offer you $250,000 with an option of 20 percent of live gate and all ancillary rights. Feel that the box will gross $5 million dollars. We will feature the greatest basketball player versus the greatest fighter."

But Super Bowl Week was less than 60 days away. I couldn't

possibly learn enough about boxing in that time—even if Herbert Muhammad would relent and permit the fight.

A week or two into 1971, the Ali people contacted me again. This time, they said, they had Herbert Muhammad's approval to make the fight—and they were prepared to guarantee me a minimum of $500,000 in cash, to be put into escrow even before I started training.

On Feb. 21, we signed the contract for the fight. I still have a copy of that contract. It said we would fight on June 21 in the Houston Astrodome. But we agreed verbally that we would only fight if Muhammad beat Joe Frazier in his upcoming title fight. I wanted to fight for the championship; if Ali got beat, he wouldn't be the champ anymore. That, of course, is exactly what happened. On March 8—two weeks and a day after Muhammad and I signed our contract—Frazier beat Ali. Our fight was off.

But Ali's people wanted the fight with me more than ever then. Muhammad needed every fight he could get, to rebuild his image and his bank account until Frazier would fight him again— if he ever would. Muhammad had contributed more money and more prestige to the Muslims than any other man in the world; the Muslim leaders didn't want to lose that either. He had to fight.

To induce me to fight an exhibition, instead of a championship bout, Ali's people sweetened the pot considerably. This time, they made me an offer that would gurantee me $500,000 *after* all taxes were paid—and I would also get a percentage of the closed-circuit television and all other ancillary rights.

It was an unbelievable offer, but my boss—Jack Kent Cooke —didn't want me to accept it.

"The fight crowd's a sleazy crowd," he told me. "You don't want to get mixed up with them."

Of course, Jack hadn't minded getting mixed up with them himself when he promoted the Ali-Frazier fight, but I guess he was just looking out for my best interests. I didn't for a minute think he might be against the fight because he had a big investment in me, and didn't want to risk seeing that investment—and the Lakers' championship hopes—destroyed in a boxing ring.

Jack didn't have much hold over me, though. When I came to the Lakers, I'd signed a three-year contract with a two-year option. The three years were up, and I hadn't picked up the option yet.

243

the sale, licensing and exploitation of such rights. Proceeds from merchandising rights shall include all items relating specifically to the Bout sold by PROMOTER or by PROMOTER's licensees other than programs and food and beverage items sold at the Astrodome. It is expressly understood and agreed that the expenses to be deducted by the PROMOTER in determining net ancillary proceeds shall be limited to One Hundred Twenty-five Thousand Dollars ($125,000.00), plus the expenses incurred in exploiting the merchandising rights to the Bout, if the gross proceeds derived from the sale or exploitation of the merchandising rights to the Bout exceed the expenses incurred thereby. PROMOTER agrees to use its best efforts to derive the maximum proceeds from the live gate and the sale, license and/or exploitation of ancillary rights to the Bout and Pre-Bout events. ALI and CHAMBERLAIN and/or the duly authorized representatives of each shall have the absolute right to inspect (during business hours) all of PROMOTER's books and records pertaining to the proceeds derived and the expenses incurred by PROMOTER in connection with the Bout, as well as any and all contracts, purchase orders and such other documents pertaining to the Bout, and PROMOTER shall keep and maintain separate records relating to the receipt of all such proceeds and the expenditure of all items of expense relating thereto.

4. PROMOTER agrees that the aggregate amount to be paid to CHAMBERLAIN under Paragraph 3 of this Agreement shall not be less than Five Hundred Thousand Dollars ($500,000.00). To secure the payment of the minimum Five Hundred Thousand Dollars ($500,000.00) guarantee to CHAMBERLAIN, PROMOTER agrees that it will deposit in escrow the said sum of Five Hundred Thousand Dollars ($500,000.00) on or before April 1, 1971. Said escrow deposit shall be made with a bank located in California to be

A page from my fight contract.

I told my attorney, Sy Goldberg, to make the fight.

Ali's people announced a big press conference, and on April 22 —just four days after the Lakers' final playoff game in Milwaukee —Sy and I flew to Houston for the formal signing ceremony and public announcement at the Astrodome. My accountant, Alan Levitt, flew in from Philadelphia to join us. The fight was going to be July 26 in the Astrodome.

But when we walked into the board room they had set aside for the signing, we saw that the contracts did not guarantee me $500,000 after taxes. The guarantee was the same as on the first contract—a flat $500,000 (taxable) for me and $1 million for Muhammad. In my tax bracket at that time, I would've had to give most of that to the government. Alan and Sy and I got mad. Muhammad's people said we must have "misunderstood" their offer; they said they had never mentioned an after-tax guarantee.

Meanwhile, hundreds of newsmen and photographers and TV people were milling around the Astrodome, waiting for the big announcement. Muhammad was out there with them, and every time he came in to our meeting room to see what was holding things up, his advisors told him not to worry, and hustled him back outside. Finally, he demanded to know what was going on. I told him. He offered to split his share of the guarantee with me, so we'd each get $750,000. His advisors kept shouting, "No, no," but he just told me, "Look, Wilt, I want this fight. It's my money and my career. Don't pay any attention to them."

Alan and Sy and I stepped into a nearby men's room to consider Muhammad's offer. We knew that $750,000 before taxes wasn't nearly as much as $500,0000 after taxes, but it was still a helluva lot of money for one 12-round fight—36 minutes of work, at the most. With all the ancillary rights, I could probably clear $1 million or so.

On principle, though, we were all pissed off at the way Ali's people had reneged on their original offer; we were afraid there might be some more problems like that before the fight actually came off. Alan, who probably knows me better than any man alive, had never been that keen on my fighting Ali anyway, and he used the occasion of their reneging as a lever to talk me out of the fight altogether.

"Look, Wilt," he said, "you've spent your whole life building

245

up a certain image of yourself. Now you could throw it all away in one night. Ali could make an absolute fool out of you in the ring."

I started to interrupt, but Alan kept talking.

"Sure, sure, I know you might win. You're the strongest and most determined guy I've ever known. You'll go into the fight in great shape, and you might land a lucky punch and knock him out. But you might not. He's been a fighter for almost as long as you've been a basketball player. Fighting is his game, not yours. How do you think he would fare against you in basketball if he trained for six months and never played the game before? You'd make him look like a big clown. And that's just what he might do to you in the ring. Is that what you've worked so hard for all these years—to be embarrassed and humiliated and laughed at like some freak in a carnival sideshow?"

Alan had a good point. It was something I'd thought about myself every time someone wanted me to fight Ali. I wasn't worried that he'd hurt me physically; I'd been pummeled enough in basketball to know I could take most anything. If he really started smashing me, I could always fall down if I thought I was in danger of being permanently injured. So that didn't bother me much. The thing Alan talked about—the possible humiliation—did bother me. I really thought I could beat Ali, but between the reneging of his advisors and what Alan said, I decided not to go through with it.

On the way back from the men's room to the meeting room, Alan and Sy and I joked about having just "flushed a million bucks down the toilet."

When I told Ali's people my decision, they didn't think it was so funny. But Muhammad quieted them down in a hurry. He'd been a gentleman throughout the negotiations, and he remained that way.

"Wilt's my friend," he said. "If he doesn't want to fight, I don't want to fight."

That ended it. There was no signed contract, no press conference, no fight.

Alan and Sy and I left the Astrodome for the airport, where we were ushered into a VIP lounge to await our flights—Sy back to Los Angeles, Alan and me to Philadelphia. And who shows up in the lounge? Muhammad. And where is he going? Philadelphia.

He lives in Cherry Hill, New Jersey, and he was going home. My mother lives in Maple Shade, New Jersey, and I was going to visit her.

The two towns are about five miles apart.

Muhammad and I joked and kidded each other throughout our hour-long wait—and the entire flight back—and we've remained pretty good friends (and mutual admirers) to this day. But every once in a while, I get a little twinge of regret that our fight never came off. Fighting Muhammad and competing in the Olympic decathlon are probably the two things I'll always wish I'd done. I think I could have done a helluva good job at both of them—maybe even won them.

But I guess I'll never know.

14

AFTER THE ALI FIGHT FELL through, Jack Kent Cooke and I fenced through the spring and early summer over how much money he was going to pay me for the next season. Then, on August 15, Jack got help from an unexpected source; President Nixon ordered the wage-price freeze. Jack couldn't give me more money then, even if he wanted to—which he most clearly did not. I thought it was ironic that Jack, a dedicated Democrat, was able to take advantage of me by using the decision of a Republican President I had helped elect. But there wasn't much I could do about it; I picked up my option for the 1971–72 season—at the same salary I'd been paid for each of the three previous years.

You would think that worrying about Jack Kent Cooke, Richard Nixon, and Muhammad Ali would be enough to keep any athlete busy for one off-season. Not me. I also went to Europe for a few weeks that summer—and supervised the design and construction of my new house.

The decision to build a house—or even just to own one—was probably the single most uncharacteristic act of my entire life.

I've always been nomadic by nature—a gypsy—and from the time I'd left home to go to college in 1955 until that summer of 1971, I'd never lived in one place for longer than two years. For me to build a $1 million house that would probably take almost two years to complete was quite a gamble. I might want to move out before I could even move in.

I thought about that a lot before I made my decision to go ahead with the house. Finally, I just decided I loved Los Angeles, and would always want to come back here, even if I traveled extensively and lived elsewhere temporarily on occasion.

Actually, I had almost built a house six or seven years earlier, in San Francisco. I bought three-fourths of an acre there for $65,000, but I got traded to Philadelphia before I could get the house started.

When I first came to the Lakers, I tried again. I found a great old house in Trousdale Estates, the most exclusive section of Beverly Hills. It was owned by some movie tycoon who was about to split up with his wife, and it had high, vaulted ceilings and a big movie theatre in the living room, and it was just a really fine house. They were asking $465,000 for it, and no one was interested in buying. I finally negotiated them down to about half that price.

I gave them a deposit and was ready to move in.

The next thing I knew, a television crew was traipsing through the place—without my permission—to do a show about "Wilt Chamberlain's house."

I demanded my deposit back, and forgot about the house.

A couple of years later, when I started looking for land to build on in Los Angeles, I looked primarily along the beach. But most beachfront property is so valuable that it's been divided into small lots, and the streets are congested. That meant I'd have neither the spaciousness nor the privacy I wanted; there would always be nosy sightseers gawking at me and watching my every move. I was renting a home in Trousdale then—a place owned by Billy Rose's sister, Polly—and with neighbors like Elvis Presley, Groucho Marx, and Danny Thomas, I already knew what that was like. People carrying cameras and maps and autograph books were always riding up and down our street and banging on doors and peering in through windows. I wanted no part of that in my house.

If I wanted to live at the beach, then, it seemed the only solu-

249

tion was to live in one of the fashionable oceanside colonies up the coast a bit, where the lots are big enough to provide some protection and insulation. I found a great piece of land in one of those colonies—right behind Governor Ronald Reagan's mansion in Pacific Palisades, about 20 miles northwest of downtown Los Angeles. Unfortunately, the owners wanted $500,000 just for the raw land! There was no way I could afford that—not with what I knew it would cost to build the kind of house I wanted.

Then I found the land I live on now—a beautiful three-acre site in Bel Air, in the Santa Monica Mountains, about seven miles inland from the ocean and 12 or 13 miles from downtown.

I'm only a mile or so off the freeway, so I can drive to the beach in ten or fifteen minutes—and I don't have the congestion and sightseers and high prices I'd have if I lived right on the ocean.

Sightseers occasionally wander by, and try to look in my windows, but I have a large iron fence surrounding my property, and I have closed-circuit TV trained on the electronically controlled front gate to discourage them from trespassing.

My house sits on a peak, with a panoramic, 360-degree view of the entire metropolitan area. On one side, I can see from downtown to the ocean (a magnificent sight on a clear day); on the other side, I can see the sprawling suburbs of the San Fernando Valley (a gorgeous, glittering sight on almost any night).

Because I love the view—and the feeling of freedom that the outdoors gives me—my house is almost completely encased in sliding glass doors. With the glass and the high ceilings—a minimum of nine feet and a maximum of twenty—you almost feel like you're outdoors in every room of the house. You can feel the sun and see the moon and the stars and the surrounding hillside and the city below. I've even brought the outdoors indoors. The swimming pool that curls around the corner of my house flows under one end of the living room, and you can actually step right into it through a good-sized hole I had cut in the living room floor.

Probably the single most distinctive feature of my house is that there are no squares or rectangles or right angles of any kind in its design. We borrowed an idea from Frank Lloyd Wright and made the house a series of interlocking equilateral triangles. The rooms, the sun deck, the fireplace, the cantilevered balcony, the breakfast table, the sunken marble bathtub in my bedroom—they're all equilateral triangles; even the front door, a 14-foot-high wedge of wood, is an equilateral triangle.

I think the triangle concept lends an added dimension, a reinforced sense of freedom to the house—you don't feel like you're moving around in a series of prefabricated boxes. I also like the basic uniqueness of the triangle concept. If I'm spending a fortune to build a home, I want it to be truly different, not just some extra-fancy tract house. But I didn't want my home to be different just for the sake of being different. I tend to be a very private person, not an exhibitionist, and I want to live in my house, not display it.

When my architect and my designers and I started planning the house, I told them I had one basic thought I wanted them to keep in mind throughout—this was to be a house in which I could feel comfortable, not cramped, but where my smaller friends could also feel comfortable, not dwarfed.

In my travels abroad, particularly in Europe, I'd always been impressed by how warm and open the people were, and by how eagerly they invited even the most casual friends into their homes for a meal or a drink or a visit. Los Angeles was the only big city in America where I'd found that same quality, and I wanted my house to encourage friends to come see me, again and again; I wanted them to be as relaxed in the house as I would be. I wanted to entertain there, as well as live there.

People who've never been to my home automatically seem to assume that it's built on some gargantuan scale. Nothing could be further from the truth. The house *is* large—8,300 square feet, built with five freightcar-loads of redwood (enough for 17 normal houses) and 200 tons of Bouquet Canyon stone. It has 16 rooms and six bathrooms. But you can't be in more than one room at a time, so that really doesn't mean much. What's important is that none of the rooms in the public portion of the house—the dining room, the living room, the pool room, the firepit—is particularly large. In fact, they're all probably slightly smaller than average. The guest bedrooms aren't especially large either. I want people to be able to sit in twos or threes anywhere in the house, and be able to feel they're in a small, intimate

251

setting, not lost in some cavernous reception hall. To accentuate that feeling, the colors in the house are almost exclusively warm earth colors—browns and beiges, in all their various shades—and I've used rich, lustrous woods throughout, rather than the more contemporary metal and glass and black plastic.

Even the furniture in the house is designed with the concept of warmth in mind. All the pieces are upholstered in earth colors, and—except for one oversize chair, tucked in a corner of the firepit area for me—all are normal size. As I told my designers, "Willie Shoemaker is a good friend of mine, and I want him to be able to come here for dinner without feeling like he's Jack visiting the giant in the beanstalk."

I've had to adapt to normal sizes all my life; I'm used to it by now. It's easier for me to continue doing that than to expect my friends to suddenly adapt to a giant's world—sitting on chairs where their feet don't touch the ground, balancing on their tiptoes to reach cupboards, standing in front of toilets that are so high they have to piss uphill.

There are a lot of other subtle things we've done with the house to make guests feel comfortable. There are seven different mini-levels in the central core of the house, for example, each separated by a small step or two or three or four. I like the feel of that—the feel of going from one place to another, not just walking around in one big room. But the different levels have a practical application, too; if you and I are standing in the house, talking, we can be right next to each other, with you a step or two above me, and we'll be eyeball-to-eyeball, instead of eyeball-to-navel.

About the only thing I've done in the public area of the house that might indicate a pretty tall guy lives there is use high door-ways—and in most places, no doorways at all. The firepit, the pool room, the living room, and the dining room are really just one large open area, but the use of different levels—and the strategic placement of the 55-foot-high stone fireplace itself—give the effect of several different, smaller rooms.

The only room in the house designed specifically to scale for me is the master bedroom. The house itself is, in effect, a two-story pyramid—another triangle—and my bedroom occupies most of the top floor. The room is 1,000 square feet—all enclosed in

252

glass—with a 14-foot ceiling. My bed is eight feet by nine feet, and my walk-in closet is eight feet by twenty feet. I have six shower heads in my private shower, three arranged vertically on each of two walls—because I was tired of showering in gyms where the shower spray only hit me in the butt.

A few magazine stories have referred to my bedroom as a "sybaritic paradise," and I guess they're right. As much as I enjoy entertaining groups of people in the public area of the house, I must admit that my favorite form of entertainment is still me and a pretty girl and a big bed—and I can think of no better, more romantic place for that entertainment than my own bedroom. The bed sits on a raised, 13 foot by 25 foot platform, beneath a triangular mirrored ceiling, 13 feet long on each leg. I can lean back in bed and flick a switch, and the mirrored ceiling slides silently back, so that all you see is the sky above. I can hit another set of switches and close all the drapes; no matter how bright it is outside, the room can be pitch black.

Some of my house guests have told me they and their dates have had as much fun in the downstairs playroom—or "purple room" or "X-rated room"—as I've had in my upstairs bedroom. You have to take your shoes off before you walk into the playroom because, instead of wall-to-wall carpeting, it has wall-to-wall upholstered foam sectionals—all wedge shaped, surrounding a circular water bed, inside fully mirrored walls. (Somehow I suspect that a few of my guests may have taken off a little more than their shoes in that room on occasion.)

With the help and guidance of some brilliant, imaginative designers and interior architects—namely Charles Gibilterra and his bosses, Korky Korkowski and Gene Adcock of KS Wilshire Inc.—I've tried to be just as selective and discriminating in putting the finishing touches on my house as we were in planning its overall structure and design. The playroom is one example of that. The artworks hung and displayed throughout the house are another. But my favorite little touch is the Arctic wolves' nose fur we used for my bedspread and to cover the furniture and floor in the firepit area. I bought an entire year's bounty of the fur —17,000 wolves—and, stitched together, they are absolutely beautiful.

253

I bought the fur six or eight years ago, and had it kept in cold storage until I could use it. But by then, everyone was worried about the threat to endangered species and our other natural resources, and the ecologists really jumped on me. I'm deeply concerned about our environment, too, and I told them I hadn't ordered the wolves killed; I just bought the fur after they were already dead. The wolves would have been killed, with or without me; a certain number have to be killed every year to preserve the ecological balance of the Arctic.

If I was surprised by the ecologists' angry reaction to my use of the wolf fur, I was doubly surprised by the general public's fascination with my house itself. Everywhere I went, people asked me about it. "That must be a fantastic house" replaced "Why do you have so much trouble with free throws?" as the opening comment of most strangers I met. Interest ran so high that I did a small picture booklet on the house, with all the proceeds going to charity.

I'm very proud of my home—and very attached to it. In many ways, my house *is* me—a reflection of all my hopes and dreams and aspirations and accomplishments. But the house was very expensive, and a lot of people seem worried that I'll be paying off some astronomical mortgage for the rest of my life. Chick Hearn, the Laker broadcaster, even held up a picture of some wrinkled, bearded old Ubangi on television one day and said something like, "This is what Wilt's going to look like when he finishes paying off his house." Well, I've got news for Chick and a few other people—I might pay off my mortgage before they pay off theirs. I paid 90 percent cash for my house.

Probably the two questions I get asked the most about my house are "Aren't you lonely in that big place all by yourself?" and "Why would you build a house like that when you're not even married?"

In a way, I guess, the two questions are almost the same—and they're both stupid. In the first place, why would I be any more lonely in a big house than a small house? You can only be in one room at a time; what difference does it make if there are three other rooms or 23 other rooms in the house? Besides, you don't have to be alone to be lonely. Loneliness is a state of mind, not a matter of numbers. I've been far lonelier, at times, in a huge crowd than I've ever been by myself—and I'll bet most people have had the same experience.

When I'm asked why a bachelor like me would build a house like mine, I tend to respond with a speech, rather than an answer. I will never understand why people think married men have some special stability and respectability and obligation that single men can't have. A single man might as well give up any hope of getting to the top—or even near the top—in business or politics in our society; why, do you know we've had only one bachelor among our 37 Presidents—and that was James Buchanan, who was inaugurated 116 years ago! I want a house—a home—for myself and to share with my friends. Why do I need a wife and children to share it, too?

"Will you ever get married and have kids?" people ask me. I'm not sure. But I do know I'll never father my own children; if I want children, I'll adopt them. As I've already said, I think the overpopulation problem is a big one, and I'm not about to contribute to it. That would be hypocritical. There are plenty of unwanted little kids in this world who could use a good home, and since I have no egotistical, masculine compulsion to produce a lot of little Wilties, I'd like to help them find one.

As for marriage, well, I've always thought that weddings—like funerals—are more for the friends and families of the principals than for the principals themselves. None of the Chamberlain boys has exactly rushed into marriage. Oliver didn't get married until he was 28, and Wilbert—who's 40—isn't married yet. I may never have a wife either, in the legal and traditional sense. I can see no reason, in 1973, for the state to have anything to say about the status of two adults who choose to live together. If a man and woman—or two men or two women, for that matter—want to commemorate the beginning of their formal life together with a religious ceremony of some sort, that's entirely up to them. But I don't think the state should be in the business of selling marriage licenses. That's just none of their damn business. If this were the old days, when laws—and custom—prevented women from working, I could understand the need for the state to provide them with some measure of security and protection. But almost any woman who wants to work today can earn a livable wage. It may not always be as much as a man would be paid for the same job—which is absolutely wrong—but it's certainly enough, in most instances, to eliminate the need for the state to use marriage as a vehicle for the protection of women.

My strong feeling about this principle isn't the only reason I've never gotten married—or never even entered into a long-term common-law relationship with a woman. The most obvious reason is that I haven't found the right girl yet—and I may not know the right girl, even if I do find her.

I tend to be very fickle. I get tired of a girl fairly quickly, and when I do, I "fire" her. Who knows—I may already have fired one or two girls who would have made ideal wives for me if I'd kept them around long enough to really get to know them.

I have had girls living with me occasionally, but I think the longest relationship like that I've ever had was three weeks, back in 1967 or '68, with an Australian girl. Maybe I'm just afraid to commit myself fully to another person; maybe I'm afraid that in a long-term relationship I'd be too vulnerable, my faults and shortcomings too evident. But I think the biggest reason I'm not married, legally or otherwise, is that I'm a gambler—and smart gamblers don't buck high house odds.

In my 14 years in the NBA, I've had almost 100 different teammates. I've probably also had pretty good relationships with almost that many players on other teams. Of all those players, there was only one—Paul Arizin—who really seemed content with his marriage, and didn't use our road trips to find new ways of cheating on his wife all the time. I'm sure a few of the other guys have been happy, faithful husbands, too—but not many of them, judging by what I've seen. I'm not just talking about the guys with playboy reputations either; some of the most active philanderers in the NBA are players who have wholesome, all-American-boy reputations.

For all my image as a swinger—and my personal disdain for the institution of marriage—I take a dim view of infidelity. To my knowledge, I have never gone to bed with another man's wife —and I never will. I think that once a person makes a commitment of love to another person—whether in legal marriage or not—that commitment should be fulfilled.

I'm not sure I could keep such a commitment myself; that's why I haven't made one. I've never actually told a girl, "I love you." I guess I like variety and change too much. I think there are too many wonderful, beautiful women in this world to commit myself to just one. Maybe, as I grow older, I'll change. But in pro basketball, the separations from your loved ones can be too frequent—and the temptations on the road too overwhelming—for a man of my appetite to try to combine basketball and a one-man, one-woman relationship.

Because I'm not married, I've been the subject of some interesting rumors and speculation. One is that I refuse to socialize with my teammates. But that's not a deliberate decision, born of animosity, on my part or theirs. Most of my teammates, on every team I've played for, have been married. They tended to have their own interests and activities, with their families and other families. As a bachelor, I've always had my own circle of friends, with different interests and different activities. So we don't see much of each other socially.

Another rumor arising from my prolonged bachelorhood is that I'm gay. I've even had girls ask me about that—in bed, immediately after I've demonstrated that, whatever else I am, I am most indisputably heterosexual. I'm more amused than upset by that rumor. It's something almost any unmarried celebrity hears, sooner or later—particularly in Los Angeles, where so many gays make no effort to conceal their sexual preferences (nor should they; so long as they don't inflict those preferences on others, it's nobody else's business).

In my case, I can see an additional reason for the homosexual rumors. Unlike most professional athletes, I don't go around giving girls free tickets to come watch me play. Except for a couple of instances during my first season in Europe with the Globies, I've never invited a girl to a basketball game. I've always considered myself much more than a basketball player, and I'd rather have her appreciate my other skills in a more appropriate setting—ordering dinner in a good restaurant, talking on a sunlit beach, driving in a fine car, making love in a warm bed.

Many of my teammates love to give free tickets to their girl friends and wives. At the Forum, in Los Angeles, you can even see the girl friends strolling back and forth along the sideline before each game, preening for the guys. That lets the guys' teammates know what big studs they are—and the game itself lets the girls see what hotshots the players are. After the game, most players leave the arena with their wives or girl friends. Not me. I'm usually by myself or with my brother Oliver, or my brother-in-law Elzie, or any one of several close male friends. People hanging around outside, waiting for autographs, see that—game after game, year after year—and sooner or later, the rumor mill swings into operation:

"Wilt never has a girl with him; he must be gay."

But I often have dates with girls after games; I just don't feel compelled to parade them before the sporting public. I'd rather pick the girl up later, at her place, or have her meet me at my house or—when I'm on the road—in my hotel room.

Generally, when I check into a hotel on the road, there are already two or three messages waiting for me from different girls I've met there on previous trips, in the airport or the hotel or a restaurant or some other place.

One time in Boston, this last February, three girls called me in my hotel room within 20 minutes after I got back from the game. I invited one of them over at midnight and the other two at 2 A.M. All four of us wound up frolicking in the sack by the time I ordered breakfast at 8 A.M. Then, the very next afternoon—in Milwaukee—a girl called me within five minutes after I checked in to the Pfister Hotel. She wanted to "visit" me during her lunch hour.

It was a very nice visit . . . even if I was a bit weary that night when the Bucks blew us off the court by 21 points.

Those incidents aren't atypical; they happen all the time. I'm always striking up conversations with strange girls, and if I like what I see and hear, I ask for her telephone number. I must have at least 10,000 numbers at home, scribbled on the backs of envelopes, newspaper articles, cocktail napkins, matchbook covers, and ticket stubs—and stuffed into paper sacks and small suitcases in my closet.

Every few months or so, I'll sort through them, and throw away the ones I don't remember or haven't talked to or seen for quite a while. Sometimes, on a quiet night, I'll dig out a fistful of numbers, and start calling them—all over the country—just to see how the girls are doing. (One of my favorite exercises with a girl I don't know too well is to call her and ask her—rather

258

casually, in the normal course of conversation—if she's good in bed. Almost invariably, the girl will say she doesn't know. So I say, "You know if you're a good cook, don't you? Or if you sew well? Why don't you know if you're good in bed? Is it because no man has ever told you you're good? That must mean you're not very good, right?" By the time we're through talking, I know a lot of things about how the girl thinks and feels—things that have absolutely nothing to do with sex.)

My friends—especially my white friends—tell me they hear a lot of speculation over whether I date mostly white girls or black girls. That, I suppose, is because of the myth about the black man's lust for white women. Well, I date a lot of black women (and brown women and yellow women)—I always have—but I probably date more white women than black women . . . and for a very simple reason: I live in America, where there are more white women than black women available to date. I've never lived in a predominantly black neighborhood or moved in predominantly black circles. In fact, the first playmate I ever had—back when I was a kid on Salford Street in Philadelphia, before I had even the vaguest idea what sex was—was a little white girl who lived next door. Today, in Los Angeles, most of my neighbors are white, and most of the people I see—in business, on the beach, at parties—are white. That's not a conscious decision on my part; it's just that the way society is structured—and the way the black man has been discriminated against—most people who have the mobility and money and opportunity to frequent the places I frequent are white. So, I meet more white women than black women—and I date more white women than black women. When I'm in France, I date mostly French women. In Italy, I date mostly Italian women. In Spain, I date mostly Spanish women. I imagine if I went to Mars, I'd date mostly Martian women. I see no reason why I should be expected to go hunting for black women—in Los Angeles or New York or Rome or Paris or anywhere else—just because I happen to be black.

In fact, as much as I respect many of the cultural characteristics of the Japanese and Jewish, one of the things I *don't* like about either ethnic group is their clannishness in that regard. That's especially true of the Jews. I used to jump on Ike Richman and Dr. Stanley Lorber, my two Philadelphia friends, about how

259

positive I was that all their daughters would eventually marry "nice Jewish boys," even though both families were as free of racial prejudice as any people I've ever known.

Sure enough, that's exactly what happened.

Ike would never have countenanced the slightest hint of prejudice against me by anyone. But when he, in his fatherly way, introduced me to good-looking girls—or gave me the phone numbers of girls he'd met—they'd always turn out to be black.

"Ike," I asked him one day, "don't you ever meet any good-looking white girls?"

I had a similar beef a few years ago with the people who run "The Dating Game" television show. Chuck Barris, the producer, and Jim Lang, the emcee, were friends of mine, and they asked me to come on the show a few times. The way the show works, there are three guys (or girls) hidden behind a screen, answering questions that one girl (or guy) asks them. Then, based on the answers, the questioner picks one of the three to go out on a date with. Well, the first time I was on, both the other guys were black, and the girl was black. The second time, I was the only guy—and all three girls were black.

There was no third time.

This happened in 1968, if I remember correctly, and the rise of "black consciousness" since then has made for some interesting changes in black attitudes toward interracial dating—as well as in white television's attitude.

It used to be that any black man who dated a white girl was looked up to by other blacks; the white girl was a tangible symbol that he'd made it and that he could thumb his nose at Whitey, and all blacks shared, vicariously, in his triumph. Now, it's just the opposite. Many blacks say you should date black girls exclusively, to prove that you're proud of being black. So, where I used to get a lot of phone calls from strange white girls who would go out of their way to let me know they were white, I now get a lot of calls from strange black girls who go out of their way to let me know they're "soul sisters."

But I just don't give a shit what color a girl's skin is. I like girls who are bright, pretty, well read, widely traveled, interested in good food and good times—and I don't care if they're white, black, red, yellow, or green. In fact, of all the superficial physical characteristics, I'm probably far more interested in height than color; I usually prefer girls about 5 foot 4 to 5 foot 6 because I've generally found that extremely tall girls just don't seem feminine enough for me. I also tend to appreciate nice legs and a nice ass more than big breasts, although I suspect that may be because I'm a pragmatist at heart, and I can't see where big breasts have any function as useful as walking or sitting.

I will admit that I like beautiful women more than ugly women or average-looking women. Looks alone is not enough, of course. It's not even the most important consideration. But I've learned over the years that it's just as easy to find a beautiful girl who has all the emotional and intellectual characteristics I like as it is to find an ugly girl who has them. People tell me I have pretty good taste in beauty; I've been a judge for several beauty contests, and I invariably pick all the winners.

In my own personal judging, I have a 20-point scale for rating a woman's looks. It's such a tough scale that I've never seen a true 20. But I have seen a few 19s—Raquel Welch and Jennifer O'Neill being perhaps the best known of them.

At one time, right after I moved to Los Angeles, I was really into the glamour-girl scene. I got to know Kim Hunter and Gina Lollobrigida and a lot of other Hollywood types—starlets and models and Playboy bunnies. But I soon realized that a girl didn't have to be Hollywood to be desirable. I think I'm over that hangup now, and I don't care what my girls do for a living. They can wash dishes or drive trucks or pump gas for all I care—so long as we're compatible.

I would imagine that compatibility is another reason I tend to date more white girls than black girls; just as the prejudicial nature of white society has created conditions in which I am more likely to meet white girls than black girls, so those same prejudices have created conditions in which I am more likely to share common interests and aptitudes with white girls than black girls. For a black man, I've been very fortunate. I have a good education and I've traveled extensively, and I've become a knowledgeable businessman; I've learned to appreciate good food and good art —the good life. Most blacks—women even more than men—

261

haven't been that lucky. They don't have my experience and my sophistication. So, understandably, many of them are not good companions—or lovers—for me.

Black women also tend to have more sexual hangups than white women do—and I don't like any sexual hangups.

Because so many black families have been forced to live in crowded hovels, with mother and father and four little kids all sleeping in the same small room, sex has often been something best done as quickly and quietly as possible—and, preferably, in the dark. As a result, many black girls grow up thinking of sex as furtive and dirty, and they can't respond as fully as they should to a man. Many of them even insist on making love quickly—and in the dark—as their mothers or grandmothers had to do. But I save my speed for the highway and the basketball court; I like to take my time in the bedroom—and I like to see what I'm doing and who I'm doing it with.

Some white girls also have sex hangups, of course—the product of our Victorian past and hypocritical present—but they don't seem as prevalent as the black hangups. Hell, just this past season, I met a girl on a plane, and ten minutes after we started talking, she buried her head in my lap and gave a performance worthy of "Deep Throat." Fortunately, she borrowed a blanket from the stewardess before she got too involved, so we had some privacy. (We thought we got away with it Scot-free, but while the girl was back in the rest room, another young lady, who had been sitting across the aisle, came over and discreetly informed me that she had seen everything—and would like to get together with me some time under more favorable circumstances. We have since become rather good friends.)

I guess I'm something of a sex symbol to a lot of girls—and I can't say I object, as ridiculous as I sometimes find their behavior. *Women's Wear Daily* even selected me as one of the sexiest athletes in the world this year. I was also named "Heterosexual of the Year" by some outfit called "Orgasm Engineers Unlimited, Home of the Great Penetrator and Multiple Orgasms." I still haven't decided if that's a legitimate organization or not, but on their letterhead, they listed officers with such impressive-sounding corporate titles as "orgasm analyst," "phallus engineer" and "copu-

262

lation counselor"—as well as "president," "spiritual consultant" . . . and "pimp."

By winning their coveted award, they said, I was joining such "distinguished heterosexuals" (and previous award winners) as "John the Baptist, Herman Goering, Billy Shoemaker, Robin Hood, Karl Marx, King Farouk, either Stanley or Livingstone, the Hunchback of Notre Dame and—perhaps the most indefatigable of them all—Rin Tin Tin."

I get boxes and boxes of fan mail every week, and—unlike most celebrities—I neither ignore it nor hire a secretary to read it and answer it. I open and read every single letter myself, and I try to answer all the reasonable ones, sooner or later. But I didn't know what the hell to say to "Orgasm Engineers Unlimited," and I don't know what to say to any of the hundreds of strange girls who write me every month, saying they'd like to go to bed with me.

They'll write me at the Laker office, and they'll send me their telephone numbers, and sometimes they'll send a nude photo of themselves—or a G-string or a piece of their panties.

I usually throw those kind of letters away before I'm half through reading them, but some of them are pretty wild. Here are a few brief excerpts from some of the better ones I received in just one month last spring:

• "I've never loved anyone so much as you in my life (except my little girl). I dream about you every night. . . . I'd leave my husband to be with you."

• "Hi, Wilt. When are you going to come out of hiding and take me to bed."

• "I admit a strong interest in seeing your new house, especially the sheets. Interested?"

• "I would really appreciate it if you would send me your oldest and rattiest jock strap."

• "Please move your mouth and your eyes and your hands up here toward mine as soon as you can because I am going crazy. I am waiting and I am moist."

Not all my female fan mail is quite so exotic. I get quite a few letters that just say, "If you're ever in my town, give me a call, and I'll show you the sights." I even got one plaintive note recently

263

from a young girl in Clarksburg, West Virginia, who said she was going to run away from home because her parents were picking on her—and she wanted to come live with me and "take care of your animals."

Why do I get such letters? I'd like to think that most girls are attracted to me because I have a good personality or good looks or a good mind or something else equally significant. But I know that some girls just want to ball me so they can brag to their friends about it. Athletes, like rock singers, have their groupies—girls who hang around all the time, hoping the star will condescend to speak to them or maybe even take them to bed. I've never liked the sports-groupie types, and as soon as I spot one, I head the other way. Probably the quickest way for me to get turned off a girl is to find out that she's already balled another basketball player. I sure as hell don't insist on virgins, but I won't take some other athlete's hand-me-down fuck.

I also realize that some girls want to get me into bed just to find out if the stories about a black man's sexual prowess are really true—or to find out if I'm big all over. (Just this last May, on the day of our final playoff game with the Knicks, I got a letter from a young lady who said she wanted to meet me because she had heard "exciting descriptions of your anatomical attributes." Her closing line was, "Baby, you have to show me.")

Do any of those things bother me? Yes and no. If I find out that a girl just wants to see me so she can tell her friends about it, I drop her in a hurry. The signs are pretty easy to spot. She'll make a point of having a few friends at her place when I come over—or she'll start asking me to "say hello" to her friends anytime I talk to her on the phone. But I'm not particularly bothered if a girl is first attracted to me because I'm famous or black or big or rich—just so long as that doesn't remain her primary reason for seeing me after we get to know each other better. Hell, most people aren't initially attracted to a member of the opposite sex by things that really count—things like brains and personality and warmth and kindness. The first thing that usually grabs you is good looks or a nice smile or a good sense of humor or maybe even a flashy car or a particular way of walking or talking. After you get to know each other, the other things come out—or else you stop seeing each other.

Of course, girls aren't the only ones who like to latch on to athletes and other celebrities to impress their friends. Guys do the same thing. I've had more than my share of "friends" who only wanted to exploit my name and leech off me. That's why I'm so suspicious now, and take so long to make new friends. I've just been burned too many times to be open and trusting with everyone I meet.

Back in Kansas, right after I signed my first contract with the Globies, a fairly prominent black couple I'd come to know during my three years there asked me to loan them a few thousand dollars. They both had good jobs, and I didn't see why they should need any money, but they were close friends, so I made the loan. They still haven't paid me back completely, and I'm sure that embarrasses them. So they never write me or call me or see me anymore. That means I've lost not only my money, but their friendship as well. The money I can afford, but I hate to lose good friends.

Another guy I became good friends with in Kansas is now a politician in Colorado. He called me in San Francisco one day in 1962 or '63 or so, and said he was in trouble and needed some money. I had $1,600 in my dresser drawer then, and I ran right down to Western Union and wired it to him.

I'm still waiting to get all that money back, too.

Probably the worst experience like that I ever had was in the summer of 1971, while I was building my house. My best friend then was another guy I'd met in Kansas—probably the most religious friend I've ever had. He went to church every Sunday, and we usually talked religion quite a bit together. I had gone to church regularly as a child, but as an adult, I'd pretty much lost my respect for organized religion; I can't take the hypocrisy and rigid structure and vast wealth of the church. I thought I might learn something from him, but it turned out that he didn't know any more about his religion than I did. It also turned out that he was using my name to borrow money from friends—and that several of my house guests had things stolen from their purses. After one burglary at my house, the police told me it was "an inside job."

One day, my friend just took off in a Cadillac he was supposed to be buying from me on monthly installment payments.

Three weeks later, I got a call from a tire store. They said he'd tried to buy some tires there for the Cadillac—and bill them to me. When he didn't have the money to pay for the tires, they just kept the car.

After 16 years of friendship, that's the last I ever saw or heard of my "friend."

15

MY MIDSUMMER RUMINA-
tions about girls and friends and money and marriage and my
house and Muhammad Ali—and assorted other subjects—were
suddenly interrupted one morning when Tommy Hawkins, an
ex-teammate who had become a Los Angeles sportscaster, called
to tell me that Jack Kent Cooke had fired Joe Mullaney as the
Laker coach.

I was shocked—and disappointed.

Despite our occasional differences, I liked Joe, and I thought
he'd done a damn good job with the Lakers—particularly when
you considered the handicaps he was operating under. Joe had
come to the Lakers as a college coach, with no previous professional experience, and he'd inherited a dissension-ridden team,
saddled with a self-perpetuating loser's image that ate away at all
of us. He thought he was getting a team with three superstars.
But because of injuries, Jerry, Elgin, and I were in the starting
lineup together only 13 times in the almost 200 games the Lakers
played under Mullaney during his two years in Los Angeles. I
missed most of Joe's first season; Elgin missed a third of his first

267

season and almost all his second season; Jerry missed about 10 percent of his first season and the most important part of his second season. Still, Joe had managed to win more games than he lost both years, and he'd taken us to the playoffs twice—and within one game of the NBA championship once. He'd overcome most of the friction van Breda Kolff had left behind, and he'd planted the seeds for several new attitudes and techniques that wound up bearing fruit for his successor, Bill Sharman.

Not surprisingly, speculation on the reasons for Joe's dismissal centered almost immediately on yours truly. "Wilt got another coach fired," the sportswriters said. "No one can get along with the big guy." Some guys even said I'd given Cooke an ultimatum —"fire Mullaney or I quit."

That was pure, unadulterated bullshit. In the first place, no one—and I mean no one—gives ultimatums to Jack Kent Cooke. He's a strong, stubborn man who makes his own decisions. I not only didn't give him an ultimatum about Joe, I didn't even give him a suggestion. And he didn't ask me for any. Besides, as I've said, I liked and respected Joe, and I was looking forward to playing for him again. In fact, as soon as word of his dismissal got out, Joe called me, long-distance, and said he knew I'd probably be blamed by some people, but he wanted me to know he didn't blame me—and he'd miss me.

As sorry as I was to see Joe go, I must admit I was excited by the prospect of playing for Bill Sharman. I knew he was a good coach, and I was sure we could have a winning season under him. But not too many of the experts agreed with me; in the pre-season predictions, no one picked the Lakers to go anywhere. Jerry and Elgin and I were all old, by basketball standards—and all coming off major leg injuries. The rest of the team was an unknown commodity. Happy Hairston, who figured to start opposite Elgin at forward, was very underrated—a solid rebounder and a good man on the fast break—but he had a tendency to get into foul trouble, and he had a reputation for causing dissension by talking about his teammates behind their backs. Gail Goodrich, our other starting guard, had averaged 17.5 points a game for us the previous year, but he had a well-deserved reputation as a spoiled kid—a selfish gunner who dribbled too much and shot too much

268

and sulked when things didn't go his way. Jim McMillian had good potential, as a shooter and on defense, but he had only been in the league one year, and he didn't look like he'd ever be much of a rebounder. Some of the other guys figured to help in spots —particularly Flynn Robinson (a deadeye outside shot) and Keith Erickson (an erratic but versatile swing man whose hustle and quickness gave us a spark that often made up for his poor shots and wild passes). Overall, though, the experts just didn't think we were strong enough to pose much of a threat to the reigning powers in the league—defending champion Milwaukee and the polished, experienced New York Knicks.

Clearly, Bill Sharman had his work cut out for him. And he started just the way a good coach should start; he talked to his players—one at a time. He told each of us what he thought about us and how we fit into his plans and what he expected us to do, individually and as a team. Most important of all, he asked each of us for suggestions and ideas, and he told us he would always welcome anything we had to say about how the team should function.

When Bill and I had our first meeting, he told me a little about his theory of "memory muscles." Muscles, he said, are just like the mind; they perform best when they remember what they did—and how they did it—the last time. To implement his theory, he said, he always had his teams work out every day, even on the day of a game—an unheard-of practice in the NBA. On game days, he said, the practices would be short—20 or 30 minutes. We'd just run a little, do some calisthenics and take a few shots —just enough to make sure our muscles wouldn't "forget" what to do in the game that night.

Bill's theory sounded a little strange to me, but he had a phenomenal success record, and I was willing to give it a chance. I had only one concern—the game-day practices would usually be at 11 A.M., and I rarely get out of bed before then.

I've had trouble with insomnia ever since I was a kid. It probably started when I played basketball until 10 o'clock every night in junior high and came home all hot and sweaty and worked up; the harder I'd try to fall asleep—so I'd be alert in school the next day—the longer I stayed awake, tossing and turning.

269

In the NBA, the problem had become acute. I usually eat my pregame meal about 3:30 P.M. or so, to give me time to digest it before the game. Then, after the game, I'm really hungry. But by the time I get showered and dressed and back to my house or my hotel, it's close to midnight. By the time I finish eating, it's probably close to 2 A.M. I can't fall asleep on a full stomach, so I lie around and watch TV until I doze off at 4 or 5 o'clock in the morning. I used to eat much bigger post-game meals than I do now. I'd have the equivalent of three or four normal dinners, and going to sleep would really be a problem. I tend to spread my eating through the day more now, always nibbling on something. It's healthier to do that than to eat everything in one or two big meals. But I still have a decent-sized dinner after a game, and the habits of my earlier years have pretty much conditioned my sleep patterns, I guess.

To make Sharman's 11 A.M. practices, I'd have to get up about 9 or 9:30 A.M. That meant I'd be getting only four or five hours of sleep the night before every game. I said I wasn't very happy about that, and Sharman said he understood.

"Look, Wilt," he told me, "why don't we give my way a try anyway. If it doesn't work for you, we'll try something else. I know you've got a lot of experience, and you always stay in good shape, so you probably don't need the practice, like the other guys do. But I can't very well let you off. That wouldn't be a good way for a new coach to build team morale."

Bill had a point. I'd be willing to bet, though, that he said the same thing to Jerry and Elgin. Bill has a habit of telling you what he thinks you want to hear, whether it's completely true or not.

As it turned out, Bill's methods produced fantastic results. Whether his practice sessions were directly responsible, indirectly responsible, or purely coincidental, the Lakers had a great season —the longest winning streak in history, the best win-loss record in history, and their first NBA championship in history.

The season began in Hawaii, where we practiced and played a few exhibition games. Bill's practice sessions were smooth and logical and well coordinated, and he began right off by passing out notebooks and diagramming plays, and telling us he wouldn't

270

accept the stories that we were an old team that couldn't run.

"I believe in running, fast-break basketball," he told us. "That's the kind of basketball I played with the Celtics, and that's the kind of basketball I coach."

I've always liked fast-break basketball, too. It's what I'd played in high school, and I'd missed it ever since. The other Lakers were equally enthusiastic, and when the season began, it quickly became apparent that the 1971–72 Los Angeles Lakers were going to be something special. We won our first four games —by an average of 20 points a game—lost three of our next five, then didn't lose again for more than two months. From November 5 to January 9, we won 33 consecutive games. And we did it without Elgin Baylor.

On November 4—after a conference with Bill Sharman— Elgin announced his retirement. He was 37, his knees were shot, and Bill didn't feel we could afford the luxury of starting Elgin every night. Bill knew Elgin would be embarrassed as a bench-warmer, so he suggested Elgin retire and make way for Jim McMillian. When Elgin agreed, Jim stepped into the lineup, and we were on our way.

The night of the game that began our winning streak, the coach asked Jerry and me if we would like to be co-captains now that Elgin was gone. Jerry said he felt he could be more valuable to the team if he could concentrate on playing, not leading. I'd been captain in Philadelphia, and I'd liked the responsibility, so I accepted the Laker captaincy.

Five games into our win streak, the whole season almost blew up. We were in Philadelphia, where we'd just beaten the 76ers by 40 points, and an old newspaper friend of mine, Jack Kiser, wanted to know what I thought of Sharman. I told him how much I respected Bill, and how he always seemed to be working, always looking for an edge, always thinking of how he could do something extra to help us win. He reminded me of the story about the college football coach who caught his star quarterback screwing his wife, and told the kid, "God damn you! If you didn't have one more year of eligibility left, I'd kick you the hell out of here."

But I also told Jack I wasn't very happy about Bill's day-of-game practices—and especially not at that particular time; we'd

271

just come from Chicago, where our practice had been in a dark, ice-cold armory, with no lights, and baskets about 100 yards apart. Still, when the coach offered us a day off after our victory in Philadelphia, I was the guy who said we should go ahead and practice. I didn't want to be responsible for disrupting our momentum.

Jack's paper ran his interview with me the way it should have been run—with the emphasis on the many good things I said about Sharman. But the *Los Angeles Herald-Examiner* picked the story up and twisted it out of context. They made it look like all I'd done was criticize Sharman. With another coach—a Butch van Breda Kolff or a Neil Johnston—that story might have ripped the team wide-open. But Bill had helped instill a togetherness and mutual respect in this Laker team that enabled everyone to shrug the story off for the irresponsible sensationalism it was. We continued winning. Seattle, Portland, Boston, Cleveland, Houston, Milwaukee . . . like tenpins they fell before us. Everyone was contributing. Jerry and Gail and Mac were all scoring. Happy and I were rebounding. Leroy Ellis and Flynn Robinson and Pat Riley were giving us good spot play off the bench. We were not just winning, we were winning big—by scores like 130-108, 139-115, 129-99, 132-106, 154-132. On December 12, we beat Atlanta to set an all-time record of 21 straight wins. Then someone checked the record books, and found that the all-time winning streak for *any* professional sports team was 26—by the 1916 New York baseball Giants. On December 22, we broke that record.

It was almost Christmas-time by then, and the players began speculating about what kind of super gifts Jack Kent Cooke might give us for our great record. A few days later, when he gave us each a pen-and-pencil set, we all started bitching and grumbling about what a cheapskate he was. Then I realized he'd given us more for Christmas than any of us had given him. I stopped bitching.

Actually, no one was really in the mood to bitch. Like my 76er team the year *we* won the championship, the Lakers were a loose, happy team. In the dressing room before and after every game, we'd rib each other unmercifully. If McMillian was in a shooting slump, we'd say, "Hey, Mac, when's your jump shot coming back from vacation?" If I missed eight or ten free throws

272

in a row, the guys would offer to bet me $50 I couldn't hit 50 percent for the rest of the year. (They won, but I won my money back this past season.) A lot of traditionalists had predicted that sports teams would lose their discipline and cohesion if they got too casual in their dress and behavior, but the Lakers certainly disproved that. I'm not sure I ever saw any of the guys in coats and ties; on a typical road trip, we'd all be wearing slacks and sweaters—and we'd hardly ever shave until game time. Pat Riley was the only guy who dressed in all the latest, mod clothes—and Keith Erickson more than made up for him; Keith always looks like a happy-go-lucky beach bum, no matter what he wears. In fact, the whole team—and Keith in particular—are proof of what I have always said about the absurdity of requiring coats and ties or any other formal dress standards. The people who insist on these standards are just insecure; they don't have enough self-confidence to feel comfortable wearing whatever they like, so they make everyone wear the same thing.

Surprisingly, there weren't any close friendships on the Lakers. You might have expected Jerry and Gail to be close, for example —the two small, white, high-scoring guards who'd lived in Los Angeles a long time. Or maybe me and Mac—both black bachelors who had spent considerable time in New York. That wasn't the case, though. But neither were there any cliques or any real tensions on the team. Just victories. And the more we won, the more superstitious some of the guys became. Jerry refused to change his ratty old sneaks. Gail always made sure his last shot in warmup was a layup. Bill Sharman always switched his pens from his inside coat pocket to his shirt pocket just before the tip-off at each game. Fred Schaus, the general manager, always parked in the same spot before every game.

But neither voodoo nor victories go on forever.

On January 9, in a nationally televised game, Milwaukee beat us, 120-104, to end our 33-game win streak. We lost three of our next five games, then regained our momentum and won our next eight straight.

On March 11, I had a party to celebrate the completion of my house. A year earlier, when Jerry had had a housewarming

273

party, I had been the only member of the team he hadn't invited. Jerry never had given me a satisfactory explanation for that, and I thought about leaving him off my invitation list, too. But that would've been childish. I invited him, and he came, and so did everyone else on the team.

The party lasted all night. It didn't seem to hurt us, though. The next night, we destroyed Buffalo, 141-102, and we went on to win 15 of our last 17 games.

We broke every record in the book that year—most wins, most wins at home, most wins on the road, most wins in a row, most 100-point games, highest winning percentage; you name it, we broke it. Our overall record of 69 wins and 13 losses broke the all-time record of 68 and 13 set by my Philadelphia 76ers team in 1966–67, and—not surprisingly—everyone wanted me to compare the two teams. I tried to be diplomatic. I said the two teams had different styles and different personnel, and it was difficult to compare them. Comparisons between players and teams from different years can never be fair to either side; there are just too many variables and too many imponderables. The performance of the Laker team was more satisfying to me than the performance of the 76er team, simply because the 76ers were picked to win the championship, and the Lakers weren't picked to win anything. But if I had to say which team was better, I'd take the 76ers. For one thing, they had a better center—I was five years younger in 1967. The Laker guards—Jerry West and Gail Goodrich—were definitely better, as a pair, than any combination of the 76ers' Hal Greer, Wali Jones, and Larry Costello. But the 76er forwards—Billy Cunningham, Chet Walker, and Luke Jackson—were all far superior to either of the Laker forwards, Jim McMillian and Happy Hairston. And the 76ers had more depth than the Lakers.

Perhaps the most important thing to consider when comparing the two teams is the schedules they each faced. The NBA was much tougher in 1967 than it is now. There were only ten teams in the league then—not 17—and the only expansion team among the ten, Chicago, was strong enough to make the playoffs. By 1972, there were seven expansion teams in the league, and the talent had been so diluted, it was easy for the top teams—like the Lakers—to fatten their percentages against the patsies. Portland

274

won only 18 games all year. Buffalo won only 22. Cleveland won only 23. Some of the older, more established teams had been weakened by expansion, too. Detroit won only 26 games. Philadelphia and Cincinnati won only 30 each. That's six patsies in the NBA in 1972—as compared with only two, Baltimore and Detroit, in 1967. Everyone could beat everyone else in 1967; only Philadelphia and Boston had great records. Almost every other team in the league was right around the .500 mark. But by 1972, there were so many terrible teams in the NBA that any good team could run up a great record. The Lakers, Milwaukee, Chicago, Boston, Golden State, and New York *all* had fantastic records in 1972. (By last season, the polarization was even greater. The patsies—Philadelphia, Buffalo, Portland and Seattle—all won less than a third of their games. Cleveland and Houston didn't do much better. The great teams—Boston, Los Angeles, Milwaukee and New York—all won more than 70 percent; two other teams— Baltimore and Chicago—won more than 60 percent.) I'm not saying the 1971–72 Lakers weren't a great team; they were. But, all things considered, I don't think they were as great as the 76er team I played on in 1967.

The Lakers were magnificent in the playoffs, though. We crushed Chicago in four straight, then beat Milwaukee four out of six and New York four out of five. The Lakers—and I—had found a sure-fire way to avoid losing a seventh game; don't play one. In fact, that's the advice I gave my teammates when I called a team meeting before the sixth game with Milwaukee. "Let's win it now," I told them. "Let's not fuck with another seventh game."

If any of us had any doubts about 1972 being our year, they should have been dispelled in the *second* game against Milwaukee. We were ahead, 133-132, with just seconds left, when Wali Jones and Kareem Abdul-Jabbar pressured Jerry into losing the ball. It bounced toward backcourt. If it crossed the midcourt line, Milwaukee would automatically get possession for one last shot. Incredibly, the referee got in the way, and the ball hit him and bounded back toward Jerry.

I've always said that no team wins a championship without luck. I said it when my teams had bad luck and lost, and I say it when my teams have good luck and win. Injuries and bad calls and last-second shots had robbed me of at least a half-dozen NBA championships; in 1972, luck was on our side all the way. The bouncing ball in the Milwaukee series was only one indication of the grace that destiny seemed to have bestowed on us that year—just as she had on New York two years earlier. Except for Keith Erickson, for example, we did not have one serious injury all season. Gail and I played every game; Mac and Happy played all but two; even Jerry missed only five games. But Chicago had three starters—Bob Love, Chet Walker, and Tom Boerwinkle—injured when they played us in the playoffs. Milwaukee's playmaker, Oscar Robertson, was also hurt.

I'm not saying the Lakers wouldn't have won anyway, with all the other teams healthy. I'm almost positive we still would have won. We were clearly the best team. But anything can happen—and it helps when the breaks are going your way.

In the final round of the playoffs, against New York—as against Chicago and Milwaukee—they were going our way. The Knick series didn't start out very well for us, of course. New York hit 72 percent of its shots in the first half of the first game, and they blew us off the court, 114-92. Jerry Lucas alone hit 13 out of 21—mostly from about 18 miles out—and there wasn't a damn thing I could do about it . . . unless I got myself a shotgun. Bill Bradley was even hotter than Lucas. He hit 11 out of 12. But Willis Reed was hurting before the series started, and Dave DeBusschere injured his hip in the second game—like I said, the breaks were going our way—and the Knicks never really came close again, even though Jerry West had probably the worst playoff series of his life.

Jerry hadn't shot well against Chicago or Milwaukee, and his slump got even worse against New York. In the first game, he hit only three out of 15 shots. In the second game, he hit only six of 21. But the rest of the Lakers played well in the second game, and we won easily, 106-92. In the third game, with De-Busschere 0 for 6 in the first half—and on the bench in the second half—we breezed again, 107-96, despite another cold night by Jerry (he hit only 10 of 28).

The fourth game—in Madison Square Garden—was the most important in the series. We led, two games to one, and a victory would enable us to return home needing only one win in the last three games to take the championship. With two of those last three games scheduled for the Forum, in Los Angeles, one victory seemed a cinch—if we could win the fourth game in New York first.

I had been playing for some time with two very sore hands, and I was particularly worried about reinjuring the hands in that crucial fourth game. I had originally broken a bone in my right hand several years earlier; the fracture had never mended properly, and it kept re-separating, from time to time. The doctors had talked about putting it in a cast near the end of the regular season, but that would have kept me out of about ten games and might have disrupted the team's momentum, so I said I'd keep playing, without a cast. I also had a fracture in the knuckle that joins the middle finger to the left hand, a souvenir of a rebound or a slam-dunk or some other play where I banged the hand on the rim or the backboard. But it was the right hand that bothered me the most; it hurt like a son-of-a-bitch every time I caught the ball or even brushed the hand against someone. So what happened in the fourth game against New York? Late in the second quarter, I went high to block a shot, and when I stretched to get the rebound, Happy Hairston came up under me and I fell on him and hit the floor hard—on my head and my right hand.

I was a little dizzy for the rest of the game, and the pain in my hand was really excruciating, but—as if I didn't have enough trouble—I picked up my fifth foul late in the fourth quarter. I've never fouled out of an NBA game, of course, and I've been accused, on occasion, of loafing—playing with my hands in my pockets—when I get into foul trouble; I'd rather preserve my record of never having fouled out than win the game, my critics say.

Well, as anyone who knows anything about basketball can tell you, the single most risky maneuver for a man in foul trouble to make is to block a shot—and I must have blocked at least five shots in the last 10 minutes of that game, despite my five fouls and two broken, swollen hands. I hit two clutch free throws —free throws! can you believe that?—in the final minute or so to put us ahead, 99-98, but Lucas hit one himself to tie the score. West was still ice cold—only nine for 25 in the game and 0 for 7

277

in the second half—but he popped in a 22-footer with 11 seconds to go and we were ahead again, 101-99. Then Walt Frazier tied the game with a tip-in at the buzzer. Overtime! And I still had those five fouls and two sore hands. Fortunately, Jim McMillian eluded Bill Bradley for three baskets, and we got the jump on the Knicks in a hurry. When the overtime was over, we'd won, 116-111, and we were going back to Los Angeles, ahead three games to one.

The doctors examined my right hand, and their first diagnosis was that it was just a bad sprain. That's all we ever told the press. But it was broken, and Dr. Robert Kerlan, our team physician, said he didn't see how I could possibly play the fifth game, two nights later, Sunday night. He thought I was probably through for the rest of the playoffs. No way, man. We had the Knicks on the run, and I wasn't about to let them get away. Besides, I knew what everyone would say if I didn't play—even if the doctor issued a sworn statement that I had *two* broken hands, a fractured skull, a bad heart and only one good eye. The Lakers had never won a championship with Elgin Baylor and Jerry West and all those great teams they had, but no one had ever called either of them a "loser." They were tragic heroes; people felt sorry for them. I was the "loser"—the scapegoat—and I knew damn well that I'd be blamed again if we lost this championship, even though I'd played well and Jerry should've been the goat for his rotten shooting.

As soon as we got home from New York after the fourth game, I started soaking my hand in the special whirlpool I had built at my new house. I must have soaked it for 30 hours, and every hour or so, I'd try to flex it, you know, close the hand, and at first, I couldn't do it at all and it hurt like a son-of-a-bitch. But I kept trying. I'd take my big Great Danes for a walk between treatments, to force myself to close the hand around their leash. I even tried to work a little with a basketball. No damn good.

Then, that night, Saturday night, I had a couple of friends from the Knicks' front office over. I was in the whirlpool when they came, but I got out and played host, and I really believed it when I told them I didn't see how I could play the next night. One of them, Frank Blauschild, watched me pour him some whiskey and just laughed. "Bullshit!" he said. "I've been watching you pour. You'll play." I honestly didn't think so, but the hand was getting gradually better. I could close it a little more, with a little less pain each time.

With Coach Sharman calling those crazy morning practices of his every damn day, I'd been sleeping less than ever all season, maybe just five or six hours a night. But that night, I only slept two, maybe three hours. I was hurting and thinking and worrying, and mostly I was taking turns packing my right hand in ice and soaking it in the whirlpool.

When I got to the Forum for the game Sunday night, I still didn't think I could play. Even after Dr. Kerlan gave me a shot of Celestone, I didn't think I'd make it. The Celestone was only to stop inflammation, not pain. Just in case I could play, we didn't want my hand so numb from painkillers that I couldn't feel the basketball. It didn't hurt as bad as it had, though, and I could move it some, so Dr. Kerlan made me a padded splint bandage, something like interior linemen in pro football use, only much bigger. My hands looked like a fighter's before he puts his boxing gloves on, and when one of my teammates, John Q. Trapp, first saw me with the contraptions on, he asked me if I was going to punch the bag. I think I was half-joking, half-growling when I told him, "No. I'm gonna punch your head." Then, all too soon, it was time to stop joking and talking and thinking. It was time to bite the bullet. Was I going to play that night or not?

Dr. Kerlan threw a basketball to me. I caught it—awkwardly, more trapping it between my two padded mitts than actually catching it. But I held it. I threw it back. Well, I didn't really throw it. I sort of pushed it. But it got there.

"I'll play," I said, nodding toward the coach. Everyone cheered, and it made me feel good inside. Now, I thought, if only my hands felt that good. . . .

Ironically, as it turned out, I couldn't have asked for a better start—or finish—to the game. We broke fast, jumping ahead 10-0 before the Knicks knew what hit them, and that took some of the pressure off me. I even jammed in a couple of slam-dunks early.

But, like anything worth waiting for, that championship game didn't come easy. The Knicks closed to 26-24 at the end of the

279

first quarter, and tied us at 53-all at halftime. We got the lead back in the third quarter, then blew them out with a 13-2 blast in the fourth quarter, and won going away, 114-100.

I suppose I could make like a martyr and tell you how much my hand hurt me every minute I was on the floor, but in all honesty, once the game was a minute or two old, I forgot all about the pain and the bandages and everything but winning that game. I played 47 of the 48 minutes, and even I was surprised later that night, in the locker room, when someone showed me the final statistics. I'd hit 10 of 14 shots from the field, got 24 points and 29 rebounds, and held my man, Jerry Lucas, to just 14 points and 9 rebounds. He hit only 5 out of 14 shots from the floor against me, and after the way he'd torn us apart in the first game of the series, a couple of my teammates told me I should always break both my hands before we play the Knicks.

I guess it wasn't really that funny, but I laughed and laughed. When you win, you laugh at anything and everything. And we had won—we, the Lakers, as a team, and me, Wilt Chamberlain, as an individual. I even got a new car for being the most valuable player in the series.

Obviously, I didn't beat New York all by myself. Far from it. We had set records as a team all year, and we won the championship as a team that night. Gail Goodrich, who had eaten Earl Monroe alive at both ends of the court in every game, got 25 points and held Monroe to a miserable 4 for 15 from the floor. McMillian got 20 points. Happy got 14 rebounds. Even Jerry—who again hit only 10 of 28 shots and wound up with a dismal 32 percent from the floor for the *entire* series—scored 23 points and had nine assists in the championship game.

But defense had been the key to our success all season—particularly in the playoffs, against Milwaukee and New York—and even though I was pleased to have won the MVP award in the playoffs, I have to admit I was a little surprised that I didn't also win it for the regular season. During all those years I was outscoring Bill Russell like crazy, he often won the MVP because people said defense was more important than scoring, and he was the defensive genius. But in 1972, I was the defensive genius and Kareem was the big scorer. In effect, I was Russell, and

280

Kareem was me. So who won the MVP? Kareem. Suddenly, defense wasn't all-important.

Bill Sharman got most of the credit for "transforming" me into a great defensive player—especially after I played so well against Kareem in the Western Division championships.

But it wasn't quite that simple.

I had experience and strength going for me against Kareem. I also had an intangible—the gut-it-out toughness I'd picked up playing schoolyard ball as a kid. Kareem had never done that, and it's hurt his game—as great as he is.

Joe Mullaney was probably more responsible for my success against Kareem than anyone, though. I'd always been a good defensive player—it just wasn't noticed until I stopped scoring—but it was Joe who first talked to me about really stressing defense. And it was Joe who showed me how to play Kareem and force him to take his shots out of position.

Joe was also responsible for about half the key personnel on our championship team. He was the coach who traded for Happy and Gail and Pat Riley, and he was the coach who drafted McMillian.

Unfortunately, he didn't have the opportunity to reap the fruits of his labors.

I'm not trying to downgrade Bill Sharman, though. There's no question about how good he is; he's the man who coached us to the championship. But I think the credit should be spread around some. Coaching, at the pro level, isn't really coaching in the true sense anyway. A big part of coaching is teaching fundamentals, and you just don't do that in the NBA. Sharman doesn't teach Jerry how to dribble, or tell Happy not to expose the ball to the defense for so long when he's driving for a layup. Sharman, like most NBA coaches, is really more a manager or a coordinator than a coach, and—like all managers, in any business—he benefits from the work of his predecessors.

In fact, the NBA Players Association had been arguing for some time that the coach really is a manager in yet another sense— a part of management—and the day after we won our championship, that concept wound up causing everyone in the Laker organization some discomfort.

The Players Association felt that management should pay the coach's share of all playoff money, rather than have him get an equal share out of the players' pool, as he always had in the past.

On the advice of Keith Erickson, our player representative, we voted to go along with that. We excluded the coach from our division of the playoff money. Instead of dividing the money 13 ways, we only divided it 12 ways; that left more money for each player.

Because I've always been the highest-paid player on my team, playoff money has never meant as much to me as it does to some of the other guys. I've made it a habit not to vote on playoff money splits; whatever the majority wants is okay with me. That's what I did this time, too. When everyone else voted to exclude Sharman —and to let Jack Kent Cooke know that we thought he should pay Sharman's share—I voted along with them, and agreed to sign the letter to Cooke.

But Jack turned the matter over to Fred Schaus, the Lakers general manager, and when we had our victory banquet the night after winning the championship, the issue still wasn't settled, and it left an ugly cloud over what should have been a festive occasion —the culmination of 12 years of waiting for an NBA championship in Los Angeles.

Jack didn't seem particularly disturbed at first, though, and he made a point of coming over to me, that night, and telling me I should have my attorney, Sy Goldberg, call him in the morning.

"I've got something special for you, something big. I think you'll like it," he said.

I assumed he meant a new contract. Professional athletes had been exempted from the wage-price freeze by then, and Jack knew I wanted to renegotiate my contract for the next season. After our great year, he sounded more than willing to give me a good raise.

But when Jack invited me to meet the people sitting at his table for the banquet, I saw that one of them was Jim Murray, the *Los Angeles Times* sports columnist who had just written some nasty things about my new house. I had been furious over what he wrote, and Jack knew it. I wasn't about to be "introduced" to Murray then—even if he was a personal friend of Jack's.

The next morning, another *Times* writer, Mal Florence, had a story about the controversy over who would pay the coach's share

282

of the playoff money. As usual, I had been the only player willing to talk about the situation. Between my comments in Mal's story and my snub of Murray, Jack was incensed. When Sy called him that morning, Jack said he had nothing to talk to him about.

"What about the special deal you told Wilt you had for him?" Sy asked.

"That offer was made to a friend," Jack said. "Wilt's no longer my friend."

For the next four months, any further attempt on our part to talk contract with Jack was met with a stiff rebuke. I already had a contract, he said—the last year of the two-year option clause on my original contract. It was not his policy, Jack said, to renegotiate "valid" contracts.

Frankly, I wasn't too concerned about Jack's apparent disinterest in me. I was seriously considering retiring anyway, and his attitude actually gave me extra time to think things out.

A lot of friends urged me to retire as soon as we won the championship. I'd done everything there was to do on a basketball court, they said; why keep playing? They had a point. I already held 64 all-time NBA records—far more than anyone else in history. I had led the league in everything from scoring and rebounding to assists and minutes played. I was the all-time NBA leader in more important categories than everyone else combined. I had been the most valuable player four times during the regular season and twice during the playoffs. I'd played on the two winningest NBA teams of all time, had been captain of both teams, and had led both teams to NBA championships. What else was there for me to do in basketball? Why not retire?

I thought about it, I'll admit. I was tempted. But that second championship had been a long time coming, and it was, by far, the most satisfying of the two. Quite frankly, I just wanted to sit back and enjoy it for a while. For once, I wouldn't have to spend the off-season answering a lot of rude, stupid questions about why we had lost, and I wanted to bask in that glow for a few months. Besides, with all those practices and the pressure of the winning streak and the injuries, it had been a particularly difficult season, and I really needed a rest, a chance to do nothing and think about nothing for a while. I knew that the minute I announced my retirement, I'd be besieged by promoters and other entrepreneurs with

283

all kinds of ideas about what I should do with my time and my name and my money, and I just didn't want to face all that right after the season. I didn't want the hassle, and I didn't want anything to detract from the glow of the championship—for me or for my fans. After all, I'd pretty much gotten used to all the criticism. I could take it, and shrug it off for the ignorant nonsense most of it was. But my fans had taken a lot of shit for a long, long time, and I felt they deserved a chance to walk in peace for a change.

Then, after I was rested and ready to think about the future, it was too late to get things formally arranged before I would have to make a definite decision about the next basketball season.

Actually, Jack thought he had an ace up his sleeve. Through intermediaries, he was trying to convince UCLA's Bill Walton to turn pro immediately, my sources told me. Only when Walton gave him a definite no did Jack show any interest in talking to me about the 1972–73 season. By then, it was late September, and I'd turned down another big-money offer from the ABA—from the San Diego Conquistadores this time. The Lakers, meanwhile, were already playing their exhibition games.

On October 10, the day before the Lakers were leaving for Omaha to play their season opener, I signed my new contract. Jack had wanted me to sign a multi-year contract again, but I'd insisted on a one-year contract this time, and I got it. I wanted to keep my options open—and I was fairly sure I would only play one more year anyway.

(I might not even have signed for that one more year, but let's face it—when a shrewd, stubborn old guy like Jack Kent Cooke starts waving a few hundred thousand dollars in your face—and saying "Please"—how are you gonna say no?)

When the press asked Jack if he'd gone contrary to his announced policy and renegotiated my contract for a higher salary, he said he had not. When they asked me the same question, I just said I was "satisfied" with the outcome of our talks. If Jack's pride required that he save face by saying he'd won his point, it was okay with me. As far as I knew, I had already been the highest-paid player in the league; my new contract just made my position that much stronger.

I've always been distressed by what owners tell the press about

284

players' salaries anyway. Either they announce figures much lower than the truth, to discourage other players from asking for too much, or they announce figures much higher than the truth to make themselves—and their franchises—look so flush that any college all-American will want to play for them.

I figure a man's salary is his own business. If he wants to announce it to the public, okay. But his boss shouldn't do it for him.

This was one time, though, that the press caught on to what was happening. Jack had said it was against his policy to renegotiate contracts, but before this last season was very far along, word got out that both Gail Goodrich and Happy Hairston had renegotiated their contracts, too—and gotten raises.

As John Hall wrote in the *Los Angeles Times:*

"You can hardly blame Wilt if he lifts an eyebrow at the sincerity of ownership."

That wasn't all I raised my eyebrows over during the first couple of weeks last season. After we bombed Kansas City Omaha, 129-94, in our season opener, we got blitzed by Boston and New York on the road. Right away, everyone was quick to put the blame on me. I was out of shape, they said; my long holdout had kept me out of the exhibition games, and I was "getting tired too easily."

But that just wasn't so. I had played volleyball all summer, ten to twelve hours a day, and I was in great shape. Hell, I played more minutes than anyone else on the team in the first three games, and I was in double figures in points *and* rebounds in all three games. New York and Boston were both great teams, though—as they proved in the course of the season—and losing to them on their home courts was hardly a disgrace. Besides, Happy and Keith had both missed part of the exhibition season with injuries, and their condition and timing wasn't sharp yet. Gail had been injured, too, and he didn't even play against New York and Boston. And Jerry was just awful in both games. He missed eight of his first ten shots against Boston, and hit only two of seven in the first half against New York.

The one man who could have set the record straight was the Laker announcer, Chick Hearn. Chick is an extremely knowledgeable basketball man and an exciting play-by-play announcer. But he has one slight problem; he thinks Jerry West is Jesus Christ.

285

Instead of talking about how cold Jerry was against New York and Boston, Chick was busy talking about how "tired" I was. That was typical. In a game a couple of months later, Chick didn't say a word when Jerry blew two layups, made a bad pass, threw another one away, and kicked yet another out of bounds. Then, when I dropped a pass in the same game, Chick said, "Wilt's having trouble handling the ball tonight."

Chick is immensely popular, and many fans accept his word as gospel. Over the course of 100 games a season, year after year, his attitude can have a helluva cumulative effect on a player's image—for good or for bad.

Fortunately for me, some discerning fans have noticed the discrepancies between the way Chick talks about Jerry and the way he talks about me, and a few of them have written to Jack Kent Cooke about it.

One guy wrote in after the New York and Boston games, and said he "just can't take it any more.

"It's been obvious for a long time," he wrote, "that he [Chick] favors Jerry West and protects him and covers up for him in his reporting, and that he really lays it on Wilt. . . .

"When Wilt goes out of a game, they're 'benching' Wilt," the fan wrote. "When Jerry goes out, it's for 'a needed rest.' "

Jerry's a great player—maybe the greatest guard ever. He doesn't need someone like Chick trying to deify him every game. In fact, I've got a hunch there are times when even Jerry wishes Chick would let up some.

The pressure of living up to an image can be unbearable at times. Chick, for example, has nicknamed Jerry "Mr. Clutch" because he's won so many games for the Lakers in the fourth quarter over the years. But no one, not even Jerry, can come through in the clutch every time. In the playoffs against New York in 1972, he shot terribly, and in several crucial playoff situations against Chicago and New York this past season, he also missed key shots and made bad plays.

In 1971, when New York had beaten us in the seventh game, Jerry hadn't even flown home with the team. He'd stayed in New York an extra day, so he wouldn't have to face the fans who met the team at the airport in Los Angeles. In 1972, he came home with us, but he tried to slip out the back door of the plane to avoid the fans; the Lakers were winning, but Jerry couldn't stand not being "Mr. Clutch."

Chick—and the other media—have perpetuated this image of Jerry as the all-American boy. To a certain extent, that image doesn't permit Jerry to admit it when he makes certain kinds of mistakes. Take one game last season, in Phoenix. Neil Walk accidentally tripped Jerry and knocked him to the floor, and the official didn't call a foul. Jerry was furious. He looked up at the official, and called him a "stupid mother-fucker."

For the first time in his career, Jerry was kicked out of a game for bad language.

After the game, Rod Hundley, one of the Phoenix announcers, was interviewing me, and he asked me what I thought of the incident. I told him I thought the official had made a mistake.

"The officials are out there for only one reason—to keep order," I told Rod. "He should've tried to calm Jerry down and warn him once before he threw him out. By throwing a guy like Jerry out so quickly, he just got all of us mad and damn near precipitated a riot."

Jerry said the same thing—in much stronger terms—when he got to the locker room. He thought the official had screwed him, and he said so. But he wouldn't criticize the official in public. When reporters asked him about what had happened, he put on his contrite, little-boy-next-door look and said, "I have never been so embarrassed in my life. I said something that nobody should ever say. I felt like crawling in a hole after it happened, and I will never let it happen again."

Jerry, like most men, had used that language before, on many occasions—including one time when Joe Mullaney was coaching us, and Jerry got tired of hearing him shout instructions from the bench during a game; Jerry just dribbled over to the bench that time, glared at Mullaney and said, "Shut the fuck up!"

Now, in Phoenix, Jerry obviously felt more like pushing the official into a hole than "crawling" into one himself, and I had the feeling that he wished—just this once—that he could have said so. But the media had given him an image, and he was trapped by it; he had to live up to it, like it or not.

Jerry wasn't the only Laker who lost his temper early in the season, though. I found myself getting angry on the court far more often than I used to. Thanks to expansion, we were playing a lot of weak teams, teams with centers who could only play me by holding me and fouling me. I started slapping their hands away, and even trying to entice one or two of them into a fight, to teach them a lesson. For a while, I was afraid I'd lose my record of never having fouled out of an NBA game. But as the season wore on, I regained my self-control and kept my record intact.

I'm proud of that record. I get paid to help my team, and I can't help them if I'm on the bench or in the shower. I've even tried to develop special techniques to avoid fouling. That's one reason I used to shoot the fall-away bank shot; if I jumped straight up or in, toward the basket, the man guarding me would come up under me, and the official—trying to protect the smaller man from "big Wilt"—would call me for charging. The same is true now with the slam-dunk. I have to bounce the ball at least once before I go up, to get my defensive man to commit himself; otherwise, I'll get called for charging.

Defense is even tougher to play without fouling than offense. Bill Russell, for example, fouled out 24 times in his career—an average of twice a year. Throughout his career, he committed about 30 percent more fouls per game than I did. The main reason is our different approaches to shot-blocking. Bill was a master at timing—the best I ever saw. He'd wait until he thought you were just about to shoot, then slam the ball back down your throat. But, occasionally, he'd miscalculate—and he'd foul you. My timing isn't as good as Russell's, but I'm faster and I jump better, so I play the ball, not the man. I wait until the shot's in the air; then I knock it down.

Probably one of the best shot-blocking games I ever had was last season in Philadelphia. I think the official statistics gave me 15 blocks; the Laker bench said I actually had 19. Either way, it wasn't a bad night's work. But, ironically, no one wanted to talk about my shot-blocking in the locker room that night.

They wanted to talk about my "skyjacking."

We'd played in Chicago the previous night, and we'd gotten to the airport in time for a 9:30 A.M. flight. But TWA kept us waiting until noon, telling us "just another 15 minutes" about 15 times. I hadn't had much sleep anyway, and I was really pissed. TWA had screwed me up several times over the years—including

288

once when I had to hire a chartered plane to make up for their foul-ups. I'd missed playing in a benefit game that time, and I was remembering the incident this time when I walked through the boarding area in Chicago, and overheard one TWA guy tell another one, "You don't have to search those guys. They're the Lakers. You don't have to worry about them."

"Oh yeah?" I said to no one in particular. "Well, you may have to worry about *me*. The way I feel right now, if I had a gun in my bag, I might shoot somebody."

A few minutes later, after we'd boarded the plane, Chick Hearn's assistant, Lynn Shackelford, came over and said someone from TWA wanted to see me. I walked out, and this officious-looking bastard told me the FBI wanted to talk to me about "threatening to hijack this plane."

I told him I didn't know what he was talking about. He said someone had heard me say I had a gun and was going to hijack the plane. Now I knew what he meant. I explained my gun remark to him, and assured him I had no gun.

"If I really wanted this plane," I told him, "I'd just buy the damn thing. Or I'd stand on my toes and slap the son-of-a-bitch out of the sky."

He didn't think that was very funny, and he said he'd have to detain me for further questioning.

I thought he was crazy—and I told him so:

"If I was really going to hijack the plane, do you think I would have come off meekly just now when you asked to see me?"

He wasn't impressed with my logic.

"You can't get back on the plane and fly to Philadelphia," he said. "Not until I check with FBI headquarters."

I told him to shove the plane, the FBI, and TWA up his ass —simultaneously, for all I cared—and I stormed back on board, grabbed my bag, got back off . . . and flew United to Philadelphia.

Jack Kent Cooke later supported my action—and said the coach should have pulled the whole team off the plane to protest the way TWA treated me. He even issued orders that the Lakers "avoid the use of TWA wherever and whenever possible" in the future.

With all the hullabaloo over my "skyjack" attempt, everyone's attention was diverted from something far more important for the

Lakers. Happy Hairston tore the ligaments in his knee during the game in Chicago—the night before my TWA fiasco—and the team never really recovered from his loss.

Happy had been an invaluable man during our 1971–72 championship season, and he and I had come to work very well together under the boards. His loss meant Coach Sharman had to start juggling our lineup. At first, we thought Happy wouldn't be out more than a few games. He was always a good actor, who loved to take sensational, tumbling falls during a game—particularly if the game was on television—and when he fell in Chicago, we all just assumed it was another show for the folks back home. But he suffered an injury similar to the one I had suffered in 1969, and he was virtually through for the season. He only played a few minutes after that—in one of the playoff games against Golden State and in the last two against New York. I'll always believe that Happy could have made it back in time to really help us if he'd worked harder during his rehabilitation program, but he didn't seem to have that kind of dedication, and by the time he finally came back, his timing and conditioning were so shot to hell, he couldn't do much for us.

Happy's loss came at a most inopportune time for the Lakers. We had started the season slowly, but by the time Happy was hurt, we'd won 22 of our last 24 games, and we were starting to jell and to play like we had the previous year. Fortunately, the Lakers had made a trade early in the season with Philadelphia, and we had Bill Bridges on the bench to take over for Hairston. Bill is a rough, rugged rebounder—one of only about half a dozen players in NBA history to have more than 10,000 rebounds *and* 10,000 points—and even though his age (34) had slowed him down a lot and had him pretty tired by the end of the season, we probably wouldn't even have made the finals without him.

But Happy's injury wasn't the only one we had to adjust to. On February 7, just when we had started to play smoothly again, with Bill in the lineup, Jerry West pulled a hamstring muscle in a game in Boston. We had won eleven straight games, but, with Jerry out, we lost to Boston, got blown out by Milwaukee two nights later and wound up playing inconsistently for the rest of the regular season—losing 11 of our last 27 games.

Jerry missed twelve games in all, and Keith Erickson and

Pat Riley were hurt several times, too—Keith in particular; he has to be the most injury-prone guy, with the lowest pain threshold, I've ever seen. He probably asks the trainer for a shot of pain-killer every time he trims his toenails.

We had a few problems besides injuries last year, too. With me concentrating almost solely on rebounding and defense, I had my lowest scoring season ever, and there were times when my teammates ignored me altogether on offense. Even when I was wide open, standing under the basket, they'd take 25-foot jump shots—especially Gail Goodrich. Finally, I called a team meeting to remind the guys that I really didn't mind putting the ball in the basket myself on occasion.

A few critics complained that I wasn't shooting more because I was selfish. I was more interested in setting an all-time field goal percentage record than in helping the Lakers win games, they said—and they longed for the days when I'd averaged 50 points a game . . . conveniently forgetting that when I did that, they had also said I was being selfish. (I had much the same problem as Muhammad Ali. When he was young, sportswriters had ripped him for "demeaning" the fight game with his childish poetry and brash predictions and blatant self-promotion. But when he refused to go into the army and spoke out against racial discrimination, the sportswriters suddenly began longing for the days when—they assured their readers—he had been "a breath of fresh air.")

I'll be the first to admit that I wanted to set a new field goal percentage record last year. But I didn't want the record *per se;* I already had more records than Elvis Presley. Establishing that record was just another one of those artificial goals I set to get myself aroused and psyched up through the long 82-game schedule. With shooters like Jerry and Gail and Mac on the team, we didn't need me to shoot more. We needed me on defense and on the boards—particularly after Happy got hurt.

When you've played more than 1,000 NBA games, like I have, it can be terribly difficult to stay "up" game after game —especially when you've run out of goals to arouse your com-petitive instincts, and when you don't look on basketball as the most important thing in your life. That's why setting goals like leading the league in assists or setting a new field goal percentage

291

record have always been necessary for me. I imagine the one criticism of me that friends say they've heard the most often in recent years is that I'm inconsistent and unpredictable, that—as more than one fan has said—"We never know if you'll *want* to play in any given game."

Of course, I *want* to play. But we all have bad games sometimes, and we all try to pace ourselves—in the course of one game and in the course of an entire season. If we didn't, we'd be like race-horses that run themselves into the ground in the first four furlongs and fade in the stretch.

Almost all the games where people have said it didn't look like I was trying have been games that weren't all that crucial, and, subconsciously, I just wasn't able to concentrate on my artificial goals enough to make myself go all out. Let me give you an example.

Late last February, we played Milwaukee at the Forum. Jerry was still out of the lineup, and we had lost four straight games. It looked like we might really fall apart if we lost again. That was more than enough incentive for me. I hit 10 of 14 shots from the floor and four out of five free throws, and outscored Kareem for the first time in two or three years. I also had 20 rebounds and four assists and a half-dozen blocked shots. I made Kareem miss 17 of his 27 shots, and thoroughly outplayed him at both ends of the court. We won, 91-82.

Then, almost a month later, we played Milwaukee again—in the next-to-last game of the regular season. If we won, we would almost certainly be assured of the home-court advantage if we met them in the second round of the playoffs. But victory that night would also mean we would have to play Golden State in the first round of the playoffs, instead of Chicago. I wasn't exactly thrilled by that. I would rather have Milwaukee play Golden State, so Kareem and Nate Thurmond could wear each other out, while the Lakers were playing Chicago in the first round and I—hopefully—could conserve a little energy for the second round.

Does that mean I deliberately played poorly in the Milwaukee game? Of course not. Does it mean I loafed? No. What it does mean is that, with all these thoughts going through my mind, it just wasn't possible for me to psych myself into believing we just *had* to win the game. Subconsciously, I had to be less than 100 percent aroused. I still played damn well on defense, holding Kareem to just 12 of 31 from the floor, but I only got 14 rebounds, and—for just the second time in my entire career—I didn't take a single shot from the field. We lost, 85-84, and I really got roasted by the press for "not trying." Of course, my teammates weren't all that sensational either. Jerry only hit 6 of 21 shots. Gail only hit 6 of 17. Mel Counts only hit 4 of 11. Keith Erickson only hit 2 of 9. In the final eight minutes, my teammates had 12 shots; they missed 11 of them. In the final seconds, Gail had an easy 20-footer and blew it. I got the rebound, and whipped it to Bridges for an easy jumper from the baseline. He missed it.

We had lost the home-court advantage, but that, in itself, is an artificial incentive—built into the NBA system primarily to keep the players motivated and the fans interested through the long regular season. The teams with the best regular-season records get the home-court advantage in the playoffs, and that's supposed to make every regular-season game important, even after the division titles have long since been decided. But to get an idea of how much the players really believe the home-court advantage is imperative to victory, look at what they did last season when we wound up tied with Milwaukee for the best record in the Western Division. We were supposed to meet in a one-game playoff to break the tie; instead, player representatives throughout the league voted almost unanimously to decide it by a coin flip.

Milwaukee won the flip—and with it, the "right" to meet Golden State, a team they had handled with ease all year, in the first round of the playoffs. Incredibly, my old friend Nate not only wore Kareem out, he—with considerable help from Clyde Lee—outplayed Kareem, and Golden State beat Milwaukee in six games. My "plan" had worked beyond my wildest expectations.

But we almost stumbled in the first round, too. Chicago, a team we had beaten four out of five times during the regular season, almost knocked us out in the first round. Playing poorly —as we had been for more than a month—we were lucky to win the first game in overtime. We won the second game easily, then lost two rough, aggressive games in Chicago to even the series. We won the fifth game at home, and they won the sixth game at home, so it all came down to the seventh game in Los Angeles.

I was worried going into that game, believe me. Gail had

293

hit only 27 percent of his shots in the last four games, Jerry wasn't shooting much better, and only Jim McMillan was really playing well for us offensively. In the seventh game, Mac turned ice cold, too; he hit only 3 of 19 shots.

That seventh game against Chicago provided a graphic demonstration of what I believe to be Bill Sharman's single greatest weakness as a coach. Bill, who is unquestionably a damn good coach, just doesn't seem to adjust well in game situations. He has a set substitution pattern, and he rarely changes it. He pulls the same guard and forward out and puts the same substitutes in at almost precisely the same time in every half of every game, regardless of the situation; you can damn near set your watch by it. In theory—and, generally, in practice—that's a good system. It enables four of our starters to rest a few minutes each half, and it saves every player the embarrassment of being yanked out just because he's playing poorly.

But sometimes a coach *should* bench someone for playing poorly. Sharman either can't or won't make that adjustment —perhaps because he's such a nice guy, he's afraid to hurt the player's feelings. In a game like pro basketball, where momentum is all-important, that kindness can be killing. In that seventh game against Chicago, for example, Sharman kept McMillian in the game for his normal 21 minutes in the first half—even though Mac missed all 11 shots he took, and got only one rebound . . . and we were falling behind.

As a team, we shot a miserable 36.2 percent in that game, and I still don't know how we won. We were behind, 92-88, with 1:54 to play, and I was sure we were done for. But we played tough defense, held them without a shot their next four times down the floor, and closed to 92-91 with 28 seconds left. Then Norm Van Lier tried a jump shot from somewhere around the top of the key. I went out and blocked the shot, grabbed the ball and fired a full-court pass that Joe Namath would have been proud of. The ball led Gail perfectly, and he grabbed it under our basket and laid it in. We didn't let Chicago get a shot off the rest of the way, and when we got the ball back, with 2 seconds left, Jerry sank two free throws to end it.

When the final buzzer sounded, the Chicago players looked crushed—especially Van Lier. Stormin' Norman had done everything you could ask of a ballplayer throughout the series. In the last game alone, he had not only led Chicago in scoring (28 points) and raced all over the court on defense, he also led his team in rebounding—and he's just barely over 6 feet!

With the Chicago series behind us, Golden State was next—and we played as poorly in the first game against them as we had against Chicago. We hit only 38 percent of our shots, and we missed 11 free throws and got outrebounded as well. Jerry was particularly bad; he missed 13 of his first 15 shots. But Mac had a great game; his 37 points kept us close. The score was tied at 99-all with about a minute to play, when I blocked a shot by Nate. Then Rick Barry threw the ball away, and Jerry hit a jump shot to win it, 101-99, with eight seconds left.

We won the next two games easily, giving the best defensive performance I've ever seen in game No. 3. We won that one in Oakland, 126-70, for the second-biggest victory margin in NBA history; the Warriors' 70 points was the lowest for any team since the inception of the 24-second clock. But Mac got hurt in the game. Mahdi Abdul-Rahman (formerly Walt Hazzard), who had been hitting guys and pushing and shoving and tripping throughout the first three games, pulled Mac down from behind on a breakaway lay-up in the second quarter. Mac hit the floor knee-first, and he missed most of the next game. We lost, 117-109, then wrapped up the series in the fifth game, 128-118, when Gail finally got hot and scored 21 points in the third quarter and 44 in the game.

I think most people were surprised by how easily we beat the Warriors after the way they had throttled Milwaukee. But the films of the Warriors-Bucks series showed that Milwaukee had been as bad as Golden State had been good. Kareem, in particular, didn't seem to be moving well. Of course, he had been playing much of the season worrying about the Black Muslims and whether he and his family were going to be killed by the gunmen who murdered those seven people in Washington, D.C., in mid-January. Kareem knew all the victims—he had even paid for the house they were killed in—and we heard there was supposed to be a contract out on his life, too. Frankly, I don't know how he was able to concentrate enough to play as well as he did after that; he had to have bodyguards everywhere he went.

Knowing that Golden State had beaten a sub-par Milwaukee gave us extra confidence against the Warriors; our confidence was further bolstered by the realization that Nate was bound to be a little tired after going all-out against Kareem. That, it turned out, was exactly the case; he hit only 37 percent of his shots against us in the playoffs. But Rick Barry was the guy who really hurt them against us—and I don't know what his excuse was for stinking the joint up so badly. He hit only 34 percent of his shots, repeatedly lost his poise, threw the ball away in the clutch —and seemed to just plain quit in at least two games. He also got in foul trouble almost every game. In the second game, he scored 29 points and displayed the brilliant skills that could make him the greatest forward in basketball, if he'd ever learn some discipline and self-control. Then he fouled out and started ranting and raving and giving the referee the finger—about as childish a public display as I've ever seen from a supposedly mature, 28-year-old man. But Rick has always acted like a spoiled brat, and he's just lucky the San Francisco basketball writers are so hard up for good copy that they don't really get on him.

While we were busy disposing of Golden State to win the Western Division championship, Boston and New York were thrashing around for the Eastern Division championship. Boston was the favorite, but we were rooting for the Knicks.

Boston had compiled the best record in the NBA, so that meant they would have the home-court advantage if we played them in the finals; if we played New York, *we* would have the home-court advantage. More important, we thought we could beat New York. Boston had beaten us four straight times, without a loss, during the regular season, and they had seemed about a step too fast for us at every position. With Happy still out and Mac not 100 percent, I didn't relish the thought of chasing their superb young center, Dave Cowens, around the court in the championship games, trying to stop him from hitting 25-foot jump shots and still, somehow, trying to stay close enough to the basket to get rebounds and keep his teammates from getting easy lay-ups.

Well, we got to play the Knicks, all right—they beat Boston in seven games—but as it turned out, that was like getting a last-minute reprieve from the gas chamber . . . only to find out you're going to be hanged instead.

We won the first game against the Knicks, 115-112, but they won the next four, in an exact reversal of the 1972 playoffs, when *they* won the first game and *we* won the next four. But our 1972 victories had been one-sided routs; their 1973 victories were all close games that either team could have won. With any breaks at all, we could have won the championship again.

In the second game, the Knicks led by ten points in the fourth quarter, but we closed to 98-95 with 26 seconds to go. Jim McMillian—our best free-thrower all year—was on the line for two free throws. If he hit them, we had a helluva chance to pull it out. But he missed both of them. I couldn't say much about Mac's misses, though. I'd missed eight of nine free throws myself, and the whole team had played lousy offensive basketball. Gail and Mel Counts, in particular, dribbled so much and played so much one-on-one basketball, you would have thought it was a schoolyard game, not an NBA championship playoff.

Still, we went to New York for the third and fourth games convinced we could win at least one and regain our home-court advantage. But the Knicks continued to capitalize on Laker mistakes and bad breaks, and they beat us twice.

Jerry, who had averaged 28 points in the first two games, pulled his right hamstring muscle in the third quarter of the third game. He had already pulled his left hamstring in the second game, and Coach Sharman decided to keep him on the bench in the fourth quarter, rather than risk aggravating the injury and perhaps losing him for the rest of the series. If we'd been able to capitalize on our opportunities in that game, the way the Knicks did in every game, we might not have needed Jerry. But even though we held the Knicks to only one field goal in the first seven minutes of the second quarter, our offense was sputtering so badly that we couldn't blow them out; we only led 47-44 at the half. Then, when the Knicks held us without a field goal for seven minutes in the third quarter, they grabbed a ten-point lead. Playing without Jerry, we still closed to 85-83 with 22 seconds left. That's when we could have used Jerry—to take one last shot and get us even. With Dave DeBusschere, Willis Reed and Jerry Lucas all saddled with five fouls, the odds certainly would have been in our favor in an overtime game. But, with Jerry on the bench, Keith Erickson took the last shot and missed it badly and we lost again.

Jerry started the fourth game, obviously hampered by his injuries, and the Knicks quickly spurted into the lead, shooting 54 percent in the first quarter, compared to 29 percent for the Lakers. I was flat and sluggish in the first half, and when the Knicks stretched their lead to 47-26 late in the second quarter, I figured we were through. All of a sudden, we started running again. At halftime, we had cut their lead from 21 points to 11—55-44.

In the second half, I was finally able to get going, and we put on a helluva rally. But Jerry missed three of four free throws and threw the ball away twice in a row—all in the fourth quarter. Then, when we closed to 94-92, with just 48 seconds left, DeBusschere came up with that big rebound and lucky basket I told you about in the first chapter.

In the locker room afterward, we all sat around shaking our heads. DeBusschere had scored 33 points in the game, but that was the first time in four games he had really hurt us. We'd also done a good job of stopping Walt Frazier. And yet, even after doing a great defensive job on their two key players, we were still behind, three games to one. That, of course, is the great strength of the Knicks; every one of their starters can kill you; there's always someone to pick up the scoring slack. In the first two games, it had been Bill Bradley. In the third game, it had been Willis Reed and Earl Monroe. In the fourth game, DeBusschere.

On the plane ride back to Los Angeles, after the fourth game, I was playing cards, and our team doctor, Dr. Bob Kerlan, came up and uttered one of the classic lines in sports history.

"The pressure," he said, "is all on the Knicks. They *have* to win one game."

Of course, we had to win three games, and—since we felt we could easily have won the last three—we still felt we had a chance to win the next three.

But there weren't three more games—only one.

The fifth and last game started miserably for us, and that seemed to follow the pattern of the entire series. Jerry missed a lay-up off the opening tip, DeBusschere blocked a McMillian jump shot, Reed blocked a Bridges jump shot and Frazier blocked a West jump shot. With Jerry hurting and everyone else cold, I had to start going to the basket myself. Contrary to what everyone thinks, you can't play defense all year, then suddenly switch to offense in the last game of the season and hit every shot right away. I took seven shots in the first quarter—more than I'd been averaging for a full game the entire season—and I hit only two of them. As a team, we hit only 25 percent from the floor in the first quarter, and the Knicks jumped ahead, 23-16. I scored our first five points in the second quarter, and even though we only hit 32 percent in the whole first half—and Jerry didn't score a point— we squeaked ahead, 41-39, at halftime.

Unfortunately, we started the second half just as poorly as we had started the first half. Jerry threw the ball away, Mac dropped a ball out of bounds, Mac took a shot that didn't even hit the rim, Gail let Frazier steal the ball from him on an in-bounds play right under the Knicks' basket, and I missed two straight free throws— all in less than three minutes.

We committed eleven turnovers in the first ten minutes, and with the Knicks hitting 67 percent of their third-quarter shots, we were digging ourselves a hole that was just too deep to climb out of. DeBusschere hit only one of nine shots, but even when he hurt his ankle and had to be helped off the court with just under eight minutes left in the game, things looked pretty bleak for us. We were behind, 79-65, and we just weren't shooting well or moving the ball well at all. As in the previous games, however, we put on a furious rally. Then, when we got to within four points, at 84-80, Bridges made a great rebound basket and the officials called him for a foul, instead of calling it the other way around. We could have been behind by just one point; now we were behind by six points (after the Knicks made the foul shots), and Bridges was out of the game, with six personal fouls. We were through. The Knicks were champs.

I suppose there are a lot of things we could blame our defeat on. Injuries, of course—losing Happy for most of the season, and having to play New York with Jerry hurting. Coaching was a big factor, too. Red Holzman had a deep bench, and he used it brilliantly. Bill Sharman hadn't used guys like Pat Riley and rookie Jim Price much during the regular season, so when we needed help against the Knicks, he was reluctant to play them. With Jerry hurt and the rest of the team cold—we were under 100 points four times and hit only 43 percent of our shots overall—we just didn't have enough firepower on the floor. Breaks played a big role, too; crucial calls and bouncing balls always seemed to go the Knicks' way. When the Knicks played Boston, John Havlicek got hurt; when they played us, Jerry got hurt. But we'd had those kinds of breaks going our way in 1972, when we won the championship, and the Knicks had Reed and DeBusschere both injured, so we couldn't get too upset about that.

Actually, neither team played particularly well in the series; the Knicks played better than we did, though, so they deserved to win. They played like a team; we didn't. Earl Monroe, who had been humiliated by Gail Goodrich in the 1972 playoffs, redeemed himself this time, averaging 16 points a game and hitting 53 percent of his shots. Willis had a good series for them, too, and he was named the most valuable player in the playoffs.

I did get a little tired, though, of answering sportswriters' questions about how courageous Willis was, coming back from his two-year-old knee injury, and how courageous Jerry was, playing with two pulled hamstrings. Both men were courageous; I don't deny that for a minute. But I played the last game with an eye swollen about half-shut, two fingers taped together, a slight hamstring pull and a heel so sore I could hardly walk on it—and, like Willis, I had also come back from a crippling knee injury a few years earlier. But, somehow, I've always been expected to play— and win—with injuries. I'm Superman and . . . Oh well. . . .

We didn't win the championship last season, and since basketball is a team sport, there isn't much solace in individual accomplishments. We did win 60 games and make it all the way to the finals, though, and people kept coming up to me in the dressing room after that last game, and saying what, in essence, one of the New York papers had headlined:

"Even Wilt Can't Do It Alone"

In the final game against New York, I had scored 23 points and pulled down 21 rebounds. Throughout the series, I had played some of the best defense of my career—as Walt Frazier kept telling all the sportswriters when they asked him why he wasn't scoring much. In the 17 playoff games—against New York, Golden State and Chicago—I averaged 23 rebounds and seven blocked shots a game.

Actually, I had been fairly pleased with my personal performance during the regular season, too. I'd played in every game again, running my streak to 294 in a row since I'd returned to the line-up on March 18, 1970, after my knee injury—and I'd just missed leading the league in minutes played. I finished second, only the fourth time in 14 years that I didn't lead the league. But I did lead the league again in field goal percentage (for the tenth time) and in rebounding (for the eleventh time). Even though my field goal percentage was an all-time record—73 percent—leading the league in rebounding again was a more satisfying achievement; it meant that I'd led the league in at least one of the three major categories—scoring, rebounding, and assists—every single year of my career. That's something no other athlete, in *any* sport, could ever say. No baseball player has ever led the league in at least one of baseball's three major categories—batting average, home runs, and runs batted in—every year for 14 years; no football player has ever led the league in one of their three major categories—running yardage, passing yardage, and points scored—every year for 14 years. Hell, I don't know much about hockey, but I'll bet no hockey player ever led the league in one of their three major categories—points, goals, and whatever else it is they do with a hockey puck—for 14 years either.

I've always thought longevity is the one true test of greatness—in anything. That's one reason I'm such a big fan of Elvis Presley's; he's been on top for almost 20 years now, and many of the people who sneered at him as a passing fad in 1955 now stand on line for four hours to see him in Las Vegas.

When anyone asks me who the greatest players in the NBA are, I always look at longevity first. I really don't like to make comparisons because of the way conditions are always changing, but if I had to pick the best guards I've seen in the NBA, they'd be Jerry West and Oscar Robertson. The best forwards would be John Havlicek and Elgin Baylor—and, possibly, Billy Cunningham (though the best of them all, to go strictly one-on-one, within the context of a regular team game, would be Chet Walker). All these guys did so much so well for so long; that's why they're all-time all-pros. At center, I'd have to hedge a little. Bill Russell is the obvious choice—particularly given what I've said about longevity. He was absolutely fantastic for 13 years—the greatest rebounder and greatest defensive center I've ever seen. But Kareem Abdul-Jabbar is so good on offense *and* defense—and he has such un-

301

limited potential—that I can't leave him off my team, even if he has played only four years in the NBA.

I'd also be tempted to put Nate Thurmond at center, because he's played so well against both me and Kareem. But he hasn't been that outstanding against the other centers in the league. I guess the easy way out is to leave Nate, Bill, and Kareem *all* off my all-time team.

Guess who my center would be then?

But all-time teams don't mean much. Better players are always coming along—bigger, stronger, faster, and smarter—to break the unbreakable records and surpass the unsurpassed superstars. Walt Frazier may soon be better than West and Robertson ever were. Spencer Haywood or Rick Barry may ultimately be better than Baylor and Havlicek. Bill Walton may be better than Russell and Abdul-Jabbar and Thurmond and Chamberlain. And some kid who's in junior high school now may be better than any of us one day.

That's good. I hope all my records are eventually broken. That's what records are for. If the players get better, that means the game gets better—and the fans have more fun.

That, after all, is what spectator sports is all about—competition and entertainment.

16

WIN OR LOSE, I'D PRETTY much decided before last season began that it would be my last year in professional basketball. After 14 years in the NBA—plus three in high school, three in college, and one with the Globies— I was fed up with the regimentation of basketball as a way of life. I tend to be a free spirit, and I was tired of building my life around airline timetables and bus departures and game times and practice schedules.

A lot of people seem to think a professional athlete's life is an easy way to get rich. You only play three or four games a week in the NBA, so they figure it must be a soft job. Well, I'll bet my work week is at least two or three times as long as the average 9-to-5 guy's, when you figure up all the time we spend practicing and traveling, as well as playing.

Take one road trip this last season. We played Sunday night in Los Angeles, then flew to New York early Monday morning and played in Madison Square Garden Tuesday night. Ideally, we'd like to leave Los Angeles Tuesday morning for a Tuesday night game. But because of the time difference, that wouldn't get us in until almost game time. So we had to leave Monday—and spend Monday night and all day Tuesday sitting around New York. Then, Wednesday morning, we flew to Boston for a game with the Celtics Wednesday night. Thursday morning, we flew to Milwaukee for a game with the Bucks Friday night. After the Milwaukee game, we took a bus to Chicago, hopped a plane, and got back to Los Angeles at 3:15 A.M. Saturday.

An extra day and night in New York sounds like fun, you say? It can be—but not after 14 years of doing that several times a year . . . and not with New York as screwed up as it is now. Boston isn't too bad a place to spend a night sometimes, but who the hell wants to spend two days in Milwaukee . . . or in Cleveland or Buffalo or Omaha or Philadelphia or Kansas City or Baltimore or any of the other cities we play in? If you add up the days and nights we're on the road, including training camp and exhibition games and playoffs, you'll find that the average NBA player spends more than four months out of every year away from his home and his friends and—if he's married—away from his family.

For the superstar, it's even worse. You're not only away from home, you're a virtual prisoner of your hotel room—particularly if your name is Wilt Chamberlain.

I saw a survey six or seven years ago—before my teams had won any world championships—and it said my name was the most easily recognized of any athlete. It's so bad that when I call people on the telephone, and their secretaries answer, I have to identify myself as "Mr. Norman" or "Mr. Chamberlain"; I know that if I use "Wilt Chamberlain," I'll have to talk basketball with them for ten minutes before they put me through to their boss.

If just my name creates that kind of distraction, you can imagine what my actual physical presence does. Wherever I go, it's instant crowd. I remember reading once that George Mikan said he'd like to be able to walk down the street, and have people say, "There goes the greatest basketball player who ever lived." Not me. I'd like to be able to walk down the street, and have no one notice me. But that's not likely to happen. So, on the road, I stay in my hotel room, watching TV and talking on the telephone and ordering most of my meals from room service. Sometimes, even my hotel room isn't much of a sanctuary. One time, last year, the Essex House Hotel in New York ordered a special, king-size bed for me, without bothering to tell me anything about it; then they invited the press up to my room to see it. When I checked in, my room was swarming with photographers.

To pass the time on the road, I often play cards with teammates or practice my French or Italian with a Berlitz course I have on tape cassettes or challenge my teammates to one of several little mental exercises I've devised. Most of the exercises are based on the laws of probability and human nature, and they can be fun —and mildly profitable—on a dull night in Cleveland. I also tend to retain most statistics I read, so I try to make a little more money from my teammates by betting them on the population of various cities or the lengths of various rivers or the production levels of various crops. But even the most fertile mind runs out of games after awhile; I'd like to go outside to get some fresh air and mix with some other people. No chance. I can't go for a walk or go window-shopping or go to a restaurant—or much of anyplace else—without causing a commotion, and being so besieged for autographs that it's really not worth it. Hell, I can't even go to a football game without disrupting things. All the fans sitting around me start pointing at me and talking about me and coming over to ask for my autograph. Then I can't enjoy the game, and the other fans sitting near me can't enjoy it either. Worse yet, I wind up stealing the spotlight from the athletes on the field—and that's rude. So I stay home and watch the games on television—if they're on. Most celebrities don't have to be celebrities around the clock if they don't want to be. Elvis can put on some old Levis and a dirty shirt and not shave, and chances are, he can go unrecognized. Raquel Welch can put a baggy sweater and some old pants on, throw a few curlers in her hair, and walk around virtually unnoticed. But I'm probably the most recognizable man in the world, and there's not a damn thing I can do about it. I'm Wilt Chamberlain 24 hours a day, like it or not. (I remember being with President Nixon a few times before he was elected, and having people come up to me for autographs, and not even notice him.) With my size and my color and the amount of time I've been in the public arena, there's just no way I can escape attention, no way I can have even the slightest semblance of privacy.

Sure, I won't deny there's some ego gratification in having people recognize you. And I realize that my celebrity status works

305

both ways; a lot of doors get opened for Wilt Chamberlain that wouldn't be opened for anyone else. I realize that the inconvenience of being a celebrity is part of the price I have to pay for that entrée—and for the wealth and fame and pleasure basketball has given me. But you wouldn't believe how rude some people can be when they see you and want your autograph.

I suppose it would be easier if I adopted Bill Russell's policy— no autographs for anyone, at any time. But I think I owe something to the fans, and I like to be cooperative. If someone asks me for an autograph when I'm on my way in or out of an arena, I'll usually sign it—if I'm not in a hurry to meet someone. I'll even sign autographs when people come up to me in restaurants or on the street or in airports—if I'm not busy. You never have enough time to give autographs to everyone who wants one, though. If 100 people crowd around you, and you sign 97, you make three people unhappy—and they tell all their friends that you're a selfish bastard who thinks he's too good for them.

A lot of autograph seekers even interrupt me when I'm in the middle of a conversation—or a meal—and then they get mad when I ignore them or refuse to sign. I've lost count of the number of times I've had people tug at my arm and stick a pen in my face while I'm trying to cut a piece of steak in a restaurant.

I think the thing that gets me the angriest is when someone comes up and says he wants my autograph for "my son" or "my daughter." Why should I care who—or what—they want it for? They're only saying that because they think I'll find it harder to say no to a child than to an adult. There's another, more subtle reason for taking that approach, though; they know how ridiculous it is for an adult to collect autographs of sports stars. By asking for it in their child's name, they're implying that they're above that sort of thing—but that I'm down there at their child's level, playing a child's game.

Sometimes, when I'm not in a very good mood, I'll refuse to sign autographs when people ask "for my son."

"Just have your son come up to me at the next game, or write to the Laker office, and I'll be glad to give *him* my autograph," I tell them.

One time last season, a woman kept pestering me for autographs for her two sons. I signed one slip of paper, and while

I was doing it, I asked her if she was a good mother who taught her children all the right things—"like how to share."

"Oh yes, of course," she said.

Then she gave me a slip of paper "for my other son."

Instead of signing it, I just looked at her, and said, "I thought you told me you taught your sons to share."

I suppose people will always notice me and bother me, whatever I do; but if I'm not playing basketball, I can be much more selective about where I go—and when. I won't have to spend so much time in airports and restaurants and other public places during the busiest time of the day—and I won't get stuck sitting in airports for four or five hours at a time, waiting for late flights, while other passengers crowd around, grabbing at my luggage and demanding my autograph.

But what will I do if I'm not playing basketball? Well, there are two things I won't do—I won't take a coaching job in the NBA, and I won't go on the lecture circuit, like so many ex-athletes do. A coach has to suffer through the same regimentation and time-consuming commitments that a player does—and that doesn't interest me at all. Nor does public speaking. I've overcome the stuttering problem that several members of my family had, but I always turn down invitations to speak at functions like high school sports banquets anyway. I think they're an artificial setting, where you're invited more for the adults' benefit than the kids'. All your presence does is give the kids false hopes; I mean, how many of them are ever likely to be Wilt Chamberlains? I'd much rather take the kids on a picnic or a hike or just play ball with them in a schoolyard—which I frequently do.

I guess there's one other thing I won't do—play pro football. That offer I had from Hank Stram to come to Kansas City and play for the Chiefs back in 1965 wasn't the only time the NFL has approached me. When George Allen was coaching the Rams, he talked to me a couple of times about switching sports. George is a real believer in specialization, and he wanted the Rams to hire me to stand in front of their goal posts on field goal situations. George figured I could jump up and block any ball the enemy kicked my way. Who knows, once I got with George, I might have become a helluva football player. I mean, man, how would you like to be a cornerback, and see me out there, as a tight end, block-

307

ing for Larry Brown? But I'm 37 years old now, and football, I'm sorry to say, is out of the question.

One thing I *will* do if I'm not playing basketball is travel in Europe a lot—at the best time of the year to travel, not during the summer, when I've always had to travel before because I was playing basketball in the spring and fall. I'll also have a lot more time to play with my dogs. I have three big, beautiful Great Danes now, and I really enjoy running with them and wrestling with them and playing with them. One reason I like Danes is that they're so independent and they have so much dignity and bearing, but I can tell they miss me when I'm gone so much—and I miss them, too.

Another thing I'd like to do is organize a world volleyball tour. (I already coach and sponsor my own girls' volleyball team.) And I wouldn't mind owning my own NBA or ABA team, or maybe taking a top executive position with one of those alphabet-soup amateur sports organizations, like the AAU or the NCAA, that are usually about as screwed up as their names.

I'm sure I'll be able to keep busy. I have several business investments to manage, and I'm already doing quite a few television commercials and sales promotions. I've also been approached about being on the advisory board for a new men's magazine and hosting my own television show.

I might like to get into the production end of movies, too. I've seen enough of them on television in my hotel rooms over the last 14 years to have a pretty good idea of what makes a movie work. For a number of reasons, I've always liked the movie world. I guess one superficial reason is that movie theaters have been one of the few public places I could go without being bothered. Once the lights go out and I slouch down in my seat, I'm just another guy with a box of popcorn. I really do love movies—particularly action movies. My all-time favorites, I guess, would be *Bridge on the River Kwai, Ben-Hur,* and *The Guns of Navarone.* I must have seen *Bridge* in seven different languages. I even rented it and showed it at my home for some friends earlier this year. My affinity for movies goes beyond being a fan, though. Some of the nicest and most genuine people I've ever met have been movie people—actors like Karl Malden, Ricardo Montalban, Charlton Heston, Anthony Quinn, Gregory Peck, and Cary Grant. and actresses like Raquel Welch, Rhonda Fleming, Gail Fisher, Jane Russell, Liz Taylor, Jill St. John, and, of course, Kim Novak. Those are the kind of people I would enjoy working with.

I realize, of course, that no matter what I do, there will be times when I'll miss basketball. You can't leave something that's been the biggest thing in your life for more than 20 years, and not feel an occasional twinge of nostalgia.

Basketball has been good to me. I love the game, and I always will. I'm probably the only superstar who still plays in schoolyard pickup games, with a bunch of strange kids, just for the sheer pleasure of the game.

There are a lot of things about basketball that I'll miss when I'm no longer playing—and good fans are one of them. The fans in Philadelphia and Los Angeles have been especially good to me. So have the fans in Detroit. In fact, the fans in Detroit just might be the best in the league. They not only know the game and are fair-minded enough to cheer good plays by the opposition, but they have remained unbelievably loyal to their team—even though they've always had a losing team. I used to think the New York fans were the best—knowledgeable, sophisticated, fair-minded. But when the Knicks made their sudden, dramatic rise to the top a couple of years ago, the New York fans lost all their perspective. The Knicks became demigods; they could do no wrong. And the opposition could do nothing right. One reason for the change in the Madison Square Garden crowds is that a lot of the seats are now filled by people who aren't true basketball fans. They come to the Garden because it's the thing to do, not because they want to see a basketball game. But there's still a special excitement about playing in New York, and I know there will be days when I'll miss that—just as there will be days when I'll miss the Forum in Los Angeles and the Boston Garden and the Spectrum in Philadelphia and . . .

Does that mean I might "unretire"? You'll probably be able to answer that question better by the time you read this book than I am today, while I'm writing it.

The Lakers certainly made their choices in the NBA draft this past April as if they thought my retirement was imminent; five of the first seven men they chose are centers. But it's early summer now, while this book is being put together, and—as usual for me

309

when the basketball season is just over—I don't even want to think about basketball. What will have happened between now and the day you buy this book in your friendly, neighborhood bookstore? Well, Jack Kent Cooke might have made me an offer I couldn't refuse. Or the ABA—San Diego in particular, since they've been calling my attorney almost constantly—might have come up with so much money that I'd be a fool not to switch leagues and play one more year. Or some NBA team might have made a trade pitch that neither Jack nor I could turn down.

I really, truthfully, don't want to play another season of basketball. But my financial advisors tell me that if I play just one more year, under the right terms, I'll be financially set for the rest of my life. That's a powerful incentive to play again.

So this book doesn't really have an ending—a *denouement,* as they say in the movies. You may be seeing me soon on the floor of your local NBA arena. Or on television, in the game-of-the-week. Or you may be more likely to find me on a movie or television set—behind a camera, not in front of one. Or on the beach, playing volleyball and running with my dogs. Or floating down the canals of Venice, in a large gondola, with a beautiful girl on my arm and a smile on my lips and a twinkle in my eye.

Ciao. . . .